MODERN
TEACHING OF ENGLISH

Nayyer Shamsi

ANMOL PUBLICATIONS PVT. LTD.
NEW DELHI - 110 002 (INDIA)

ANMOL PUBLICATIONS PVT. LTD.
Regd. Office: 4360/4, Ansari Road, Daryaganj,
New Delhi-110002 (India)
Tel.: 23278000, 23261597, 23286875, 23255577
Fax: 91-11-23280289
Email: anmolpub@gmail.com
Visit us at: www.anmolpublications.com

Branch Office: No. 1015, Ist Main Road, BSK IIIrd Stage
IIIrd Phase, IIIrd Block, Bengaluru-560 085 (India)
Tel.: 080-41723429 • Fax: 080-26723604
Email: anmolpublicationsbangalore@gmail.com

Modern Teaching of English

PRINTED IN INDIA

Printed at Balaji Offset, Delhi

Contents

Preface

Education is a vast discipline and Teachers' Training is a vital part of it. The responsibilities of the educationists and educators are focused on the task of providing better training to the future teachers for their better learning and proper development. Needless to say that this responsibility can only be exercised, if the trainers are equipped with the required knowledge of the subject concerned. That's why it becomes essential for making adequate provisions for each course to the student-teachers or teacher trainees. The present series is designed for providing a solid workable base for all course-papers. It has been prepared strictly according to the syllabus of the B.Ed class, prescribed by the UGC for different universities.

No doubt, there are so many other books on the subject, available in the market, written by worthy authors. However, every writer has his or her own style and way of presentation. The present work also has its own features and characteristics.

In preparation of this series of texts, the editor had to refer to the works of other authors and information sources. The editor feels a deep sense of gratitude for incorporating their ideas in the text. Hopefully, this series would serve as a 'ready to refer' tool for all teachers, teacher-students and others.

— Editor

1

Introduction

The language is a means through which a child contemplates the past, grasps the present and approaches the future. It goes without saying that the language plays an important role in the mental, emotional and social development of a person. Though English is a foreign language yet it occupies a unique position in our country. Whether we are at home, in the state or out of it, in the country or away from it, English is important and it continues to hold a unique position. How much is that importance? It is a very pertinent question. In order to understand it fully, we shall have to study the history of this language in our country.

Undoubtedly, Hindi is one of the most important languages of the country. But as a link language, Hindi has not been accepted on the whole by people in the South. Hence English has been given the status of the Associate Official Language of the country.

Professor P. Gurrey writes in his book "Teaching English as a Foreign Language'- "All languages are used for the same purpose ....they are used, for insurance, for communication, for expressing anything that we have attended to, for recording information, for thinking, for getting what we want, and so on." Whatever may be the language, say English, Hindi, Punjabi, Chinese, Russian, French, Germany or any other, the purpose of each is the same i.e. communication, expressing, recording, thinking etc.

In our country, English was introduced about two centuries ago. It is rather interesting to know how this language gradually got prominence. In the Charter of 1813, article 433 was a pious clause which changed the whole lot of the people. The said clause authorised the Governor-General in Council to spend a sum of not less that one lac of rupees in each year on the revival and improvement of literature ....for the introduction and promotion of a knowledge of the science.... among the British territories in India. With this, a background for British education was prepared. Later with the coming of Lord Macaulay, the man behind modern education in India, it was clarified how the sum of one lac of rupees was to be spent. That was the time when the foreign plant of English' was sown in Indian soil. Lord Macaulay clarified the meanings of the words like literature, medium of instruction, agency of education etc. Thereafter the study of English was made compulsory. Soon English became the medium of instruction. The supremacy of English led to many controversies. After 1857, the common feeling was to oust the Britishers from the Indian soil.

On seeing the plight of Indian students, Gandhiji wrote, "our boys think that without English they cannot get Government service. Girls are taught English as passport for marriage. The canker has so eaten into the society that in many cases the only meaning of education is a knowledge of English. All these are for me signs of our slavery and degradation." He condemned the study of English at the cost of the study of mother tongue. M.K. Gandhi further said, " I would have our young men and women with literary tastes to learn as much of English and other world languages as they like...... But I would not have a single Indian to forget, neglect or be ashamed of his mother tongue ....

The Pre-independence Scene

During the pre-independence period, English enjoyed the privileged position. During that time it was:

Queen of Languages

During the British rule over India, English enjoyed the top-most position. It was the first language in the whole country. It was the lingua franca of the literate. It was considered to be the queen of the languages. In every walk of life, it was the vehicle of thought and activity. The importance given to it was the envy of every one and in no way it created any jealousy. It was the pride of all.

Medium of Instruction at Different Levels

English used to be the medium of instruction at school and college levels. In some of the elementary schools also, English was used as a medium of instruction. Every body loved to study different subjects through this language.

Englishmen Teaching English

The study of English was meant for all the children who joined the school. Our elders speak English very nicely. The main reason behind is that they were taught mostly by the English men. All subjects whether English, History or Geography were generally taught by the English men. Thus the students were under the impact of the English men for a good deal of time. They listened to spoken English of the native speakers. That is why our elderly persons whose schooling careers belong to that era, can speak 'A Class English.'

Introduction of English from the Day of Schooling

The study of English was introduced on the day the child entered the school. Every body was proud of it because the study of this language was considered a passport for employment.

Thus we find that English was of great importance before the freedom of our country. But with the passage of time, there have come about a number of changes in the position of English in our country.

Scene

In 1947, India became free and the English people left India for good. The whole administration, the language policy etc. came into the hands of Indian authorities. The very question regarding the place of English in India became controversial. Some leaders argued that English should be uprooted from the country, whereas some others favoured the retention of English. Mahatma Gandhi said, "It is my considered opinion that English education, in the manner it has been given, has emasculated the English educated Indians. It has put a severe strain upon the Indian students and made us imitators." He further said, "all the superstitions that India has, none is so great as that, a knowledge of the English language is necessary for imbibing ideas of liberty and developing accuracy of thought." But other persons like C. Rajagopalacharya say that English should be retined in the country. Their considered opinion was-" We in our anger and the hatred against the British people should not throw away the baby (English) with the bath water (English people)."

Maulana Abul Kalam Azad, soon after taking over the education portfolio in the Interim Government, said at a press conference: "So far as general studies are concerned it was never my intention to suggest that there should be any fall in the standard of English." In the words of Pt. Nehru "One hundred and fifty years of intimate contact has made English an integral part of our educational system and this cannot be changed without injury to the cause of education in India. In addition English has today become one of the major languages of the world and Indians can neglect its study only at the risk of loss of themselves. I am convinced that in the future as well, the standard of teaching English should be maintained at as high a level as possible. "

In fact, for the first two or three years of independence, so much was said but nothing concrete could be decided. In 1950, when Indian constitution was framed, it was unanimously decided to continue English as the official language of the country for fifteen years. During this period all efforts were made to develop Hindi-the national language of the country. The Indian authorities, thus, hoped to replace English by Hindi in due course of time. But there was great opposition by the people living in southern part of the country. The result was that in 1963, the Parliament passed a bill according to which English was declared to be the Associate Official Language of India for an indefinite period. In 1968, the National Policy on Education adopted by the Govt. of India stressed, "Special emphasis needs to be laid on the study of English and other international languages. World knowledge is growing at a tremendous pace, especially in science and technology. India must not only keep up this growth, but also make her own significant contribution to it. For this purpose, study of English deserves to be specially strengthened." With the passage of time, some of the states adopted their regional language as the official language. But they could not make Hindi as the link language between the different states. The reason is that Hindi is not understood in the different states of free India. So in order to continue links between various states of India, English continues to be the unifying factor.

Reddy T. Prabhaker writes in the Journal of English Language Teaching (1977), 'The number of Indian writers who use English for creative writing is increasing gradually. It looks as if it has become one of the languages of India and its long and wide use by the Indian intelligentia has given it a distinct identity.'

In School Curriculum

In school curriculum, English occupies an important place. In some states, English is introduced in class I in Govt. schools and Govt.

aided schools. Its study is compulsory for all the students. Pass in the examination in this subject is essential. In the case of central schools, English as one subject is introduced in the standard 1. In schools affiliated to C.B.S.E. also, English is introduced in standard 1.

Now when the regional languages are becoming important day by day in every state of the country, the status of English can be considered from the following points of view:

(i) English as an international language.
(ii) English as our major window on the world.
(iii) English as a link language.
(iv) English as a library language.

Problem of Language Study

Language is a means of communication without which the society is not able to make progress. In some countries, there is no language problem. In India, the language problem exists because there are many languages used in different states of the country. Due to different social groups in our country, the language problem has been there due to one reason or the other. Every body loves mother tongue and every body likes his regional language. Then interest of the national language i.e. Hindi cannot be sacrificed. There are some parts of India where people are not ready to accept Hindi. Therefore, the language problem in our country has to be cared for and proper solution has to be thought of.

Before independence and immediately after independence, the medium of instruction in secondary and higher education was English. Gradually shift in the medium of instructions at all levels was made from English to mother tongue or the regional language of the area. Officially all that was done and the problem with regard to the medium of instruction was solved at Government level. But the hard fact is that during the last two decades, a large number of English medium schools have cropped up. Keeping the ever growing demand of the people for English medium schools, more and more English medium schools are being established not only in cities but also in rural areas. Its effect on Government schools have also been felt by all concerned. Recently some state Governments have announced the introduction of English from first standard. Some other state Governments are considering the issue of introducing English from first standard. Rather it has become a serious problem with them. Discussions and debates are going on there.

Three Language Formula

Different committees and commissions have given their suggestions to solve the language problem in the country. The Central Advisory Board of Education (1956) designed a three language formula and recommended it for the school children. Then in 1961, the Chief Ministers' Conference endorsed the three language formula for the schools. According to the three language formula, every school going child was required to study the following three languages.

(i) Mother tongue or the regional language

(ii) English

(iii) Hindi for non Hindi speaking areas

(iv) If mother tongue is Hindi, then another modern Indian language. Thus if mother tongue of the child is Urdu, he/ she will have to study Urdu, English and Hindi. On the other hand, if the mother tongue of the child is Hindi, he will be required to learn, Hindi, English and one more Indian language. Thus in Punjab, the students learn Punjabi, English and Hindi and in Haryana, the students learn Hindi, English and Punjabi. In U.P., the students learn Hindi, English and Sanskrit.

Kothari Education Commission (1964-66) modified the dum language formula. According to the commission, regional language should be taught at the lower primary stage (class I to class IV). At the higher primary stage (class v to class vi) mother tongue or Hindi/ mother tongue or English should be taught compulsarily and the third language should be taught on optional basis. In classes VII to X, the students should study three languages. Thus in Hindi speaking areas, the students will study Hindi, English and a modern Indian language. In non-Hindi speaking areas, the pupils will study regional language, Hindi and English.

Thus we find that English has to be learnt by one and all in the schooling period. Now in this age of science and technology, every one is conscious of making improvements. Without English, it is not possible. Now more and more people are getting ready to learn English.

Significance of English

"We in our anger and the hatred against the British people should not throw away the baby (English) with the bath water (English people)".

In the history of English in India, we find that English has dominated the teaching learning programme from the beginning. Never was there any hatred or grudge against this language. It has been taught and learnt with affection and love. It has definitely enjoyed a privileged position. The persons not studying it might have felt some sort of inferiority complex. There have been good teachers of this subject not only foreigners alone but Indians as well. Some of them came out to be more sincere and dedicated to the teaching of this language. With them, a study of the subject was always a point of inspiration. They have not only done their duties but in addition they have also contributed a lot.

It goes without saying that English is a language borrowed from six thousand miles away and it belongs to an entirely different nation. But that does not mean that it has no relationship with us. Every human being is free to study any language. English is not only a national language of the English men, it is an international language. It may be called the language of the world civilization. Its richness, its flexibility, its elegance, its dignity seem to have made it universally popular. Even M.K. Gandhi said' in 'Thoughts of National Languages' "I hold its knowledge as a second language to be indispensable for specified Indians who have to represent the country's interest in the international domain. I regard the English language as an open window for peeping into western thought and science.' In other words, Gandhiji accepted the importance of this language for the selected few people who are to hold the reigns of the motherland. In this age of democracy, every one can dream of holding the charge of the country. Naturally none can be denied the study of this language. Pt. Nehru said, 'English language is our's by-historic necessity."

The different points explained here below show very clearly that English has its unique importance in our country. We can hardly bear dispensing with it from our mother land.

A Link Language : In our country, we have different states with different regional languages. People living in these states use their own languages for conversation, discussion etc. But English is a language which links them together. The leaders from different states meet sometimes formally over a common platform. By using this language, they can convey to one another their heart felt desires and thus they can share the views of one another. In the words of Pt. Nehru, "The language link is a greater link between us and English speaking people than any political link or common wealth link or anything else. It is so because we can see how their thoughts are functioning, much more than in other European languages." Thus, we find that the use of English in our country has been a unifying factor.

Pt. Nehru once said, "If you push out English, does Hindi fully take its place? I hope it will. I am sure it will. But I wish to avoid the danger of one unifying factor being pushed out without another unifying factor fully taking its place. In that event, there will be a gap. The creation of any such gap must be avoided at all costs. It is this that leads me to the conclusion that English is likely to have an important place in the foreseeable future." Besides, we can keep our links with the outside world by using English language. Prof. R.S. Trivedi points out, "India's connection with the Common Wealth, the U.N.O. and its agencies, her needs of foreign trade and economic aid from different countries, her need for the technical know-how for her development and her role in the affairs of the world, all conjointly enjoin upon the framers of her educational policy to give due weight to English so that her interests do not suffer and she does not detract from her rightful place in the world policy."

Educational Importance : From educational point of view, English played a prominent role in the past. Before independence it was the medium of instruction both at the school stage and the college stage. Higher education in Science, medicine, engineering, technology etc. was not possible without English. Even now advanced studies in these areas are not possible without the knowledge of English. Good books in all these subjects are available in English only. But Indian languages have not been developed enough to meet the demands of the difficult subjects. If we decide to give up English altogether, we would cut ourselves off from the living stream of ever growing knowledge.

Role in Trade, Industry and Commerce : English plays an important role in the industrial and commercial life of the country. All correspondence is done mainly in English. National and international trade, development of industry and the working in commercial establishments take place in English. Efficiency and success in these fields depends upon an adequate knowledge of English. Their maintenance of accounts, issuing of instructions and correspondence with others are mainly conducted through English medium.

International Status : As English is spoken and understood all over the globe, so it has got international importance. It is the first language in U.K., U.S.A., Canada and Australia and the second language in India, Africa, Russia, France, Pakistan etc. The number of people speaking this language is about 350 million which is next to the Chinese language. Thus it is English and other language which can serve the purpose of linking together people of different nations of the world. Chinese language is confined to that country only whereas English is popular with people living in different countries of the world. Naturally its popularity on the basis of its utility all over the globe determines its strength. It is English language which can bring greater and greater number of people in closer contacts with one another. It helps every nation to study the culture and civilization of the other nation. It is through English that we can establish political, cultural, intellectual and economic relations with the rest of the world.

F.G. French in his book, 'Teaching English as an International Language' says : "By accidents of history and by the rapid spread of industrial development, science and technology, international trade, and by something like an explosion in the speed and ease of travel and by all factors which have broken down frontiers and forced nations into closer interdependence, English has become a world language. It is the means of international communication: there is no other."

So English language is indispensable for us. Even Mahatma Gandhi had to say, "English is a language of international commerce; it is the language of diplomacy and it contains many a rich literary treasure ; it gives us an introduction to western thought and culture."

The following points indicate very clearly the international importance of English language :

- (i) It helps in international trade and industry.
- (ii) It leads to better understanding between the different nations of the world.
- (iii) The latest and up-to-date information in the field of science and technology is available in English only.
- (iv) A person knowing English stands opportunities of employment almost in every country.
- (v) It helps in bringing people of different nations in closer contacts.

Cultural Values : English helps in bringing people of diverse cultures closer to each other. It also assists us for our inter-cultural understanding inside the country. It is through the medium of English that we are able to keep the different cultural groups of India united. In fact, English has helped us in building new cultural traditions. It has also resulted in the process of modernisation of Indian society.

The study of English cuture has dispelled ignorance and superstitions from the minds of the Indian people. English language has imported the wealth of the Indian people. English language has imported the wealth of knowledge and experiences in India. To abolish it will be to shut the doors of the western culture and civilization for Indian students. Thus from the cultural point of view English has great importance. It has become the next powerful vehicle of our thought and activity. It is, undoubtedly, a language of modern scientific culture.

Window on the World : The study of English by Indians serves the purpose of a window. Just as we can peep through the window and see what is happening all around us. In the same way, by the study of English we can come to know the progress being made by the people of different nations oil the world in the different areas of life. F.G. French rightly observed. "A traveller who can speak English will find some body who can understand him wherever he may go: anyone who can read English can keep in touch with the whole world without leaving his own house."

In fact, in Pt. Nehru's words "Our major window on the modern world" regarding English language are quite apt. Radhakrishnan's University Education Commission remarked, "It (English) is a language which is rich in literature-humanistic, scientific and technical. If under sentimental urges we give up English, we would cut overselves off from the living stream of evergrowing knowledge. Unable to have access to this knowledge, our standards of scholarship would fast deteriorate and our participation in the world movements of thought would become negligible. Its effects would be disastrous for our political life, for living nations must move with the items and must respond quickly to the challenges to their surroundings. English is the only means of preventing our isolation from the world and will act unwisely if we allow ourselves to be enveloped in the fold of a dark curtain of ignorance. Our students who are undergoing training at schools, which will admit them, either to university or to vocation must acquire sufficient mastery of English to give them access to the treasures of knowledge and in the universities no student should be allowed to take a degree who does not acquire the ability to read with facility and understaning works of English authors."

Thus we find that English informs us about the advancement or progress having taken place or taking place throughout the world. It may be the field of science, technology, machine or it may be any human activity we come to know about it through this language. It is a highly developed language and it mirrors to us everything in the true sense. Our country cannot afford to close the window because it gives us true picture of the various facets of life-political social, religious, cultural, agricultural etc. Here the words of Mr. Nehru, our late Prime Minister are worth quoting. He said, "All regional languages must be developed and promoted. But that did not mean that English should be discarded. To do that will amount to closing a window on the world of technology. Foreign languages served as window in the world of technology. Foreign languages served as window on it and to suppose that translation could take their place was a mistake. It was no use getting into an intellectual prison after achieving political independence.

Role in our Social Life : English is playing an equally important role in the social life of Indian People. Majority of educated people use this language for correspondence. They find it more convenient to converse in English. It is the means of social and intellectual communication in the highly educated sections of society. In marriage parties or at the time of some social ceremony, the invitation cards are mostly printed in English. In our daily conversation we use a large number of English words. It has become such a habit with us that in our speech we use English words and find dearth of words of our own languages.

English at the Administrative Level : English has been the official language in our country, for more than 150 years. Even now, this language has almost the same position in the offices of the country. No doubt, some states have made strong efforts for developing their own regional languages and propagated its use in the offices. But the hard fact is that in majority cases, they have not been able to replace English. Almost at every level of administration we find that English alone is being used. In the District courts, High Courts and the Supreme Court, cases are presented in English. So it remains a proved fact that English dominates in our country at the different levels of administration.

Already Known to Indians : In this age of competitions, every one wants to excel the other. Some people are interested in learning more languages. The need to learn some foreign language is there. Now the question arises which foreign language should be learnt. English is a language already prevalent in our country since long. We have people who can teach this language and also we have English literature produced by our own country men. So instead of thinking about some other language, it would be better if we learn this very language, We have a suitable climate for it already created in our country. Regarding English language Pt. Nehru once said, "We know it a good deal and we have people who can teach it."

Knowledge of English-a successful Passport for Employment: The knowledge of English provides a privileged position to a person. People with good knowledge of English are given preference for selection to good posts. The prospects of employment for a person knowing English are bright anywhere whether India or abroad. S.K. Chatterji rightly says. .'It (English) is, therefore, pre-eminently the language which opens to us prospects of employment at home and abroad and offers means of cultural communication with other parts of the world. Knowledge of English is an asset with any person post."

A person with knowledge of English stands good chances of employment anywhere and everywhere in the world. F.G. French rightly says in this connection- "English is rapidly becoming a world language. It is the mother tongue of more than two hundred million people; and, in addition, it is spoken and read by many millions of Europeans, Africans, Chinese, Indians, Japanese and South Americans as a second language."

The Radhakrishnan Commission emphasized; English is the means of preventing our isolation from the world and we will act unwisely if we allow ourselves to be enveloped in the folds of a dark curtain of ignorance. A sense of oneness of the world is in the making and control over a medium of expression which is more widespread and has a large reach than any of our languages to-day will be of immense benefit to us."

Thus we find that English plays quite an important role in our national life. Almost from every angle, it is significant for us. In the past, it enjoyed a privileged position in our country. Now also its position is in no way less as compared to other languages. Inspite of the bare fact that mother tongue as medium of instruction almost at all levels of learning has been accepted at Govt. level but the hard fact means that more and more English medium schools are coming up and greater and greater number of people are becoming interested in those English medium schools. All this speaks clearly about the dominating position of English language in our country On this basis, we can calculatively fore see that the future of English in our country will be as bright as ever.

A Library Language

Whatever has been said in *Kothari Education Commission Report* regarding the place of English is perfectly true because they have taken into consideration its present position in the country. The point is that at present everybody is talking against this language. The conditions prevailing in the schools are not favourable. The politicians, the parents and the public in general are saying rot about this language. Their inner desire is to uproot this language from the country. Many teachers are seen finding faults with the students. Sometimes they say that it is next to impossible to show good results in English. The authorities have also expressed the view that it would be difficult to progress without the knowledge of English. So Kothari Education Commission has suggested that English should be made a library language in our country That way our scholars who are doing advanced studies in the field of Science, Medicine, Engineering etc. will be able to consult library books. Advanced knowledge and excellent literature of the world be in the books which are in English medium. Indian readers must have at least as much knowledge of English as is required to understand the books lying in the library. Without the study of English books, there can be every possibility of duplication in labour. Only the study of English books reveals the degree of advancement that has taken place so far in the world. Our scholars by the study of those books, can acquaint themselves fully with the subject matter and they may think of going ahead in that direction or a new era of researches may be found out by them.

Thus Kothari Education Commission has said that it is rather advisable to make it a library language. In fact, making English a library language in the country will be nothing short of accepting defeat in the teaching-learning of this language.

By library language, we mean that the carriers must study that much English which should help them to understand the subject matter contained in library books. They may not become fluent speakers of the language. They may not even acquire the ability of writing nicely in correct English. But they must learn English which should ensure them comprehension of the reading material. So the ultimate aim here is to teach reading. Now the question arises whether reading cart be taught without giving practice. No, it is not possible. For all purposes, we must begin with speech. Practice in listening is needed -which will help in speaking. Speech is important for learning reading of the language. The ability to recognise the written symbols comes through continuous practice and for reading out those very symbols, speech is required. So by starting writh speech, language should be learnt and the ultimate aim should be reading with comprehension. Only then a person will be able to use English as a library language.

English is, therefore, an important language and it must be studied. *Prof Gokak* has rightly observed that "it was in the English classroom that the Indian library renaissance was born." A few words from *Kothari Education Commission Report* are worth quoting," English as an important library language would play vital role in higher education. No student should be considered as qualified for a degree, in particular, a Master's degree unless he has acquired a reasonable proficiency in English."

So it is a decided fact that English is an important library language. If some people say that it is a difficult language and hence cannot be taught well in our country, it is their weakness. As a teacher of English I am of the opinion that English can be taught and it should be taught as a living language in the country. If all teachers of English determine and fight against the bad situations, there is no reason why they will not be able to succeed in this direction. The newly evolved approaches may be made use of and by applying sincere and honest efforts, the English language can be taught as it should be taught for its success and bright future in the country.

ASSIGNMENTS

1. "English has been playing, is playing and will continue to play a significant role in India's national life." Discuss.
2. "English has become one of the major languages of the

world and Indians can neglect its study at their own risk." Examine critically.

3. "English is a language of international commerce; it is the language of diplomacy and it contains many a rich treasure; it gives us an introduction to western thought and culture. " Discuss.
4. "In free India, the importance of English is more than what it used to be in British India. " Discuss.
5. "We cannot be overselves alone in this world of internationalism. In the light of the statement discuss the importance of English in India.

2

Principles of Teaching

Being complex social and cultural phenomenon, teaching is not as easy to teach as it appears. While teaching, a teacher has to keep in mind the aims and objectives of his subject, needs, interests of his pupils, the environmental situation suitable for them etc. Success of this profession depends upon good planning and mastery in the subject to be taught. Hence for helping the teacher, some principles have been designed on the basis of general experiences, traditions and researches. These principles provide guidelines to the teacher as to what methods should be adopted in the class-room to increase the teaching efficiency.

A good teacher always wants that his teaching should be effective. He wants that all the students of the class should properly attend, listen to him and try to grasp what he teaches in the class. The principles evolved help the teacher to carry on his routine of teaching efficiently. They provide him guidelines and keep him on the right track. They check him from going astray. They ensure the achievement of the teacher in the process of teaching.

General Principles

A few principles of teaching which are of general nature are explained below:

Principle of Definite Objectives. While teaching anything, the teacher should first of all fix up some objectives. Then he can select the material, use the appropriate methods and then ultimately ensure the attainment of those objectives. In the absence of definite objectives teaching may not remain purposeful activity. The learners may also deviate and may fail to achieve anything solid.

Objectives may vary from subject to subject and from time to time. Behind teaching English, the objectives usually are listening, speaking reading and writing. But at present in free India, the objective of reading for comprehension is being emphasized. So in teaching, the objectives should be fixed and then efforts be made to achieve them.

Principle of Model Presentation. The teacher who presents the material while teaching should see that his presentation is really a model one in every way. The personality of the teacher, his behaviour actions etc. should be model. The learners imitate the teacher to the maximum. So the teacher should present all excellences of life in him which he ultimately wants the learners to acquire in life. The pronunciation of the language that he uses for teaching should be reasonably good. Through his behaviour he should reflect regularity punctuality, honesty, truth, sincerity etc. Then only he will be able to make his learners reach the goals of ideal life. That way only his teaching will come out to be worthwhile and profit yielding for the humanity.

Principle of Selection of Material. In teaching whatever material is to be presented by the teacher should be well selected. It should be in accordance with the aims and objectives of teaching. It should also be according to the likings and the mental level of the learners. Then only it will be digested by the students properly. The right selection of material will result into proper teaching and hence desired results.

Suppose the teacher wants to teach composition. For this he selects topics keeping the syllabus in view the mental level of the learners, their teachability, their learnability etc. This type of material will make the teaching efficient.

Principle of Gradation. The material which is selected should be graded properly. By gradation we mean which item will come at serial No. 1, which item after that end which item at the end. While grading the material, easy and simple things will come first and difficult and complicated things will occur afterwards. Thus placement of material in graded form will make teaching-learning process more effective.

Suppose the teacher has selected 10 essays of English for teaching some class. By gradation these essays will be numbered as I 2, 3 etc. which means that essay No. I will be taught first and essay No, 2 will come afterwards.

Principle of Activity. The traditional methods of filling up the minds of the children with a lot of information are useless now. The learners sitting passive in the class are not considered good students. Teaching-learning is a bipolar process. Both the teacher and the students should remain active. The more the activity of the children, the better is the teaching-learning process.

Every subject every-topic within a subject can be taught through activity method. An intelligent teacher tries to involve the maximum number of students in his teaching. That makes guaranteed learning by the students. Moreover, the students do not feel any type of lethargy or boredom.

Principle of Correlation. Good teaching makes the students feel everything for better life. The learner in the class-room feels as if he is being prepared for better life. A good teacher tries to correlate his teaching with life. He also tries to correlate one subject with various other subjects which the student is expected to study.

According to *John Dewey* "Education and life are two different names for the same phenomenon. Education which does not prepare the student for life is meaningless. Suppose the teacher is teaching arithmetic to the students, he should enable the students to apply that knowledge in his day to day life situations. While making purchases in the market the student can apply the knowledge of mathematics and thus he feels happy and satisfied. The teacher of English should also teach English in such a way so that the student feels that he is becoming a better social being by the study of this subject. He should be enabled to speak English with his parents, relatives, teachers or friends. He should also be able to listen to TV Programmes telecast in English. It will give him a lot of confidence.

While teaching one subject the teacher should try to correlate that subject with some other subject which the student studies. It will make his whole studies interesting for him. The child may also get the sort of feeling that the different subjects are preparing him for better life.

Principle of Child Centredness. Teaching should be made child centred as far as possible and it should not be allowed to remain teacher centred as it has been so far. By child centredness we mean interest and liking of the student should be given priority while teaching. No subject matter should be made meaningful for the child. It should be taught to the child as per his liking and in no case it should be thrust upon him. Thus the child who is not interested in studies should not be compelled to study. He should first of all be mentally prepared for studies. Then only any teaching done for him will be of any use.

Suppose the child wants to study English. In that case teacher should teach him that subject and not some other subject which the teacher wants to teach. An intelligent teacher is able to deal with this type of situations very wisely. In the above situation, he initiates teaching English to the child as per his desire but gradually he makes the child shift to the other subject which the teacher wants to teach.

Principle of Co-operation. Teaching-learning is a co-operative venture of all concerned. For the best teaching, the teacher, the students, the Head of the institution, the parents and everyone else concerned with it co-operates. Then only there is efficient teaching and good learning by the students. Sometimes the Head of the school does not cooperate with the teachers, the result is poor teaching. Thus, co-operation of the teacher, the taught and the Head of the Institution forms the basis of efficient teaching-learning.

Principle of Planning. The principle of planning is the *sine qua non* of efficient teaching. The teacher comes prepared with everything planned before entering into the class. He tries to foresee the problems and he thinks of their possible solutions. Thus the principle of planning helps him to perform his duty of teaching excellently. A good teacher keeps his planning flexible throughout. He may mould things here or there according to the need and requirements of the learners in different situations.

Principle of Individual Differences. In any group of students, no two individuals are exactly the same. There are always variations as far as likings and dislikings, attitudes and aptitudes are concerned. The teacher teaching the whole group by using one and the same method and dealing with everyone in the same way will fail miserably. A good teacher expects the individual differences among the students. He tries to deal with the students according to their individual differences. He tries to satisfy one and all by using different tactics and strategies of teaching.

Implications

General principles of teaching affect the teacher and the learner in many ways which are briefly explained below:

(a) In every teaching-learning activity, aims are fixed up. A good teacher always keeps these aims in view while teaching. Thus the teacher remains on the right track and he works meaningfully. Both the teacher and the taught are able to make right efforts for the attainment of goals already fixed up.

(b) The teacher tries to present the subject matter to the learners in the best possible way. He tries to put up his best before the learners so that they also come out very good as a result thereof.

(c) A good teacher selects the material very carefully and then only he presents it before the learners. Surely he keeps in mind certain principles for the selection of material. In this way, the subject matter does not pose any problem to the learners. The teacher is able to handle the selected material, well while teaching. The students are also able to understand the subject matter fully.

(d) Gradation of material helps a lot in the process of teaching-learning. So the teacher grades the material after its selection and then only he presents it in the class-room. This makes the teaching-learning process successful.

(e) The teacher keeps in mind the principle of variety. He tries to bring in variety in a number of ways so that no student finds teaching-learning a drudgery or boredom.

(f) The teacher tries to correlate the subject matter with the different life-situations of the students. Many a time, the teacher correlates the topic with other subjects being taught to the students. It helps the teacher to teach the subject matter effectively and the learners are also able to learn it well.

(g) The teacher tries to make his teaching child-centred. He sees everything from learner's point of view. Thus the students find it useful for them and they do not feel any type of imposition on them.

(h) The teacher co-operates with the students during the process of teaching-learning. Then naturally all students co-operate fully with the teacher. This creates healthy environment and makes teaching-learning more effective.

(i) The teacher always plans the lesson before teaching. Naturally, thus his teaching will be systematic and will be liked by all concerned with it. Systematic teaching helps in better learning by the students.

(j) When the teacher knows that no two students are of the same type in liking, interest, attitude etc., he tries to teach in such a way that majority of them are benefitted. He becomes interested in programmed learning. Thus there is better teaching-learning so as to benefit every one.

Psychological Principles

A psychological principle is one in which teaching is made effective by taking into account the psychology of the child. These principles are framed by keeping in mind the abilities, aptitudes, capacities and potentialities of the learners. They are formulated from the students point of view only. They would always create interest in the child for learning. The desire to learn not only makes his learning more effective and easier but it also helps him to retain the subject matter in mind for a longer time. These principles include every psychological method which will help to improve the learning of the child. For example, principle of feedback and reinforcement is based on the laws of learning where reinforcement has always been given a lot of importance for learning. Further psychology has told that in a group a child will always learn better, thus the principle of utilizing group dynamics has been framed. Similarly, Psychology has always laid emphasis on rest and recreation and on it also a principle has been formulated.

The Difference

1. General principles are followed by the teachers to make teaching-learning process effective whereas the Psychological Principles take the help of motivation of the students.
2. General Principles cover a wide range as compared to the Psychological principles which work within limited range.

Further Explanation

A few Psychological principles of teaching are explained here below:

Principle of Motivation. Teaching is a tripolar process which involves the interaction of the teacher, the taught and the subject matter. For this, co-operation between the teacher and the taught is a must. Now the concept of teaching-learning has changed. It is no longer a process of teaching only. The emphasis has now shifted from the teacher to the learner. The important thing is to see whether the learner co-operates, whether his interest is there. The teacher's job is to motivate the learner by creating different situations of his interest. Motivation, therefore, is of supreme importance. How to motivate the learners is the pertinent issue.

The children are interested in their surroundings. The teacher should, therefore, provide to them that type of material. Some problems linked with their life situations may be put forth. The learners will try to be inside that problem and make all efforts to find out its proper solution.

The students should, therefore, be motivated towards the topic. The teacher has to teach. It is motivation which will make them interested in the topic and they actively participate in the class. Better learning on the part of students will be there if they are motivated towards that topic. Environment of the class can be changed to break the monotony of the class. Aids can be used for the smaller children and for the matured students. Previous knowledge testing can be a potent motivation. For example, while teaching English grammar, the teacher should first explain the importance and need of learning English in present day world-how English can help them choose a better career and how it can be helpful for securing a good job. In this way, the students will be motivated to learn English well. Undoubtedly, motivation and interest are the two central factors in any process of teaching and learning.

Principle of Repetition and Exercise. The teacher should repeat several times what he teaches in the class so that the learners are able to grasp and understand the subject matter well. It also helps them to retain it in their minds for a longer time. Exercises for further practice may also be given as class work or as home assignment. It was Thorndike who put experimental evidences in favour of utility of repetition and exercise in the learning process.

Practice makes a man perfect. The students will fully grasp a thing when they are in a position to do it themselves. It needs a lot of practice on the part of the students. The teacher who makes use of exercises like revision, recapitulation, application of what has been taught to the students etc. can teach the students efficiently.

While teaching Geometry, the teacher asks the students to draw various triangles (isosceles, equilateral and right angled). He then asks them to measure the angles of those triangles and find out the sum of all the three angles of a triangle. It will obviously be equal to 180' in all the three cases. He will then repeat by giving some more examples of other triangles with different angles. Then the teacher may give more questions of similar type as home work.

Principle of Feedback and Reinforcement. During teaching the teacher should try to give positive reinforcement to the students. Some sort of feedback helps the students to learn things better. The knowledge of results should also be given to the learners side by side and as quickly as possible. Thus a weak student is able to know his drawbacks and then he can re-learn things and prepare himself again for further studies. By giving immediate results to the students, the teacher can also judge about his own teaching. Accordingly he can improve his teaching. During teaching, the teacher should try to encourage students as far as possible. It helps in developing a congenial environment.

Suppose the teacher during teaching has put a question to the class and no student is coming forward to give the response. The teacher should encourage the students and make them think and give the answer. The teacher in no case should discourage the child even if the answer is totally wrong. He should never say that the class is dull or the students are hopeless cases. He should show leadership in class and try to imbibe the qualities of leadership in the students.

Principle of Variety. The principle of variety is the foundation for better teaching-learning process. The teacher should try to bring variety in the class-room teaching. He should not use the same method of teaching always. For teaching, different methods at different times may be used. Suppose the teacher wants to correct the note-books of the students he can use different methods of correction work at different times.

Principle of Rest and Recreation. Fatigue decreases the speed of learning. There is need of giving rest after some interval of time. Study followed by rest and recreation refreshes the mind and prepares the learners for more studies. So the teacher should see that during teaching there should be provision for rest and recreation. Off and on some recreation activities may be organised in the class. That way class-room boredom will be ended.

Principle of Readiness. If a person is not ready to learn anything then teaching whatever it may be, cannot take place effectively. Readiness on the part of the learner is essential. As soon as the teacher enters into the class he should try to judge the readiness of the students. In case they are not ready then it is the duty of the teacher to make them ready. If the teacher takes care of this principle, then only his teaching comes out to be effiective.

Principle of Fostering Creativity. During teaching the teacher should foster creativity among the students. He should always discourage cramming or reproduction of the material by them. In the class-room situations there are some students who cram the material, reproduce it and try to win the applause of the teachers. The teacher should be able to judge about this type of students. There are some other students who are of creative type. He should encourage them to the maximum. In fact, the best teaching is one which always fosters the creativity among the carriers.

Principle of Sympathy and Co-operation. During teaching the teacher should possess sympathetic attitude and a co-operative bent of mind. Usually the students are afraid of the teacher. A good teacher is affectionate and tries to understand every student. He shows fatherly affections and motherly co-operation to his students. Whatever may be the situation, a good teacher remains sympathetic and affectionate.

Principle of Self-learning. A good teacher encourages the self-efforts made by the students for learning anything. He teaches in such a way so that the learners acquire the habit of self-learning. The teacher no longer believes in spoon feeding while teaching. He may start with lecture method but gradually he takes the students to self-learning situations. He remains there in the background helping and guiding them wherever they need some help or guidance.

Principle of Group-dynamics. The teacher should understand group-dynamics. He should try to inculcate among the learners a suitable type of group-behaviour. For this purpose he does his job of teaching in such a way so that he succeeds in making his students well behaved in every type of situation-may be as individual or in a group.

The children learn better in a group. They are also able to develop qualities of tolerance, co-operation, sacrifice etc. The teacher should therefore, encourage group learning.

The Implications

All the psychological principles effect the teaching-learning process considerably. A good teaching always keeps those principles in mind and thus ensures good teaching-learning. Here below are given the implications of the different psychological principles.

(a) The teacher motivates the students in the class and that makes everybody interested in the process of teaching-learning. Through motivation, the teacher becomes a source of joy for the learners. When the carriers are interested in the teacher, then they also like his activity of teaching.

(b) A good teacher is not always busy- in just finishing the prescribed course of study. He repeats matter and also gives sufficient practice so that it is fully understood by them.

(c) Feedback and reinforcement are very important in the process of teaching-learning. If a test is held, the teacher should tell the students about their results as early as possible. Immediate feedback helps them to learn more.

(d) The teacher should keep in mind the principle of variety. A good teacher uses different methods of teaching and that keeps the students fully interested in the process of teaching-learning.

(e) The principle of rest and recreation changes the attitude of the teacher. So a teacher while teaching takes care of the fact that the students have some rest in between. He also recreates them. All this helps the teacher to teach better and the learner is also able to learn more.

(f) A good teacher prepares the students first for his teaching and then only he starts teaching. This is bound to improve teaching-learning.

(g) Creative teaching is good. The teacher should teach in such a way as the learners become creative.

(h) A sympathetic type of teacher is able to win the hearts of the learners. The teacher should always be co-operative with the students. Let co-operation flow from the teacher first. That will make the whole teaching-learning quite effective.

(i) The teacher should not give spoon feeding to the learners. He should arouse their interest and develop in them love for self-learning. This practice reduces the load of work of the teacher. The student is also able to learn really.

(j) While teaching a group, the teacher should keep in mind the group behaviour of learners. Then only he will be able to teach well.

Principles of teaching are, undoubtedly effective tools in the hands of a teacher. Only a good teacher is able to put them to right use. The saying a bad workman quarrels with his tools is perfectly true. The different principles of teaching can work wonders in the hands of a good teacher. The teachers under training are, therefore. advised to keep the principles of teaching in mind while teaching. It is bound to make them better and better teachers in due course of time.

The Maxims

The Oxford Dictionary defines Maxim as a general truth drawn from science of experience. Over the years various educationists have given numerous rules of conduct for teaching which may be called maxims. These maxims are the true facts found out by the teacher on the basis of experience. They are of universal significance and are trustworthy. Every teacher is expected to familiarise himself with the time honoured maxims of teaching. The knowledge of different maxims help the teacher to proceed systematically. It also smoothens his way of teaching especially at the early stages of teaching.

The different maxims of teaching are briefly explained below. The teacher should always proceed keeping them in view:

Known to Unknown. This maxim is based on the assumption that the student knows something. We are to increase his knowledge and widen his outlook. We have to interpret all new knowledge in terms of old. It is said that old knowledge serves as a hook on which the new one can be hung. Known is trustworthy and unknown cannot be trusted. So while teaching we should proceed from known and go towards unknown. For example, while teaching any lesson, the teacher can link the previous experiences of the child with the new lesson that is to be taught.

Suppose the teacher is teaching English to the children and he is to teach the word 'book.' He reminds them the Hindi word '*Pustak*' which they already know and then he tells them that in English we say 'book'. This way of teaching helps the learners to understand things fully.

Simple to Complex. Class-room teaching is formal where the teacher tries to teach and the students try to learn things. In this process of teaching-learning, the teacher should see that simple things are presented first to the students- That way they will start taking interest. Once they become interested, then gradually complex type of things can also be learnt by them. By learning simple things, they feel encouraged and the also gain confidence. On that basis, they become further receptive to the complex matter. On the other hand, if complex type of things are presented to the learner first he becomes upset, feels bored and finds himself in a challenging situation for which he is not yet ready being immature and unripe.

Simplicity or complexity of the subject matter should be determined according to the viewpoint of the learners. Gradually more difficult items of learning may be presented to the students. It will smoothen teaching being done by the teacher and make learning convenient and interesting for the students.

For example, while teaching sentences of English simple sentences should be taught first and complex type of sentences may be taken afterwards.

Concrete to Abstract. Concrete things are solid things and they can be visualised. But abstract things are only imaginative things. So it is rather difficult to teach the children about abstract things. The students are likely to forget them soon. On the other hand, if we teach the students with the help of concrete objects, they will never forget the subject matter. *Froebel* said, "Our lesson ought to start in the concrete and end in the abstract."

For example, when we teach counting to the students we should first take the help of concrete objects like, beads, stones etc. and then proceed to digits and numbers. The stars, the moon, the sun etc. being concrete should be taught first whereas the abstract things like plants, satellites etc. should be taught afterwards.

Analysis to Synthesis. Analysis means breaking a problem into its convenient parts while synthesis means grouping of these separated parts into one complete whole. A complex problem can be made simple and easy by dividing into units.

"Analysis is the approach for understanding and synthesis is for fixation." Analysis of a sentence is taught to the students, that helps the students to understand the different parts of a sentence. Later on, synthesis of sentences should be taught.

Particular to General. While teaching, the teacher should first of all take particular statements and then on the basis of those particular cases, generalisation should be made. Suppose the teacher is teaching present continuous tense while teaching a English, he should first of all give a few examples and then on the basis of those make them generalize that this tense is used to denote an action that is going on at the time of speaking.

Empirical to Rational. Empirical knowledge is based on observation and first hand experience. It is particular, concrete and simple. We can see, feel and experience it. On the other hand, rational is based on our arguments and explanation. The stage of arguments is the last whereas seeing things or feeling them is the first stage. Empirical is less general statements whereas rational is more general statements. So the safe approach in teaching is that we should proceed from empirical to rational. It is less mental maturity to more mental maturity.

Induction to Deduction. Induction means drawing a conclusion from a set of examples whereas deduction is its opposite. The teacher should proceed from induction to deduction. For example, in English while teaching conversion of active voice into passive voice. 'The teacher should first convert a few sentences of active into the passive voice and on the basis of those conclude the general rule for conversation of active voice into passive voice.

Psychological to Logical. While teaching, the teacher should first keep in mind the interest, aptitiudes. capacities, development level etc. of the children during selection of subject matter and then on to its logical arrangement.

In teaching English, the structures are selected as per needs and requirements of the students and then arranged in a logical way. The psychological appeal of the thing is more important at the early stages. Then the logic behind it should be seen.

Actual to Representative. For teaching excellently, actual objects should be shown to the children as far as possible. It gives them concrete learning which is more desirable. The learners are able to retain it in their minds for quite a long time. Specially in the lower classes first hand information to the students impresses them a good deal. Representative things in the form of pictures, models etc. should be used for the grown ups or the seniors who are already familiar with the actual objects.

For example, the teacher should show the elephant, the camel, the horse, the railway station, the post office etc. and thereby he should make them understand about these things. The representative of these things in the form of pictures or models may be used at later stages.

Near to Afar. Every child is able to learn well in the surroundings to which he belongs. So the child should be acquainted fully with his immediate environment. Gradually he may be taught about those things which are a far from his immediate environment. This principle, if kept in view ill smoothen the teaching-learning process considerably. Thus the child should be taught the home, followed by the street, the bazar, the school and then the distant environment of the city to which he belongs. In the same way acquaintance with the city should lead to acquaintance with the Tehsil- the District, the Division, the State and then the Country as a whole. This type of teaching will be incremental and will be step by step learning. The text book writer who writes books for the small children should also place the different chapters in his book keeping in view of this principle. Then only his book will stand better chances of approval by all concerned.

Whole to Part. In teaching, the teacher should try to acquaint the child with the whole lesson first and then the different portions of it may be analysed and studied intensively This principle holds good while teaching a thing to the small children. At the early stages, the child loves to speak full sentences because in daily life situations, full sentences are used. The child should be given a full sentence. Then he may have full familiarity with the different words contained in that sentence. Later he may have the knowledge of words. Then he will have the knowledge of different letters forming the words.

Suppose a poem is to be taught to the students. They should be acquainted with the full poem first. Gradually they may be asked to grasp the poem stanza by stanza. In the case of average students, their first attempt may be on a full stanza, taking it as a whole and then to the different lines contained in the stanza as parts. It will help the teacher to teach better and the learners to learn things conveniently.

Definite to Indefinite. In teaching, definite things should be taught first because the learner can easily have faith in them. Gradually he should be given the knowledge of indefinite things. Definite things, definite rules of grammar help the learner to have good knowledge. Gradually he can be taught about indefinite things.

The above given maxims are only hints and guidelines for the teacher especially at the initial stages. He may use them if he finds some of them useful in his teaching situations. In some situations of class-room teaching, he may not use them if he feels so. The teacher should keep the maxims in his hand and he himself should remain their master. Then only the different maxims will remain tools and yield better results.

Language Learning and Teaching

Teaching learning of a language is a matter of practice. The language teacher can teach the language any way he likes. But the knowledge and application of certain principles help him to teach the same language effectively. While teaching, the teacher must keep in mind the learner, his capability and capacity to learn and above all his environment of learning. Some teachers knowingly use difficult words of English while teaching. They forget the mental ability and the grasping capacity of the learners. That type of teaching is not good. Effective teaching of a language is based on certain principles. Some of the basic principles for teaching the language effectively are explained below:

Imitation: Learning of any language is based on the principle of imitation. In fact, imitation is natural to man. From childhood, language is best learnt through imitation. It is especially true in the case of small children. Whatever they see all around them, they mutate those things in the same way. Sometimes even the wrong habits of the teacher are carried on by the small children. If a teacher has poor pronunciation, his students at the early stages of learning the language will pick up the same poor standard of pronunciation from him. The bad handwriting of the teacher may also have adverse effect on the learners. It has been seen that if some teacher is in the habit of writing with left hand, the students under his charge also acquire that habit of writing with left hand.

So the teacher who is given the charge of teaching the small children must be good through and through. He should have a model type of pronunciation. His handwriting should be very good. He must possess good habits. All this will have very good impact on the growing personalities of the small children. It is, therefore, very strongly recommended that really good teachers should be recruited for teaching the small children in the schools.

Practice and Drill: Learning of language is a habit formation process. Habits are formed through repetition. Continuous practice and drill work are needed for it. All aspects of language learning i.e. listening, speaking, reading and writing can be acquired after a lot of practice. They should learn to use the language correctly though they may not know the rules of grammar. Robert Lado says, "To know the language is to use its patterns of construction with appropriate vocabulary at normal speed for communication."

Practice makes a man perfect. Learning a language is more a matter of skill rather than of knowledge. Robert Lado rightly says, "The student must be engaged in practice most of the learning time. This principle has a psychological justification since other things being equal, the quantity and permanence of learning are in direct proportion to the amount of practice." In this regard, Fries recommended eighty four percent of time be devoted to practice and fifteen per cent time be utilized for explanation and commentary.

Thompson and Wyatt write in their book The Teaching of English in India'. "The power of expression in a language is a matter of skill rather than of merely meanings or rules." In the learning of a language the students require a lot of practice and drill work. Only then they will be able to learn it properly. Language learning or teaching is not a knowledge subject, it is rather a skill subject like swimming, dancing painting etc. So the learner will have to repeat and revise things in order to have mastery over the language. The various skills of language learning i.e. listening. speaking, reading and writing will be properly- learnt through practice and drill work. *Otto Jesperson* says, "He who gets the tip of his finger dipped in the water three times in twenty weeks will never lean, how to swim." There is need of continuous practice for acquisition of every skill.

Oral Approach: Language is more connected with ears and tongue than with eyes. So in the teaching of English, oral work should be given topmost priority. If a students is good at spoken language, he will automatically be good in reading and writing of the language. Moreover, whatever is learnt orally is remembered better. So due emphasis should be laid on this aspect of the language.

Selection and Gradation: In the teaching of a language, selection and gradation of language items are very important. Selection may be done by the teacher, in respect of grammatical items, vocabulary and structures. Selection and gradation should involve frequency, leachability, range of applicability, usefulness etc.

Selection

The selection of language items should be based on the following principles:

1. Frequency of language items-its occurrence.
2. Range of applicability i.e. in how many contexts it is applicable.

3. Coverage-a word conveying a number of meanings e.g. meals stand for dinner, breakfast etc.
4. Availability-the items which can be conveniently taught e.g. actual objects available in the class-room like table, chair, chalk etc.
5. Teachability-items which are easy from teaching point of view.
6. Learnability-items which are easy for the students to learn should be taken up first.

Gradation

Gradation means putting the language items in order of presentation. Thus simple items having more utility and better teachability will be taken care of. Gradation involves grouping and sequence. The basic principle of grading according to W.R. Lee is : "Teach first there sentences structures the use of which can be made clear by means of visible actions in the class room.

(a) Grouping
   (i) Group according to the sound e.g. pay, bat, say, sat etc. This is called phonetic grouping.
   (ii) Grouping according to words used in the same situation e.g. words connected with post office-post master, postman, dak, letters, it is called lexical grouping.
   (iii) Patterns of sentences which are similar should be taught together e.g., This is, that is my book. your book etc. called grammatical grouping should be taught together.
   (iv) Semantic grouping words that convey similar meanings are grouped together e.g. shelter, hut, house, tent etc.
   (v) Structure grouping-bow the selected items fit with each other sounds into words, words into phrases, phrases into sentences and sentences into contexts.

(b) Sequence-What comes after what.
   (i) Lexical sequence-which words follow which e.g. sit, stand, come, go.
   (ii) Grammatical Sequence-means which structure follows which.

S.V.O. For example,
I am throwing a ball.
I am throwing a ball to you.

(iii) Semantic sequence-Every word has a number of meanings. They are put in order and are taught at different occasions e.g., the word 'there'

(a) The pen is there. (Place)

(b) There are many pens. (Introduction)

Motivation or Interest: Motivation or interest is of great importance in the teaching-learning process. Language is learnt quickly if interest is created in it. So the language teacher should make use of different types of aids for this purpose. Some interesting methods like activity method, playway method can also be used. Thus the learners remain captivated and learn things very actively They are also able to retain those things in their minds for a longer time.

The general poor standard of students in English is due to the lack of interest. Many students learn English half heartedly. They consider it a neccessary evil. The teachers themselves are seen criticising English in their class rooms. How can there be good teaching-learning of English when both the teacher and the taught lack interest '? The teacher who cannot make his teaching interesting, should better quit the teaching profession. He should be able to deal with the solutions in such a way that the learners should become interested both in their teacher and the subject matter.

Natural Way of Teaching-Learning: Natural process of learning the language should be followed. Listening and speaking should precede reading and writing. The teacher should lay more emphasis on the first two aspect i.e., listening and speaking. Then the learners will automatically be good at reading and writing of the language. Some people are of the opinion that listening to some other language, unless mother tongue is fully learnt, is dangerous. But it is not true. In this regard, *Dr. Penfield* rightly says, "A child who hears three languages instead of one, early enough learns the units of all the three without added efforts and without confusion." *Jesperson* says "The very first lesson in a foreign language ought to be devoted to initiating the pupil into the world of sounds."

Language should be Learnt in Context and Situation: Language is taught so that the learners are able to make use of it in their day-to-day life situations. Different language items-say vocabulary structures etc. should be dealt with in the context of some appropriate situations so that the learner may find them very near to life. In the words of *Eugene A. Nida* "Language learning means plunging headlong into a series of completely different experiences. It means exposing oneself to situations where the use of language is required." It is, therefore, very essential that vocabulary items should be learnt in the context of a sentence or sentences and the sentences should be learnt in situations. Only then teaching-learning will be more effective and meaningful.

Adoption of Multiple Line of Approach: While teaching a foreign language, the multiple line of approach should be followed as it helps the learners and the teacher in many ways. Suppose a class is to be taught an essay on 'Diwali'. First of all, there should be oral work and after that the students may be asked to write a few sentences on that topic in their note books. Spelling practice is given out of the same topic. While doing translation, sentences on the topic 'Diwali' be given. Thus our approach to language would be many sided. By correlating the different aspects of the language, we can certainly make the learning of language easy, interesting and useful.

Balanced Approach: While teaching the language. the teacher should see that the different aspects of it are fully taken care of listening, speaking, reading and writing should be equally emphasized. Each aspect has its own importance. It is not proper if a teacher -teaches grammar and ignores other things. In the same way, emphasis on written work alone does not help much. In this regard *Palmer* says, "The principle of proportion does not necessarily imply quality of treatment nor even a fixed standard of ratio ; it simply means that all items in the whole range of subjects and aspects must receive an appropriate degree of attention so that the student's knowledge of them may ultimately form a harmonious whole."

There should be proper co-ordination in teaching different aspects of the foreign language. Thus in teaching a prose lesson, grammar aspect may be discussed side by side. While doing written composition, oral aspect should also be covered. Thus a sort of balance between the different aspects of language should be maintained.

Swami Vivekananda says, "Arise, awake and stop not till the goal is achieved." A good teacher is ever in search of new principles of teaching. He is always keen to make use of them in his teaching. Thus his aim is to make his teaching better and better. He works for the satisfaction of his inner wish of having excellence in teaching.

He, therefore, finds inspiration in every type of situation and then he works with full zeal and vigour and thus ensures better outcomes of his teaching. He works for excellence oriented education and having applied the different principles, he is able to have quality based education.

ASSIGNMENTS

1. Discuss the main principles of teaching English. How do they affect the language teacher?
2. Discuss briefly the general principles of teaching and learning English.
3. Discuss briefly the various principles of teaching and learning English. Of what practical use are they to a class room teacher'?
4. State the general principles of teaching a language. How are those useful in teaching of English?
5. Enumerate the broad principles of teaching a foreign language.
6. What is the importance of oral approach in teaching English?
7. How will you apply 'Multiple Line of Approach' in teaching English? Explain briefly.
8. Explain briefly what do you mean by Selection of language materials?

3

Different Methods

In the process of learning and teaching, a method of teaching is very important. The teacher with a good method of teaching is liked by the students. A good method of teaching results into good learning. A good teacher is always in search of an effective method of teaching. A method tells the teacher how the matter should be taught. It is a tool in the hands of a teacher. A method is a servant and not master. A good teacher tries to take out best out of it. Selection of the right method ensures success of the teacher. It helps in the achievement of goals.

Let us first of all know what is a method? In a method, the word 'how' is important. Thus in a method we come to know how should something be presented. According to *W.F. Mackey*, "A method determines what and how much is taught (Selection), the order in which it is taught (Gradation), how the meaning and form are conveyed (Presentation) and what is done to make the use of the language unconscious. Thus we find that a method deals with form of things that is selection, gradation, presentation and repetition."

If we go back to the old days, we find that nobody was so particular about the method of teaching. But this does not mean that at that time no method was being used. They followed certain methods surely. But a method has become a problem in this age of scientific approach. The questions, what should be taught and how it should be taught, are intimately connected. "Methods are meant for us and not we for the methods. The methods are to serve us in our teaching process and hence to be our servants and not our master."

Translation Method

The Translation Method is better known as the Grammar-Translation Method. It is also called the classical method of teaching English. In the teaching of English as foreign language, it has enjoyed a great reputation in the past. At present also, many teachers prefer to teach English by this method. It the past Greek, Latin, French, German etc. were taught by this method.

Translation method means teaching the target language by translating it into mother tongue-may be Hindi or Punjabi. Here each phrase or sentence of English is taught by translating it into mother tongue. The philosophy behind this method is that the foreign language can be best taught or learn through translation. The learners, however, have to make use of set rules and principles of grammar.

The Principles

The Grammar Translation method is based on the following principles:

(a) Teaching of a foreign language through translation is easy, quick and economical.

(b) The structural patterns of the two languages are compared and this comparison makes learning more clear and firm.

(c) The fundamental principle of proceeding from known to unknown is followed throughout.

(d) The knowledge of rules helps the learners to avoid any type of mistakes.

The Advantages

The grammar translation method has a number of advantages which are given below:

(1) This method is very successful in the present day class-rooms, where there are a large number of students in each section.

(2) By telling the meaning of a word or sentence in mother tongue, the teacher can at once make the students understand. Thus it is less time consuming.

(3) It is very reliable for giving the students practice of reading with understanding.

(4) In this method, the teacher as well as the learners are able to facilitate the teaching-learning process.

(5) Teaching English by using this method does not require lot of labour on the part of the teacher. Thus many teachers who are not habitual of working hard feel happy.

(6) By using this method, the comprehension of the students can be tested very easily.

(7) The learners are able to learn many items of English by comparison with mother tongue. That makes learning more clear and firm.

The Disadvantages

1. This method ignores the practice of oral work to the students which is the most important aspect in the teaching of any language.
2. In this method, reading comes first and speaking afterwards. That is very unnatural,
3. This method wastes a lot of time of student because everything has to be translated compulsorily.
4. The translation work is always approximate. So the learner is not able to learn things accurately.
5. Through translation work, the real spirit of meanings contained in the sentence is missed.
6. It does not provide opportunity for silent reading.
7. It lays more emphasis on rules of grammar which is not very sound in teaching-learning of a language.
8. This method makes the students think in mother tongue and then translate the same into English. In many cases, it may lead to funny expressions for example:- The road began to walk.
9. It is a dull and mechanical method because the learner remains passive mostly.
10. It does not help the students to learn correct pronunciation of English.
11. The learners can remain absent minded while being taught by this method. Many a time they just try to show their teacher that they are listening to him.
12. This method does not help the students to learn the language.

Thus we find that the grammar translation method has a few merits and more draw-backs. But even then we find that it has gained universal popularity. It is being used by a large number of teachers. One of the reasons of deteriorating standards of English is the use of this type of method. The best thing would be not to use translation method as such in the class rooms. It may be used only when the class-room situation demands it.

Direct Method

Direct Method of teaching English means teaching English directly through English medium. In this method, mother tongue is not used at all. This method came as a reaction against the translation method. It is also called the natural method of teaching. No doubt, large number of teachers are in favour of translation method but even then, there are many others who like to follow the direct method. The main philosophy behind this method is that the learner learns a foreign language in the same way as he learns his mother tongue.

According to Webster's New International Dictionary, "Direct method is a method of teaching a foreign language, especially a modern language through conversation, discussion and reading, in the language itself, without the use of pupil's language, without translation and without the study of formal grammar. The words are first taught by pointing to object or picture or by performing actions." Some language experts are of the opinion that the direct method is not a method at all. *Prof Gurrey* says, "But essentially it (The Direct Method) is a principle, not a teaching method, a system that operates through many methods; a way of handling the new language and of presenting to the class. It demands direct bond, that is, a direct association, between word and thing and between sentence and idea instead of an indirect one through the mother tongue."

Basic Principles of the Method

The basic principles on which this method is based are briefly given below:

(a) ***Direct Association between Thought and Words.*** In this method, the learners think and speak by using the same medium.

(b) ***Oral Practice.*** 'A lot of oral practice is a must for even, one, is the basis of this method.

(c) ***Functional Grammar.*** In this method, stress is laid on functional grammar and not on theoretical grammar.

(d) ***Inhibition of Mother Tongue.*** This method propagates the teaching of the foreign language without using mother tongue.

(e) ***Sentence as the Unit of Speech.*** Here the unit of speech is a sentence and not a -word. Emphasis is laid on speaking full sentences.

(f) ***Limited Vocabulary.*** This method favours the presentation of limited vocabulary, based on needs and experiments of the learners.

The Advantages

The following are the advantages of this method:

1. This method lays more emphasis on oral work. That ensures good pronunciation to the learners.
2. For teaching the idioms of English, this method is more suitable.
3. There is direct bond between thought and expression. So it helps the learner to have fluency in speech. It helps the students to have good command over the language.
4. Psychologically, this method is very sound because the teacher proceeds from particular to general and from concrete to abstract.
5. It makes the teaching of English easy and pleasant.
6. It helps the teacher and the learner to cover up more syllabus in less time.

The Disadvantages

(1) There is need of really competent teachers for teaching English by using this method. But we have dearth of such teachers. Sometimes the teacher fails to make the students understand the meaning of a particular word because the use of mother tongue is not allowed.

(2) In this method, there is over emphasis on oral work. Reading and writing process of the language get less attention.

(3) This method, cannot be used successfully for the average and the below average students.

(4) It is an expensive method because the teacher has to use some aids for teaching.

(5) This method does not lay emphasis on the selection and gradation of language material which is very important.

(6) At the early stages, sometimes this method may fail miserably.

The students may not be able to learn anything.

Thus we find that the direct method of teaching has some shortcomings, but its merits cannot be ignored. On the whole, it is considered to be a good method for teaching English. The best thing for the teachers would be to modify it according to the needs and requirements of the learners.

Bilingual Method

Bilingual method means a method where two languages i.e., the mother tongue and target language are used. Here the mother tongue is used to achieve the target language. This method is based on the similarities and differences which exist between the two languages. The similarities and differences may be of situation, sounds, vocabulary, structure etc. If these differences or common things are known well, then learning of a foreign language is facilitated considerably when the child is learning his mother tongue, he becomes familiar with the situations and picks up the language correctly. While learning the foreign language, the situations are created again in order to make the child learn the foreign language. The advocates of bilingual method believe that it is merely wastage of time as there is duplicity of, the same thing. Of course, mother tongue equivalents he told but there is no need of re-creating the situations. It is suggested that the time thus saved may be utilised for giving practice in sentence patterns.

Comparison with Translation Method

In comparison with translation method, the bilingual method stands unique because in this case, we have some modification of translation method. In this method, mother tongue is used by the teacher only, and that too for explaining the meaning of difficult words and not by the students. Secondly, the students get a lot of practice in patterns which is not taken care of in translation method.

The Advantages

1. The teacher is able to teach English to the entire satisfaction of the learners.
2. The students are able to understand English well.
3. Judicious use of mother tongue by the teacher does not spoil the environment of teaching English. It only helps in teaching English.
4. It helps in giving proper training for different skills i.e., listening, speaking, reading and writing. Pattern practice given to the learners is essential in acquiring a skill.

5. The use of mother tongue saves a lot of time otherwise the teacher will have to make use of number of devices for giving meanings of words. Meanings and conncepts conveyed in this way are better understood by the learners.
6. It helps in developing fluency in spoken language.

The Comparison

In Indian situations, many a time the Direct Method of teaching English creates problems. Sometimes the teacher finds it difficult to make the student understand and sometimes the student fails to follow properly. Bilingual method is, that way, a very good remedy. In Direct Method, no body is allowed to use mother tongue in any situation whereas in the Bi-lingual method some freedom is there for the teacher. He/She may use mother tongue where the situation demands it. In some situation where the student has failed to follow the teacher inspite of the best efforts made by the teacher, mother tongue may be used. Thus the glaring drawbacks of the Direct Method have been put to end by the use of the Bi-lingual method. Moreover, the merits of the Direct method continue in the Bi-lingual method.

7. This method does not need special facilities or equipment. It can be successfully used anywhere and everywhere.
8. Teachers of English also love to teach by this method as it does not burden their mind with extra tabour.
9. It fully makes use of the language habits already acquired by the learners while learning their mother tongue.

The Disadvantages

(1) In Bi-lingual method, the teacher teaches English through English medium and in certain situations he starts using mother tongue. It diverges the attention of the learners.

(2) A teacher of English may not be good in both the languages. Whatever mother tongue he uses in the class while teaching English, may not be upto the mark. It may leave bad impression of the teacher on the learners.

(3) The use of mother-tongue while teaching English spoils the continuity and fluency of language.

(4) A few students in the class may be more attentive to mother tongue sound and less attentive to English sounds. Their pronunciation may become defective.

(5) While contrasting the features of the two languages, there is possibility of confusion.

(6) The bad habit of learning everything by filtering through mother tongue may be formed.

(7) This method may degenerate into pure translation method if the teacher fails to handle it properly.

Which Method is the Best? Having discussed the various methods of teaching English in India, we come to the conclusion that there is something good, something bad in each method. None of the methods is perfect in every respect. This does not mean that we shall give up the use of all these methods. We must use one method or the other but the point to be taken care of is that a teacher should use the method as long as it (method) is a slave to him and he is able to do well with it. But when the teacher becomes a slave to the method, the whole teaching work becomes a hotch-potch. So it is rather advisable that the teacher should adopt eclectic and pragmatic approach because no single approach is useful in all the situations.

The technique of teaching is important but at the same time we must say that the material is not of less importance. The success of teaching-learning depends upon the technique as well as the choice of material. The material required and the method to be used for it always depend upon a number of factors which are mentioned below:

1. The learner-his age, level of learning, capacity, interest etc.
2. The teacher-his efficiency, insight, training etc.
3. The objectives of teaching English.
4. Class in which its study is introduced.
5. Availability of different types of aids.
6. Size of the class.
7. Location of the institution.
8. Social background etc.

ASSIGNMENTS

1. The best method of teaching English is the translation method as it is governed by the maxim 'proceed from known to unknown'. Discuss this statement giving reasons. Why do you agree or disagree with?

2. How does the Bilingual Method of teaching English differ from the Grammar Translation and Direct Methods of teaching English? Elucidate with examples.
3. What do you mean by Translation Method of teaching English? Discuss its merits and demerits.
4. Compare the Translation Method with the Direct Method of teaching English highlighting their advantages and disadvantages.
5. What are the underlying principles, advantages and disadvantages of the direct method of teaching English as second language (TESL) in India?
6. "Direct method ensures fluency, Grammar-Translation method measures accuracy, but Bilingual method answers both." Discuss
7. What are the principles of 'Bilingual Method' of teaching English? How is it an improvement over the other methods of teaching English?
8. Is there any foolproof method of teaching English to Indian students? Give your comments on having an eclectic and pragmatic approach to the teaching of English in India.
9. Write notes on
   (a) Principles of Direct Method
   (b) Merits of Translation Method
   (c) The Bi-lingual Method
10. (a) Compare the merits of translation method with the merits of Direct Method.
    (b) What are the demerits of Direct Method?
11. (i) Write five sentences on the use of Direct Method.
    (ii) What are the demerits of Bi-lingual method?

4

Effective Teaching

In the school curriculum English as a subject is given great prominence by the authorities. Its study is compulsory for every one. Naturally there are good many teachers of this subject in the schools. But it is rather sad to me that there is something wrong with the teaching of English in Indian schools. *Prof V.K. Gokak* says, "The study of English in our schools is in a chaotic state today- Pupils are taught English for about six periods a week for six years. But it has been estimated that they hardly know 1500 words by the time they join a university. This means that they have hardly been able to learn English words at the rate of one word per period. They do not know how to use the commonest structures of English."

Many a Problem

Will it be right to say that there is something wrong with the teaching of English? No. The reason is that there is also something wrong with the learning of English in Indian schools. In this context, *Michael West* said "A language is not a subject which can be taught ; it is a subject, which must be learnt. " We should make efforts to check the defects. In the words of *Harold Palmer*, "What has been badly assimilated must be eliminated consciously".

If we mirror the whole situation, we are rather astonished to see the sorry state of affairs. Everybody these days is after the examinations. A student does not bother about knowledge or learning of the language. He makes all efforts to get the diploma or degree, no matter what way he is able to get it. For that he follows short-cuts to knowledge. He does not want learning rather he wants prize, money, status etc. On the other hand, the teacher is after enabling the students to pass the examination. He is always careful that his pass percentage may not go down. Thus there is no real teaching by the teachers or learning by the students in the schools.

The standards of English are fast deteriorating: What makes us feel like that? If we compare the graduate of today with the graduate of a few years back, we notice the marked difference. That graduate was much better. Shall we say that there is something wrong with the learning of English? The fact is that the standards are rather disappearing. The conditions under which English is being taught in the schools are far from satisfactory. The following point highlight the facts:

Short of Purpose

The teachers in the schools teach English and the learners learn English but none of them is fully clear about the real purpose of teaching-learning English. The different items of the syllabus are covered in the class. Every time the teachers as well as the learners consider it as a knowledge subject and not as a skill subject. They are not clear about the aims of teaching English. The teacher is like a sailor who does not know his destination and the pupil is like a rudderless vessel which may be drifted along anywhere ashore.

Incapable Teachers

Many teachers of English who are teaching the subject are not competent. Very few of them are really competent for teaching this subject. They have defective pronunciation. They have hardly a satisfactory command over English. At the time of selection thy are taken up as Social Studies master and mistresses and not as English masters or mistresses. Moreover, in the selection, no body gives any weightage to the subject. Teaching of English, studied at B. Ed-level. They are selected on the basis of their subjects studied upto B.A. level.

In this context, the *English Review Committee* appointed by U.G.C. in 1965 said, "There is a shortage of teachers. Those available have just passed the school final examination, having themselves studied English in a village school for 4 or 5 or 6 years. They have little idea of correct usage, and not at all of correct pronunciation. Their vocabulary is limited as is their reading."

With the lapse of some more time, we find that now better qualified teachers are available. But in basic qualifications, they are lacking all the more. Their knowledge of English is inadequate. *Prof V.K Gokak* in his book, 'English in India, its Present and Future' has righty said, "The foundational years for the teaching of English in school are in the hands of teachers who neither know enough

English nor are familiar with the latest and far reaching developments in the pedagogy of English."

Faulty Methods

The methods of teaching English adopted in the schools are quite defective. The translation method of teaching is used almost in all the schools. The teachers do not show any interest in acquiring knowledge about the lates methods of teaching the subject. They simply enable the students to pass the examination. For this purpose, they use any cheap method. Even all the aspects of learning a language are ignored. The teacher feels that his job is finished as soon as he has translated something of English into mother tongue. Then they encourage the students for cramming the material. In short, the composition is dictated by the teacher, the textbooks translated into mother tongue and the entire emphasis is on passing the examination through that magic wand of cramming."

Examination System

The students as well as the teachers have become examination minded. They do every thing just for the sake of examination. The paper setter, the examiner, the teacher etc. don't bother about real teaching-learning of language. The paper setter sets the question paper and only tests the crammed knowledge of the learner The teacher and the students do their work keeping the examination system in view. Things important from examination point of view are taken up. There is no examination for spoken English. So every body ignores this important aspect of learning the language. The fear of the examination remains taxing for the teachers and the students. There is hardly any learning in the real sense of the word.

Crowded Classes

Another thing that hampers learning of English is the over crowded classes. The number of students sitting in a class vary from sixty to eighty. In the case of private aided schools, the number sometimes touches ninety. In such over crowded classes, the teacher cannot pay individual attention to the learners. In such situations, the teacher cannot do full justice to his duty and work.

Poor Conditions

The physical conditions under which English is being taught are unfavourable. Sometimes there are no good seating arrangements, the room is dark and is not airy. In some cases, the rooms are separated by using bamboo screens. The noise from the neighbouring classes disturb the students. Neither the teacher nor the students are able to concentrate properly.

Short of Audio Visual Aids

For teaching English well to the students, there is need of audiovisual aids like linguaphones, tape recorder, film strips, epidiascope etc. But usually we find that these aids are not available in the schools. In the absence of these aids, the sound of English and correct pronunciation cannot be taught.

Textbooks

The prescribed textbooks of English suffer in many ways. No doubt, these textbooks have been written by CIEFL and NCERT. The same have been adopted by the school boards of different states. The textbooks have many defects in them. A number of students find themselves in troubles while reading these books. The subject teachers also find many shortcomings in them. These books in the hands of average English teachers fail to deliver the goods. The students hardly feel any attraction for the subject matter contained in the books. The subject matter is hardly related to the surrounding environment of the learners. The vocabulary, the structures also present difficulties to the learners. They are not according to the mental level of the learners. *Guy-Boas* writes, "The only persons equipped to choose these books are school masters who really know the fodder suited to their flock." But the teachers working in the fields are not given chances for writing or editing the books.

Syllabus

The prescribed syllabi of English for different school classes are not satisfactory. They are not related to the surroundings of the learners. The students are able to pass the examinations but in their real fife situations, they can hardly make use of anything learnt by them. In their schools, they learn many essays, stories, letters/applications but in real life situations, they find it hard to write a simple application. Sometimes they are able to write but their mistakes amuse others.

Correction Work

In the teaching of a language, correction work is of great importance. For teaching a foreign language like English, correction work becomes all the more important. But we find that very little attention is paid to it. The school authorities don't care for it. The teachers of English have the same number of periods as teachers of other subjects. Their load of work on account of correction work is not taken into consideration while distributing load of work. In their over busy schedule of work, the teachers are not able to do justice to their duty of correction work. All this results into deterioration in the learning of English by the students.

Supervision

Supervision of English teacher's work lies in the hands of the Head of the school. Sometimes the Head is conservative. He tries to poke his nose into the class affairs of the English teacher. He is not acquainted with the techniques of teaching English but being a boss, he interferes unnecessarily. His criticism of English teachers' work disheartens the teacher. This type of situation discourages the teacher for doing any work with more interest.

Interference by Parents

Interference by the parents in the work of the teachers hinders the progress. When the teacher makes efforts to apply the new ways of teaching English, he faces a set back due to the interference of the parents whose children are studying there. The parents may be of orthodox type. They themselves were taught in same way. If the teacher spends time on giving the learners just listening and speaking practice, the parents feel as if nothing has been taught. They judge the work on the basis of written exercises only. Under such circumstances the teacher has to change himself, his methodology and teach the way the parents like. Thus undue interference of the parents deteriorates the situations.

Lack of Research

Teaching-learning process needs continuous overhauling. The drawbacks in the teaching-learning of English may be many, but their solutions need be thought of. Who should do this? The teachers of English, the research minded scholars can do it. A good teacher does not teach the same thing in the same way year after year. He is always on the look out for introducing new things in new ways. In this fast changing age of science and technology, research on the part of the teachers is very essential. But we find that the teachers are not able to carry on any research. The lack of research deteriorates the situations.

Thus we find that the conditions under which English is being taught in the schools are not satisfactory. The different factors be checked properly. All efforts should be made to remedy the draw-backs. Only then the deteriorating situations will improve. *Ronald Mackin* has summed up the defects. "The old-fashioned type of benches and desks which restrict movement, the bad light ; the noise from neighbouring classes which may he separated from them by nothing more than a bamboo screen ; insufficient provision for their subject in the time-table, lack of aids of all kinds interference from parents or a dominating, conservative Headmaster; and finally the requirements of an examination system which places a premium on the written language and consequently seems to favour the grammar-grinder of the old school."

Mother Tongue

Learning of mother tongue takes place in a very natural way. From the birth of a child it is surrounded by an atmosphere where mother tongue is spoken Thus listening by the child goes on and after a few months some meaningful cries are uttered by it. If any error is committed by the child in speaking it is constantly corrected because there are many teachers who are helping it. For learning mother tongue, there is unlimited time and equipment. And above all, everything is learnt quite unconsciously, without straining the mind. In every case, listening and speaking are learnt at home and then the child is sent to school for learning, reading and writing of the language.

A Foreign Language

The process of learning a foreign language is the same because listening and speaking precede reading and writing. In each case, language is a habit to be got at, activity to be developed, a skill to be practised and enthusiasm to be caught.

Learning a foreign language is an artificial process. The atmosphere of listening or speaking is created for some time but that is not as natural as we have in the case of mother tongue. According to *David Abercrombie,* " The infant has little else to do, has the strongest social compulsion to learn, is continually surrounded by the language it is learning, and has no old habits likely to interfere with what it is doing. But the foreign language learner, whether school-child or adult, is at a disadvantage compared with the infant in so far as he has many other things to do, has sometimes little urge to loam, encounters the language he is learning only at intervals, and finds the native language habits in continual conflict with those needed for the new language. But he is also at an advantage compared with the infant in so far as he possesses a developed intelligence, and is also literate."

When the child learns mother tongue, his mind is a clean slate but at the time of his learning a foreign language, he has already learn his mother tongue. *Robert Paul* says, "When we learn our first language, face the universe directly and loam to clothe it with speech when we learn a second language, we tend to filter the universe through the language already known. Thus the knowledge of mother tongue helps and it also interferes in the learning of a foreign language. *Prof. Frisby* is of the opinion that, "The process of learning of all languages is almost alike." Thus the skill acquired in the learning of mother tongue helps in acquiring the skill of a foreign language.

Two Processes

Learning a language is a habit to be got at, an activiity to be developed, a skill to be practised and enthusiasm to be caught. It holds true in the learning of any language whether mother tongue or second language or some foreign language, may be English or any other. Another thing needs to be classified here. When mother tongue is learnt the whole process is very natural. While learning English, the process remains artificial whatever may be medium of the school-English or mother tongue. In case of English, the atmosphere of listening or speaking is created for sometime but that is not as natural as we have in the case of mother tongue.

Prof. Frisby put forth the opinion that "The process of learning of all the languages is almost alike. Thus the skill acquired in the learning of mother tongue helps in acquiring the skill of a foreign language. *Ryburn* says, "Any emphasis laid on the mother tongue will have a good effect on the standard of English." *P Gurrey* is of the view, "The teaching of mother tongue and the teaching of a foreign language can support and assist each other."

Interference of Mother Tongue in Learning English

(a) Since no two languages are alike, it is rather difficult to find but exact equivalents of English language in Hindi or Punjabi. If a learner is doing some translation work, it will always be approximate.

(b) The alphabets of English are 26 as compared to the alphabets of Punjabi and Hindi which are respectively 35 and 33. These alphabets are used to produce all the sounds. It confuses the mind of the learner.

(c) Punjabi and Hindi are phonetic languages- that is their spoken system and writing system are the same. But English is not a phonetic language. So the learner of English faces a number of problem while reading or writing it.

(d) A few, consonant sounds of English are not found in Punjabi or Hindi e.g. the initial sound in the words think-, then ; the sound occurring in the middle of the words, measure, treasure. Thus the sound of this type create problems for the learner.

(e) Stress, intonation and rhythm of the two languages differ widely. That also creates problems for the young learners of English.

(f) The sentence patterns of English and mother tongue (Punjabi or Hindi) are quite different. In Punjabi and Hindi, we use Subject, Object and Verb pattern but in English it is 'subject+verb+object.'
For example:
It is a table

(g) Interrogative sentences of the two languages are different. In English, the internrogative sentences start with a question word, but in Punjabi or Hindi, such a sentence starts in a simple way.

(h) In Punjabi or Hindi, an adjective undergoes a change according to the number or gender, in English it does not change.
For example
Good brother.
Good brothers.
Good sister.

(i) In Punjabi or Hindi, the verb undergoes a change according to the gender, but in English it does not change.

For example :
The boy sings.
The girl sings.

(j) The structural words of English and Punjabi/Hindi are no equivalent.
For example:
She is a good girl.
The girl is sitting in the chair.

(k) In mother tongue, the students form a habit of producing some sounds. For example, they produce sound in some way. While learning English, they come across two sounds. V, W which are different but the learners produce those sounds like mother tongue sounds.

Thus we find that the knowledge of mother tongue helps in learning the language. In many ways, it hinders the effective learning of English. The language teacher should make efforts to overcome the problems in an interesting way.

Suggestions for Improvement

The poor standards of teaching English in the schools is a problem which needs proper solution. It is high time now that some ways out to tackle this issue be thrashed out. A few suggestions in this regard are given below:

- The teacher should understand fully the different aims of teaching English. He should teach the language keeping the fundamental aims in view. All the aims i.e. listening, speaking, reading and writing are important. He should lay due emphasis on each and teach the learners really. The learners should be enabled to use the language in their day to day life situations.
- The teachers of English should be given training for the improvement of their own English. Some refresher courses should be organised for them. Attendance in those refresher course should be made compulsory for the teachers. For new recruitment of teachers posts of English teachers should be separated from teachers of social studies. Those who are good in English and have also studied teaching of English at B.Ed. level should be

selected. The teachers who have passed some courses in teaching of English from R-I.E. or CIEFL should be given preference in selection. All this will improve the situations.

- It is undoubtedly right that the teachers in the schools use faulty methods of teaching English. Through orientation programmes, they can be acquainted with the latest techniques of teaching English. They will also come to know the effectiveness of various methods in teaching English. Moreover, the teachers-may be asked to attend special training courses in pronunciation.
- The examination system should be improved keeping in view the aims of teaching English in India. Examination should discourage cramming. There should be examinations for testing the different abilities such as listening, speaking, reading and writing. Then there will be real teaching and learning of the language.
- No doubt, India is a poor country and we shall have to adjust more students in the classes. But effort should be made to decrease the number of students. For grammar and composition work, groups comprising lesser number of students may be formed. That will make correction work easier on the part of the teachers. For text book teaching, the classes may have more students.
- The physical conditions in the schools should be given special attention by the school authorities. Every school is inspected periodically by the Govt. agencies and by the supervisors. The authorities concerned should check up the deteriorating situations and make special efforts for improvement. Improvement can be possible provided right type of efforts are made for it.
- The different types of audio-visual aids should be made available in the schools. No doubt, some grants for this purpose have been sanctioned to the schools but more in this direction is needed. The school teachers should also be given training for the handling of different type of sophisticated aids. The teachers should also be

acquainted with the libraries from where tapes can be borrowed by the institution for the teaching purpose.

- Text Books which are prescribed in the schools these days have been nationalised. They have been written by CIFEL and NCERT experts. Even then, some drawbacks in the books continue to be there. The good teachers of the subject and the research workers, should be associated with the task of writing. That will improve things further.
- The curriculum of the school should be carefully planned. It should be made less burdensome and more useful for the learners. It should help the learners to learn things really. The text-books and other activities in the school fulfil the need and requirements of the children- The curriculum should be practical type.
- Correction work should be understood in its right perspectives by the school authorities. Keeping the total correction work to be done by the teacher in view, load of work should be decided. It will certainly improve the whole situation and help the teacher to teach better and in an effective way.
- As far as possible, the teachers should be encouraged to carry on research in their day to day working in the schools, Research mindedness on the part of the teachers will certainly improve things.

On the basis of suggestions given above, the critical situations in the teaching of English be checked from further deteriorations. Who is to take the initiative in this direction? Decidedly one or two persons can't do anything solid. Let everyone concerned with it shoulder the responsibility and help bringing a better environment. Only then we could be able to achieve appreciable results in the teaching of English.

ASSIGNMENTS

1. "The conditions under which English is being taught in our schools are far from satisfactory." Discuss.
2. "The teaching of English in our schools is said to be in bad shape". Suggest some practical steps to improve it.

3. a) Only good teachers can improve poor standards."
   Discuss.
   b) "Neglect of regular correction work leads to poor standards.
   Discuss briefly.
4. Explain briefly.
   i) Effect of over-crowded classes in Teaching English.
   ii) A good method of teaching English can improve the position of English in the schools.

5

Secondary Level Teaching

In the hands of a good teacher teaching of any language is a very interesting activity. An effective teacher is able to put life in the teaching -learning programme. Who is a good teacher and how can one become a good teacher are good questions. Good teachers are made through the process of teaching-learning. Such a teacher loves teaching and he is able to come out as a good teacher on the basis of his learning in different situations.

Every good teacher fixes up aims of teaching learning. Then he/she makes all efforts to achieve those goals. Such a teacher does not hesitate in rethinking, reframing or rewriting the goals. And above all, the effective teacher follows the general principles of teaching-learning the language. The different principles and aims of teaching keep the teacher on the right track. Never for a moment even does the teacher feel astrayed.

The Objectives

Are aims and objectives one and the same thing or are they different terms? Generally the students of Education use them for one and the same thing. But that is incorrect. The fact is that aims are the ultimate goals-the destination, the target but the objectives are immediate-they are the immediate concern of the teacher and the learners. Objectives surely help in achieving the aims.

Teaching at Different School Levels

There are two types of schools where English is taught to the students. First the schools where English is introduced from the beginning when the child enters the school, Secondly the schools where English is introduced in the sixth class. The objectives of teaching English differ in both types of schools at different school levels.

Teaching in the First Type of Schools

In the nursery, K.G. and First standard classes, listening and speaking of English are the most important objectives. The teacher should keep these objectives in view. Reading and writing should be given secondary importance. In reading, loud reading by the student is strongly recommended.

In second and third standards, listening, speaking and loud reading should be given top most importance. Writing should be secondary. In fifth and sixth standards, listening, speaking, reading and writing are important. All the four skills should be equally emphasized.

At the middle school and high schools levels again listening, speaking, reading and writing should be given equal importance. Of course, at high school level, silent reading by the students should be given top most importance. They should be asked to read extra books like supplementary readers. They may also be asked to read for pleasure and entertainment.

In the second type of schools where English is introduced in the sixth class, the objectives of teaching English are as under :

In the sixth class, listening, speaking and loud reading should be given primary importance and writing may be of secondary importance.

In seventh and eighth class, listening, speaking, reading and writing should be equally emphasized. At this stage, loud reading is of greater importance as compared to silent reading.

At high school level, again listening, speaking, reading and writing are important objectives. Of course, at this stage silent reading by the students should be encouraged. The learners may be asked to develop the habit of reading extra books. They may read for pleasure or for entertainment. In the schools, the students of high school stage should be made library-minded. Proper guidance by the teachers will help in achieving the goals rightly.

Thus we find that objectives of teaching English vary from level to level and from learner to learner. Surely brilliant students may be encouraged to have different objectives of studying. English as compared to the average ones. Firing up the appropriate objectives is half-way through the game. It guarantees good achievement on the part of the learners.

Aims and Objectives

Aims are very important in the teaching-learning process. For teaching any subject to the learners, aims are fixed up. Then effort are made to attain those aims. In the teaching-learning of English as a foreign language, some aims have been fixed up by the authorities. But the sad thing, at present, is that nobody bothers about those aims. Everybody is after the examination. The students feel that passing the examination is the actual aim of learning the language. The teachers also feel that their aim is to enable the students pass the examination. This is all very sad on the part of the teachers and the learners. The actual aims should be well considered and cared for. Only then something useful and satisfying can be achieved.

Regarding aims of teaching English, *Thomson* and *Wyatt* say, "It is necessary that the Indian people should not only understand English when it is spoken or written, but also that he should himself be able to speak and write it." The teacher of English should aim at linguistic aims only. According to *Palmer*, "To aim at literature is to miss the way to language. To aim at language is to pave the way to literature."

Before taking up anything—say a lesson on prose, poetry, composition etc., aims should be decided first. *Prof Gurrey* remarked: "In teaching, it is highly desirable to know exactly what one is hoping to achieve as it is in all great undertakings. If this can be clearly seen then the best way of getting to work usually becomes evident. We ought, therefore, to consider carefully what we are trying to do, when we are teaching a language." Once the destination is fixed up, then all efforts should be made to achieve the fixed aims. Plans are made, means and ways are thought of and then efforts to achieve them should be made. Ultimately assessment is made to see how far the aims have been achieved. In case, something is lacking, what and why of it are traced out. Then again efforts in the right direction are made so as to achieve the targets. According to P. Gurrey, "With careful thought, Puzzling out precisely what he wants to achieve and what are the immediate needs of his pupils, a teacher of language can soon become expert in noting the objective that he should strive for and once he is aware of the advantage, he very soon forms the habit of directing his efforts and those of his pupils on to selected objectives."

The special aims of teaching English in India are as under:

1. Every learner should understand English when it is spoken and written.
2. He should also be able to speak and write English.

The different aims of teaching English can also be written as,:

(1) Reception. (2) Expression.

Mainly the language is taught to the students so that they are able to receive it. In reception we can include listening and silent reading with comprehension. Then the teachers should be able to express themselves fully. In expression, we can include speaking, loud-reading and writing.

Reception

Listening: In the learning of a language, listening is the basis of everything. When the child learns mother tongue, listening-skill comes first. In the teaching of English as a foreign language the students should be given a lot of listening practice. For this Radio, Tape Recorder, Record player etc. can be used. The learners are helped to recognise the sounds correctly. If some body talks in English, the learner of the language must be able to listen to him correctly. The speaker may be native speaker of the language or any one else.

Practice in listening is the first and foremost principle in language learning. Without it the whole foundation of language learning will be weak and defective. So due stress must be laid on it while teaching English.

Silent Reading for Comprehension. Reception includes silent reading of the language with full understanding. The learner of the language should be able to read the subject matter of that language silently. Here reading means reading with full understanding. In reading he should have a reasonably good speed of reading.

Expression

The learner of the language should be enabled to express himself using that language. In expression we can include (a) speaking (b) loud reading (c) writing.

Speaking. Every language should be learnt as a living language. By living language, we mean the person should be able to speak well by using that language. But the sad thing about teaching English in the school is that speaking of the language is not given any importance. It is not given any weightage in the examination. So the teacher and the students do not bother about it. They don't care for producing the sounds correct,,-.

Speaking ability of the student depends considerably upon his listening ability. The learner who gets a lot of listening practice becomes good in the spoken aspect of the language. So the teachers should give due importance to spoken English. The learner should have fluency in speaking. His pronunciation should also be reasonably good.

Loud Reading. Loud reading is one mode of expression. Every learner of the language should be taught how to read the subject matter of that language loudly. In this way, his fluency of the language can be seen by others. His pronunciation also is judged by the other person.

Writing. Writing is another aim of teaching English. Through writing, a person is able to express himself. The teachers teaching the language should give full importance to it. No doubt, writing ability is given sufficient importance in the schools these days. The fact is that the students hardly express themselves. They only cram something and express themselves in English. The teacher should give due importance to original writing of the students. They should be encouraged for it.

Writing, therefore, is one of the important ways of expression. Without the writing aspect, learning of a language remains incomplete. A good writer is he who has clear understanding of the language. He should be in a position to write it.

Every learner of a language is expected to express himself clearly. He should be in a position to write composition on simple topics of day-to-day life including letters, applications etc. whenever need arises thereto. It is an equally important aim and it should not be taken up lightly by the learners.

So real teaching of English depends upon the acquisition of all the four skills. Each skill is important in its own way. The teacher should give training for all the skills. He should teach the language in such a way that the learners should be able to achieve the aims of teaching English.

Now the question may arise which aim out of these is the most important. We can't say that only the first or the second aim is the most important. In fact, all the aims are important because in language learning, we need reception ability as well as expression ability. *Dr. Michael West* is of the view that for Indian children, the ability to read is more important than the ability to write because they have less opportunities to speak that language. In the words of *H.A. Cartledge*, of the four skills involved in language learning-listening, speaking, reading and writing—the one which is likely to be the most useful for students of a foreign language is reading. Most of them, unless they are able to visit the country where it is spoken, will have little opportunity of speaking or hearing the language themselves, nor will most of them have occasion to write in it. All of them, however, once they are able to read it without difficulty, can go on improving their knowledge of it indefinitely."

So whenever we are teaching English and in whatever situation we may be, we should try for linguistic aims. *P. Gurrey* says, "Our chief concern should not be about the difficulties of pronunciation, growth of vocabulary grammar and structure, but with language abilities."

It is the duty of the teachers that they should make the study of this language as interesting as possible, *V.K. Gokak* is right when he says, "Language teaching is not such an unpleasant task as it is imagined to be. With proper training and equipment, it can even be delightful."

In each lesson, the teacher should make a precise and to the point selection of aims. That will help him to work better on it. In this context *P. Gurrey* says, "The technique of choosing a very limited objective for each lesson is the most fruitful aid to better teaching. It gives focus and therefore, concentration, it gives clarity and therefore, better understanding, it gives precision and the fore more firmly established progress. The careful thinking out of a comprehensive and well defined objective for the lessons will do more than almost anything else to improve a teacher's work and to make it effective."

ASSIGNMENTS

1. What are the objectives of teaching English as a second language at secondary school level? Discuss briefly.
2. Discuss briefly the aims and objectives of teaching English in Indian schools.
3. Discuss reception and expression as aims of teaching English.
4. Which aim of teaching English do you think is the most important and why?
5. What are the aims of teaching English at the junior and senior levels?

6

Planning of Lessons

In every walk of life, the planning is important. The success of a work is ensured if the work is properly planned. Without planning we shall be loitering about, aimlessly, applying means without aiming at the achievement of ends. In case of a language, planning certainly means selection and gradation of the language material. It is foreseeing success or failure of a work, or a lesson that we are going to teach to a class.

Teaching-Learning Process

Just as planning is important in our daily life, likewise planning is of unique importance in the teaching-learning process. The academic session comprises of a number of terms-say April to May August to September, October to November and January to February. It is known before-hand that there will be summer vacation for June ana July, Dussehra holidays, December house test, Christmas holidays, and annual examination in March. All these item are taken into consideration at the time of planning.

Purpose of Planning

It is a very important question whether we should plan for the teaching or we can do without it. The obvious answer to this is that planning is important everywhere. It is important not only in the class room teaching, but also at home where the student is to learn anything or he is to do some other work. Planning smoothens the work because a person is able to foresee the hurdles that he may possibly face in times to come. Thus he can think of possible solution to any problem coming to him.

The Advantages

1. By planning we are able to emphasise the different aspects of language equally, otherwise it is just possible that one aspect may be over-emphasized and some other aspect may be just touched upon and another one may be completely ignored.
2. It enables the teacher to do full justice to the different portions of the syllabus. He is able of maintain interest of the learner throughout. He is also able to teach everything systematically. There is no at once rush of finishing the work and hence there is nothing to burden the minds of the teachers.
3. It gives sufficient time and an opportunity to the teacher for the preparation of the lesson before hand. The teacher knows what he is to teach at what time and so he prepares himself accordingly and goes to the class well prepared.
4. It helps in keeping the teachers as well as taught on the right track.
5. The teacher can find out what has been taught and what has not been covered so far. So he can proceed further without any sort of duplicacy or confusion.
6. Permanent record of work finished or to be finished can be kept.
7. Once the habit of planning is formed, then the teacher gets a lot of time for preparation. He can easily think of the ways and means of making the lesson all the more interesting.

Present Scene

At present, we can say that in most of the schools, planning for teaching is not done at all. In some of them if it is done, that is not very systematic and is not rigidly followed.

At the time of training period, the pupil teachers are given all sorts of training how the lessons are to be planned before going to the class room for teaching. In spite of the best efforts made by the teaching personnel, we find that some of the trainees plan just to finish up the required lesson plan work. In most of the cases, we find that the same old plans based on Herbartian steps are being followed. The lesson plans hardly show any difference between the knowledge subjects and the skill subjects. Moreover, the lesson plans are very lengthy. Some of the steps are there which seem to be artificial and old but still they are continuing there. Moreover, preparation of that type of lesson plans consumes a lot of time which is not generally liked.

Later on when the trainees join the profession and start working as teachers, they forget all about lesson planning. They teach according to their own full freedom without taking into consideration any thing of lesson planning. There may be many reasons behind it. But the major reason is that they are made to handle very lengthy lesson plans and they develop a sort of negative attitude for them. So they do not plan at a for their lessons.

The Procedure

Before the start of the academic session, the teacher is to plan everything. He should see the syllabus and know the language material, text-books, supplementary readers that he is to take up in the classes for teaching purposes. Then he divides the whole work into a number of sections depending upon the terms of the whole year which are not equal. The work of different terms is spilt up into work for each month and that is further sub-divided into work for each week and then into daily work. In doing so, the teacher should see that different aspects of language learning i.e. listening, speaking, reading and writing are given sufficient time for practice.

The different lesson plans for the whole week should be based on the books. Thus we have lesson plans for teaching structures and vocabulary contained in a particular lesson. It does not matter, if we have more than one or two lesson plans on these language items and spend more than 2 or 3 periods for teaching. Then lesson plans for reading comprehension on the same lesson can be prepared. Teaching of composition should also be based on the same lesson. That will enable the students to learn everything in context and real language learning takes place.

Lesson Planning

In the planning of a daily lesson, there are three different stages:

(i) Pre-Teaching Planning
(ii) Planning during Teaching.
(iii) Post-Teaching Planning

Pre-Teaching Planning. Before teaching a lesson to some class, the teacher prepares notes at home. Then he thinks over everything of the lesson i.e. what he is going to present, how he is going to present, what techniques he is to use, which audio-visual aids he is going to make use of etc.

Planning during Teaching. Planning is important at each step of a lesson. It is a well known fact that planning is of unique importance before going to the class-room, and planning at the time of actual teaching is all the more important. While actually teaching in the class, the teacher is to plan the black board writing in a systematic way, plan the activities of the students etc. The teacher also knows before hand what type of mistakes will be committed by the students and he thinks of their solution. Whatever is presented to the students and whatever is to be done by them-all that needs to be very systematic. The point is that planning is very much needed even when the lesson is in progress.

Post-Teaching Planning. Post-teaching planning is that stage when the teacher has finished the class-room teaching. At this stage, he is to see how far he has been successful in teaching. He also brings to his mind the good and bad points of his teaching. He plans about the correction of written work enlisting the errors of the students, preparation of exercises for improvement etc.

Thus we find that all the three stages are very important from planning point of view. The success of a lesson depends upon a number of factors. A good lesson plan alone does not ensure its excellent teaching. There is need of a good teacher and a good lesson plan. Only then we can have satisfactory execution.

Good Lesson Plan

A good lesson plan is like a clock. From the lesson plan, we can guess somewhat about the teacher, his method of teaching provided the lesson plan is made by the teacher himself. A good lesson plan has the following characteristics:

1. Objectives in Behavioural terms are given in it.
2. From the lesson plan, we at once come to know about the different audio-visual aids which are going to be used in its teaching.
3. It shows the activities done by the teacher and the students in the class-room,
4. It tells us about the general procedure adopted by the teacher for teaching. The method of handling the language material is also revealed.
5. There is no mention of assignment or home work which is to be given to the students.

6. From the lesson plan we come to know the reference books consulted by the teacher while preparing it. In a good lesson plan, there is always a mention of it.

The Observation

Observation of a lesson is as important as writing of it. A very good observer of a lesson is he who himself knows the art of writing lesson plans. In fact, only an efficient lesson plan writer can prove to be an excellent observer. The main duty of the observer is to appreciate the good points, point out the drawbacks and then suggest steps for improvement. Sometimes the observers just criticise and they go on finding faults with the lesson plan; method of teaching, class discipline etc. But that is not a right approach. The observer, in the real sense, is there to guide the trainee and his ultimate aim is to improve his method of teaching and wake him a good teacher. So he should not continue criticising things just for the sake of cricism.

Important Points

An English lesson is widely different from a lesson of Science or Mathematics. But we find that it is generally observed like the knowledge lesson. While observing an English lesson, the following points are more important and so they should be properly considered and credit be given for them :

1. Lesson plan is the basis of a good teaching. So the observer should see whether it is correctly prepared or not. He should also see whether the fundamental principles of preparing a lesson plan have been taken into consideration or not.
2. The teacher who can speak correct English fluently in the class deserves credit.
3. How much time does the teacher speak in English in the class?
4. Are the students able to give responses in English? If not, do they understand the fundamentals of the languages?
5. Has the teacher made use of the different drills in the class-room? How far was he effective? Were the drills monotonous, dull and boring or they were made interesting through a variety of situations?

6. Whether practice in reading and writing was given to the students or not? Was it satisfactory?
7. Was he class interested in the lesson? How far was the teacher able to motivate the class?
8. Other general points like black-board writing by the teacher, class discipline etc. should also be taken into consideration.
9. Were the questions put in the class appropriate? Were they nicely put to different students in the class?
10. What type of home work was given? Was it satisfactory?
11. Overall delivery of the lesson should also be taken into consideration.

Plan vs Plans

Lesson plans of one subject can hardly be compared with the lesson plans of other subjects. Especially the lesson plan of a skill lesson is different from that of knowledge lesson. The Herbartian steps have been going on in lesson plans without any re-consideration of the steps. In case of English, it is no good to use those steps blindly without knowing their utility. We find that a number of English lessons become artificial when they are based on Herbartian steps. Those old types of lesson plans are being used in the colleges of education, but a few years back, under the guidance of R.I.E. Chandigarh, those lesson plans were changed. Now the lesson plans of English are decidely different from the lesson plans of other subjects. Moreover, they are based on the basic facts which hold the significance otherwise also.

Further in English, we have various aspects of it, say teaching of grammar points, composition, reading for comprehension, teaching a poem etc. The same steps of lesson plan do not fit into all these aspects. Though the main purpose of all the lesson plans of English is development and practice of the various. skills i.e., listening, speaking, reading and writing, yet the steps of lesson plans for one aspect 'say composition' do not befit the lesson plan on intensive reading or teaching a poem or some other aspect of English.

Few Model Lesson Plans

LESSON PLAN NO. 1

Pupil Teacher Roll No .... Date: ....
Subject.- English Duration of Period: 35 min.
Class: IX
Topic: Child or Adult (A poem)
Margaret Lawrence

Instructional Aids to be Used

Chalk Board, Pieces of Chalks, Duster, Eight Flashcards on which difficult words are written, eight flash cards on which meanings of difficult words are written.

Instructional Objectives in Behavioural Terms -Knowledge

(i) The students are able to recognize the ideas contained in the poem.

(ii) They are able to recall the thoughts given in the poem.

Understanding

The students are able to understand the state of mind of an adolescent. An adolescent is not able to describe whether still he is a child or he has become an adult.

tudents are able to develop the different linguistic skills ...ning, speaking, recitation and writing.

Application

The students are able to apply the art of reciting a poem in their different life situations. They can entertain themselves and others through recitation.

Subject Matter

Am I a child or an adult?
No ! Not a child now-my dools are gone :
My dream world has rippled away.
I am tall, I understand adult talk.
But does that mean that I am an adult?

Am I an adult or a child?
No ! Not an adult-I couldn't look after myself.

The understanding is just not there.
I pay a half fare on a bus to school,
But does that mean that I am a child?

Am I a child or an adult?
No ! Not a child now-it's not a teddey I love:
His cherished position is taken.
Just because my toys have lost their value,
Does that mean that I am an adult?

Am I an adult or a child?
No ! Not an adult-I do not see
The reason for adult disputes ;
I am safe in non-understanding
But does that mean that I am a child?

Well am I a child or an adult?
No ! Not one or the other now ;
One pace in front of childhood,
And one behind an adult.
Soon I shall stride into a new world,
The world of adult life.

Thought Content

In this poem, the state of mind of an adolescent is shown. She is confused. She does not know whether still she is a child or she has become an adult. She again and again asks this question from herself. In this poem an adolescent asks herself if she is a child or an adult. She tells that her days of playing with the dolls have gone. She loves a teddy bear no more. Toys have lost attraction for her. Her dream world is also gone.

After thinking over the matter, she thinks that she is one step in front of childhood and one step behind adulthood. She is thus in the middle of the two stages. But she shall soon grow into adulthood. This type of questions will not trouble her then. 'Me world of adult life, then will be new for her.

Previous Knowledge Testing

In order to test the previous knowledge of the students, the pupil teacher will ask the following questions :

(i) Name some of the poems that you have read?
(ii) Which poem have you liked the most?
(iii) Have your read the poem 'Child or Adult'? by 'Margaret Lawrence'

Announcement of the Topic

Finding the students unable to answer the ' last question, the Pupil teacher will say, "Dear students, today we shall study the poem-"Child or Adult?

Presentation

Step I: The pupil teacher will tell something about the poem in simple English. She will use mother tongue wherever she needs its assistance. In this way, proper atmosphere will be created for teaching the poem.

Step II: The pupil teacher will give a model recitation of the poem. She will use gestures wherever possible. At this stage, the students will keep their books closed.

Step III: Now the students open their books and second model recitation of the poem will be given by the pupil teacher.

Step IV: A few difficult words contained in the poem are already written on the flash cards will be shown to the class.

(1) Adult-a grown up person.
(2) Rippled away-mould in small waves
(3) Understanding-insight
(4) Cherished-much love
(5) Disputes-quarrels
(6) Pace-Step
(7) In front of-ahead of
(8) Stride-walk.

Step V: A number of students will be asked to recite the poem one by one depending upon the availability of time. If some student mispronounces a word or a line, it will be got corrected with the help of other students sitting in the class.

Step VI: The pupil teacher will ask the class if they have any difficulty in the poem. Difficult line or stanza pointed out by the students will be explained by the pupil teacher.

Step VII: In order to test their comprehension of the poem, the pupil teacher will ask the following questions from the class :

(i) Can you predict the age of the speaker of these lines?

(ii) What are the three things that have been disappeared from the speaker's life at this moment?

(iii) Name the poem and the Poetess?

Home Work

The pupil teacher will ask the student to learn anyone stanza of the poem by heart at home.

LESSON PLAN NO. 2

Pupil Teacher's Roll No .... Date ....

Subject-English Duration of Period-40 mts.

Class-IX

Topic-For Kalpana

(A Poem)

by Nissim Ezekill

Instructional aids to be Used

Chalk board, pieces of chalks, duster, flash cards on which comprehension questions are written, a chart depicting the picture of Kalpana.

Instructional objectives in behavioural terms knowledge

(i) The students are able to recognize the ideas contained in the poem.

(ii) They are able to recall the thoughts given in the poem.

Understanding

The students are able to understand that how parents are worried about their children.

Skills

The students are able to develop the different linguistic skills i.e. listening, speaking, recitation and writing.

Application

The students are able to apply the art of reciting a poem in their different life situations. They can entertain themselves and others through recitation.

Subject Matter

How parents worry

When a child is thin

What shall we do
What shall we do
they whisper in the night
their voices grey
in the anxieties of love
till the luminous
angel of sleep
leads them softly
(their souls and bodies intervening)
to her own open city
where they see again
the big bright advertisements
for tonic and vitamins ABC
DE unto infinity.
And they watch their child daily eating breakfast
greesy egg-yolk egg-white
jams jellies toast and porridge
fat with the milk of human kindness
or dinner
of curry-drowned rice
and momentus salad
eat eat my child
how thin you are
So the child looks down
distastefully
and eats and eats.

Thought Content

Kalpana's parents worry about her health. She remains thin. They do not understand what they should do. They talk about it in a low murmuring voice at night. Their voices show love and anxiety for the child. Even in dreams they see various bright advertisements of tonics and vitamins. They think of giving these tonics and vitamins to their child.

They watch their child eating daily a rich diet. The child is unwilling to eat all these. They ask her to eat more and more.

Previous Knowledge Testing

In order to test the previous knowledge of the students, the P.T. will ask the following questions :

(i) Name some of the poems that you have read.
(ii) Which poem have you liked most?
(iii) Recite that poem.
(iv) Have you read the poem—For Kalpana?

Announcement of the Topic

Finding the students answer to the last question in the negative, the P.T. will say "Dear students, to-day we shall study the poem—For Kalpana.

Presentation

Step I: The P.T. displays the chart and tells something about the poem in simple English. She will use mother tongue wherever she needs its assistance. In this way, proper atmosphere will be created for teaching the Poem.

Step II: The pupil teacher will give a model recitation of the poem. She will use gestures wherever possible. A pointer will also be used to indicate the different aspects of the chart. At this stage, the students will keep their books closed.

Step III: Now the students open their books and second model recitation of the poem will be given by the pupil teacher.

Step IV: The P.T. will write the few difficult words contained in the poem on the B.B. Meanings will be taught with the active participation of the students.

(i) Whisper-To speak in a low voice.
(ii) Grey-Voice like those of the old.
(iii) Anxieties-Worries
(iv) Luminous-bright.
(v) Porridge--Softwood made by boiling a cereal.
(vi) Milk of Human kindness-love and kindness.
(vii) Curry drowned rice-Rice soaked in curry.

Step V: A number of students will be asked to recite the poem one by one depending upon the availability of time. If some student mispronounces a word or a line, it will be got corrected with the help of other students sitting in the class.

Step VI: The P.T. will ask the class if they have any difficulty in the poem. Difficult line or stanza pointed out by the students will be explained by the P.T.

Step VII: In order to test their comprehension of the poem, the following questions will be put to the class:

(i) Why do Kalpana's parents worn?
(ii) What do they think of doing for the child?
(iii) What happens to the girl who eats such a rich diet?
(iv) What effect does the poet intend to produce in writing of vitamins from 'ABCDE' unto infinity'?

Wherever the students find it difficult to answer, the P.T. will provide guidance.

Home work: The P.T. with ask the students to write the summary of the poem at home.

LESSON PLAN NO. 3

Pupil Teacher's Roll No........... Date ....
Subject-English Duration of Period-40 mts.
Class-IX
Topic-The Umbrella Man
(Intensive Reading)

Instructional aids to be Used:

Chalk Board, pieces of chalks, duster, flash cards, a chart showing the picture of pavement.

Instructional objectives in behavioural terms:

Knowledge

(i) The students acquire knowledge of new words and phrases.
(ii) They can recognize and also recall those words.

Understanding:

The students are able to understand the ideas given in the prose lesson.

Skills

The students are able to develop the different linguistic skills such as listening, speaking, reading and writing.

Application:

(i) The students are able to make use of a few words in their day to day life situations.
(ii) They are able to read the newspaper and other such reading materials in a better way.

Subject Matter:

Lesson No. 1 -The Umbrella Man- (Paragraph 1-9)
I'm going to tell-on about a funny thing ....
.. .. This man had beautiful brown shoes.

Thought Content

The narrator is a girl of twelve years. She is narrating the incident that had happened with her and her mother yesterday. Yesterday she went with her mother to a dentist. Her tooth was to be filled. The dentist filled her tooth and then they went to a cafe. The mother had coffee and the girl took ice-cream. Just when they came out of the street, it began to rain. They looked for a taxi and the mother wished they had a car of their own. Just then an old man of about seventy, came upto them. He looked rich and had a costly silken umbrella over his head. In a very polite and gentle way, he said he was in trouble and he wanted a small help. The mother was always suspicious of strangers. So she looked at him with suspicion. As a rule she did not trust strangers.

Previous knowledge testing:

In order to test the previous knowledge of the students, the pupil teacher will ask the following questions-

1. Name the lessons that you have read from your book.
2. What is the meaning of the word 'Umbrella'?
3. Have you read the lesson 'The Umbrella man I'?

Announcement of the Topic:

Finding a negative answer or the students, the P.T. will say, "Dear students, to-day we shall study the lesson 'The Umbrella Man'. from your books.

Presentation

Step I: The P.T. will give the model reading of the paragraph. While doing so, she will take care of pronunciation. The students will keep their books open.

Step II: Then she will draw the attention of the students to the difficult words occurring in the paragraph. Those words will be written on the B. B.

Step III: The pupil teacher will create situations with the help of pictures- flash cards, black board drawings and teach the words and phrases. Wherever need arises there to he will create verbal situations. The students will be asked to use them in sentences. Grammar work will be done side by side.

(1) funny:"

He is telling .... incidents of his childhood.

(Asking the student to tell some funny incident of his childhood.

(2) Yesterday.

(Asking the student where did they go yesterday)

(3) Already:

Is it 8.30 ....

(Ask one of the students what is the time in your watch)

(4) Gorgeous (By creating verbal situation):

Gorgeous .... extremely beautiful.

(Sushmita Sen looks very gorgeous)

(5) Pavement:

(By showing a chart)

Pavement .... a hard level path at the side of a road for people to walk.

Step IV: The P.T will ask some individual students to do the loud reading. Corrections if any, will be made with the help of students.

Step V: Silent reading by the class.

Step VI : The P.T. will ask the students if they have any difficulty. The problems will be solved. Mother league will be used if the P.T. feels its necessity.

Step VII: In order to test the comprehension of the students, the P.T. will ask the following questions :-

(Flash cards will be displayed one by one).

(1) How old is the narrator?
(2) Yesterday where did they go?
(3) What did the narrator take in the cafe?
(4) Describe the physical appearance of the man they met yesterday?

Wherever the students find difficulty in understanding the questions, the pupil teacher will use mother tongue.

Home Work: The P.T. will ask the students to use the following words in your sentences at home.

Beautiful, Moustache

LESSON PLAN NO. 4

P.T's Roll No.: Date: ....

Class: VII Duration of Period: 35 minutes

Subject : English

Topic : 'The Greedy Dog' (A Story)

Type of Composition: Guided

Instructional aid to be Used:

Four stages of the story depict on a chart, black board, pieces of chalks, duster, pointer, four flash cards on which four incomplete sentences are written and four flash cards on which answers are written.

Instructional objectives in behavioural terms :

Knowledge : (i) The students get knowledge about the story "The Greedy Dog."

(ii) They are able to recognize and recall the story and the sentences used in it.

Understanding : (i) The students are able to understand how necessity motivates some one to do, new things.

(ii) They are able to give more sentences of that type.

Skills : (i) The students get listening practice.

(ii) They get practice of proper reading.

(iii) They get practice of writing English Correctly.

Application: The students are able to apply moral of the story in their day to day life situations.

Previous knowledge testing

In order to test the previous knowledge of the students, the P.T. will ask the following questions:

(i) What is on the table? (By putting toffees)

(ii) Which side of table with toffiees do you want?

By putting two toffees on one side and many wrapped stones on the other side. The P.T. will call one students to choose one side of toffees. He will choose the side in which many wrapped stones are placed. The P.T. will say, "Greed is a curse."

Have you ever written the story "The Greedy Dog"?

Announcement of the topic :

Finding the students answer in negative, the P.T. will say, "Dear students, to-day we shall develop the story "The Greedy Dog".

Presentation :

Step I: Oral Development of Composition by the P.T.

The P.T. will display the chart showing the pictures in different stages and start oral development of composition. She will be speaking sentences by pointing towards the various aspects of the story. She will also write the outline of the story on the blackboard side by side.

Once there was a dog. He was very hungry. He went here and there in search of food. But he did not find food anywhere. At last, he reached a meat shop. He stole a piece of meat. He wanted to eat it alone. So he ran to the jungle.

There was a river on the way. When he was crossing the bridge, he looked into the water. He saw his own reflection. He thought that it was another dog with a piece of meat in his mouth. The greedy dog wanted to get that piece also. So he barked at him. As he opened his mouth. his own piece of meat fell into the water. He was very sad. But it was too late.

Moral: Greed is a curse.

Step II: Oral Development of Composition by the students

The aids used by the P.T. will continue there and the student will be enabled to develop composition orally. For this, the pupil teacher will use various devices which are explained here below:

By putting questions to the class.

(1) Where did a dog go in search of food?

(2) What did he do when he saw a piece of meat?

(3) What did he see into water?

(4) What was his reaction when he saw his own reflection into the water?

Where-ever the students find difficulty in answering the questions, the P.T. will give them key words. In case the students still find it hard to answer half of the sentence may be given and for the remaining half 2 or 3 answers may be written, out of which the students may pick up one to complete the sentence correctly.

Complete the following sentences by consulting (i), (ii), (iii).

(1) Once there was .... He was very hungry.

(i) a fox (ii) a crow (iii) a dog.

(2) He went here and there in search of ....

(i) house (ii) food (iii) clothe.

(3) There was a river on his way. When he was crossing the bridge, he looked into the water. He saw his own ....

(i) reflection (ii) face (iii) shadow.

(4) The greedy dog wanted that piece also. So he barked at him. As .... his mouth.
    (i) closed (ii) opened (iii) down.

(5) He was very ....
    (i) Happy (ii) Sad (iii) Upset.

In this way by putting questions, composition will be developed by the students. Wherever they find some difficulty, all guidance will be provided by the P.T.

Step III : Writing of composition by the students.

All guidelines will continue appearing on the black board. The students will be asked to write composition in their note books. All efforts will be made by the P.T. that the students complete the composition in the class-room. The P.T. will see that none of them copies the other students.

Step IV : Correction work

Then the note books of the students will be collected by the P.T. for correction work.

Homework : The students will be asked to write the story again at home.

LESSON PLAN NO. 5

P.T's Roll No ....
Subject: English
Topic: A Morning Walk
Class : IX
Type of Composition: (A Guided Composition) Dated:
Duration of Period : 35 minutes

Instructional aids to be used:

(i) Chalk, Chalkboard, Duster Pointer, Coloured Chalks.
(ii) Flash Cards on which previous human books testing questions are written.
(iii) A chart showing various aspects of nature in the morning.
(iv) Another chart on which some questions are written.

Instructional objectives in behavioural terms:

Knowledge :

(i) The students will come to know about the beauty of nature.
(ii) They will also come to know about pleasure which a morning walk provides us.

Understanding:

The students will be able to understand the benefits of morning walk and then they can make their own habit of morning walk.

Skills:

(a) The students will be able to develop their listening and speaking skills.
(b) The students will be able to develop their reading and writing skills.

Application

The students will be able to apply the art of writing composition in their daily life situations.

Previous knowledge testing

The P.T. will ask the students the following questions by showing flash cards one by one:

(i) What is your name?
(ii) When do you get up in the morning?
(iii) Do you go for a walk in the morning?
(iv) Speak a few sentences on the topic 'A Morning Walk.'

Announcement of the topic:

Finding the students unable to speak, the P.T. will say, "well students, today we shall develop a composition on 'A Morning Walk.'

Presentation:

Step I: Oral Development of Composition by P.T.

The P.T. will start oral development of composition by showing the chart. He will be speaking the sentences by pointing towards the various aspect shown in the chart. He will also write the outlines of composition on chalk-board side by side.

Morning time is the best time of the day. Morning hours are very refreshing. Nature is at its best. It is calm and quiet. A cool breeze blows. The atmosphere is free from dust and smoke. A walk at this time is very useful.

It refreshes the mind as well as body. It is good for health. There goes the maxim: "He who walks a mile will surely smile." The morning walk provides us with a store of energy for the day's work. It sharpens our appetite. It purifies our blood. It keeps us fit healthy and gay. It makes us cheerful and happy throughout the day. It is the secret of good health.

Step II: Oral Development of composition by the Students

Now the aids used by the P.T. continue lying there and the students will be enabled to develop composition orally. For this, the P.T will show the chart on which some questions are written. The P.T. will ask a few students to read the questions one by one and then they will be asked to answer those questions.

Q.1. Which time is the best time of the day?
Q.2. How is the nature in the morning?
Q.3. How is the atmosphere in the morning?
Q.4. What refreshes our mind and body?
Q.5. What maxim is used for 'morning walk'?
Q.6. What does a morning walk provide us?
Q.7. What is the advantage of morning walk?
Q.8. What is the secret of good health?

Whenever the students find difficulty in answering the question, the teacher will give them key words. If need arises, half of the sentence may be written and then they may complete it.

In this way, the composition will be developed by the students. Whenever they find some difficulty, all guidance or help will be rendered by the teacher.

Step III: Writing of Composition by the Students

All hints or guidelines continue on the black-board or chart. The students will be asked to write down composition in the class. Every effort will be made that the students complete the composition themselves. The teacher should see that none of them copies the other students. In case, the composition remains incomplete, the teacher may ask the students to complete it at home.

Step IV : Correction Work

Then the note-books of the students will be collected by the pupil teachers for correction work.

Homework : The students will be asked to write a composition on "An Evening Walk" at home.

Note: A few lesson plans are given in the relevant chapters of this book. These chapters are (i) Teaching of Grammar (ii) Teaching of Prose (iii) Teaching of Poetry (iv) Teaching of Compositions. Please consult those pages of the book.

ASSIGNMENTS

1. Prepare a lesson plan on one of the following:
   (a) "too much' and 'too many'-for class VII
   (b) A Poem of your choice-for class X
   (c) Guided Composition on "The Republic Day'-for class IX
2. Prepare a lesson plan to teach one of the following.
   (a) Picture composition on 'The Grapes are Sour' (class VIII).
   (b) 'Under' and 'Over' (class VIII)
   (c) Change from Direct to Indirect speech (class IX)
3. Prepare a lesson plan on any one of the following.
   (a) Use of; 'either-or' to class VIII,
   (b) Composition on : -'My Favourite Teacher' for Class VII.
   (c) Change from Direct to Indirect speech for class IX.
4. Prepare a lesson plan to teach any one of the following :
   (a) Active-Passive Voice (Past Indefinite Tense) Class IX
   (b) No sooner .... than and speakingClass VIII.
   (c) Write 20 sentences on 'My Teacher' suitable for class VIII and prepare a lesson plan to teach the same as a prose lesson intensive reading.
5. Prepare a lesson plan on any one of the following:
   (a) The use of 'Neither .... nor' for IX class.
   (b) Composition on 'My Pet Dog' for VII class.
   (c) Change of Active into Passive Voice for IX class.
6. Prepare a detailed lesson plan for teaching composition on the topic 'Books: Our Best Friends' to X class.
7. Write an essay on 'Increasing Indiscipline Among the Students', in about 300 words. How will you teach that essay in IX class? Write briefly the different steps involved in it.
8. Write one stanza of any poem that you remember from the school syllabus. Prepare a detailed lesson plan for teaching it. You may take up any class of Hindi medium or English medium school.
9. (a) Write one exercise of guided composition.
   (b) Take up any three action words and prepare lesson notes for teaching the same to students of VIII class.

10. (i) For teaching the poem 'Daffodils' write the objectives in behavioural terms.
    (ii) How will you teach just two interrogative sentences of past indefinite tense to VII class?
11. Prepare a lesson plan for teaching the use of the words 'for' and 'since' to VIII class student. Write by taking up one example of each word.

7

Concept of Evaluation

The teaching learning process has been going on but its results have not been very effective. Tests and examinations have been conducted but very good results have not been seen. Evaluation which is a broader term than tests and examinations is expected to serve the purposes better. English language teaching needs better application of evaluation. That is likely to improve the teaching learning process.

In evaluation, the work of the students is assessed continuously. All round assessment of the learners is made throughout the year. It involves objectives of teaching, methods to achieve them and then finding out how far they have been achieved. The ultimate objectives of language teaching are comprehension and expression. The four skills of language learning i.e. listening, speaking, reading and writing ultimately achieve these objectives. Evaluation certainly aims at improving the abilities in the acquisition of four skills.

Comprehensive Evaluation

External examinations, as a technique of evaluation, have failed to meet the desired ends. Let us see how far the technique of continuous comprehensive evaluation will be useful.

Evaluation is continuous and comprehensive. When we have it fully internal without the help of the external agencies, it is called Internal Evaluation. In that case, the teachers preparing the students in the class rooms are to judge fully and finally the performance of their own students. All types of achievements of the students, scholastic and non-scholastic are evaluated continuously for the whole session. The whole record of the student is maintained properly in the cumulative record register and on that basis, pass or fail of a students is determined by the teaching personnels of the school.

Continuous comprehensive internal evaluation is different from internal assessment. In case of internal assessment, external examination and its fears hang like a sword in the minds of the learners as well as the teachers. Internal assessment is just a part of external examination. Some people might argue that in internal assessment, our educational institutions have no good experiences and that way internal evaluation may not prove a farce. Continuous comprehensive internal evaluation seems to be the panacea of all the ills that are being faced through the process of traditional examinations. It is high time that we make evaluation an integral part of the total teaching learning process. That way our testing will become comprehensive as it will take care of all the three domains for all-around development of the learner in both the scholastic and the non-scholastic areas. The current system of giving divisions in the examinations and thus classifying the learners into classes should be ousted. It should give place to unit tests which should be administered regularly to judge over all personality of the child in the light of objectives fixed up.

Objective Based

Objectives of teaching English are framed in the light of over all environment of the child which includes social, political, national, cultural and economic aspects of life. Those objectives naturally include scholastic and non-scholastic areas. Through continuous evaluation judgement about the child is made continuously. The objective and the efforts to achieve those objectives remain in the process of review and revision till the desired ends are achieved.

Comprehensive

Evaluation is comprehensive in the sense that the over all personality of the child is assessed. In all spheres of life. learner's acquisition of four skills of language i.e. listening, speaking, reading and writing are taken care of in evaluation.

Continuous

Continuous evaluation helps the teachers in knowing about their effects side by side and so they improve accordingly. The learners also come to know their deficiency with regard to different things and thus they can remedy the same by taking proper guidance and making more efforts.

Need

The need of the times is to make evaluation an integral part of the total teaching learning process. Testing should also be comprehensive so that all the three domains for all round development of the learner in both the scholastic and the non-scholastic areas are fully covered. Unlike the traditional system of testing which takes into consideration only the academic side, evaluation aims at testing all the aspects of the personality of the learners.

Evaluation of Scholastic Achievement

In order to evaluate the scholastic achievement of a student, the following tools which supplement each other will be used:

Written Examination

Written examination includes questions of essay type, short answer type and objective type.

(i) *Essay Type Tests* have law validity and reliability but still we cannot dispense with them. We need them for measuring the essential skills such as application of knowledge, solution of problems, expression etc.

(ii) *Short Answer Type Tests* have more validity and reliability as compared to essay type. So those will be used.

(iii) *Objective Type or New Type Tests* are still more reliable. They are comprehensive, easy to score and less time consuming. By using these we ran measure the ability to organise knowledge, express things and narrate facts.

All the three i.e. essay type, short answer type and objective type tests supplement each other.

Oral Test

These are used for testing skills which are not tested by written tests, for example, pronunciation, speed and accuracy of reading a book, comprehension and verbal expression, reciting a poem, answering questions orally etc. All these are possible through oral tests. Formal tests, interview, observation may also be used.

Evaluation of the Sessional

Sessional work done by a student is also important. Apart from written and oral examinations, sessional work is also to be assessed.

Assessment of sessional work includes the following:

(a) Home assignment done by the student.
(b) Impression of the teacher formed on the basis of class discussions etc.
(c) Use of library.
(d) Practical work done in language laboratory.

Evaluation of Personality

Education helps in the over-all development of a person. So the different traits of personality and character of an individual should be assessed. The different traits are expressed by an individual in day to day's behaviour. The teacher should record the behaviour of a student inside the class room and outside the class room, in the library, in the laboratory, in the playground, in the field of other activities etc. It can be better done in the following ways:

1. The pupil's diary which he himself maintains should be assessed.
2. Assessment of the diary maintained by the teacher for recording the behaviour of the students be made.
3. Personality test may be given from time to time.

Evaluation of the Social Development

Though education, the social aspect of an individual is developed. The teacher is expected to test the sociability of every pupil. It can be done in the following ways:

1. The teacher takes into consideration the work being done by a student daily, his participation in games, social service, cleanliness etc.
2. Proficiency in various co-curricular activities should be seen. For this a five point scale may be prepared. A variety of opportunities may be provided to the students in which they may freely display their qualities like sociability, co-operation, sympathetic attitude, self-help etc.

Evaluation of the Physical Development

Education helps in the development of good health and right habits. The pupil is able to develop himself physically. It is the duty of the teacher that he should assess the physical development of the pupils from time to time. He should try to diagnose the disabilities. Physical handicaps etc. with the assistance of school doctor and help in the immediate cure. programme for assessing the physical development will be as under:

(1) A doctor should be engaged in the school for part time or full time duty.

(2) Arrangements be made for physico-medical test after every 3 or 4 months.

(3) A record of medical check-up should be kept. Remedial measures accordingly should be used.

(4) Students' participation in games and athletics should be recorded.

(5) Physical efficiency of each pupil should be measured by using a rating scale.

Unit Approach

To make the programme of continuous and comprehensive evaluation a success, unit approach in teaching and testing will hold good. The whole of the syllabus which is to be covered in the whole of the year is divided into some units. Each unit consists of material which is almost of similar type. The total duration of the academic session is also divided into some parts-say a unit of syllabus for every month or for two weeks or three weeks. Thus teaching is done for the syllabus given in the unit and after covering that much of the syllabus, test is given to the learners out of the syllabus marked for that unit. This type of approach is called unit approach.

Unlike traditional testing at the end of the year, unit teaching and unit testing make the instructional work more meaningful. The teacher is able to do justice to his duty of teaching. The learners are also able to prepare well. This approach does not allow the teacher or the students to skip over certain portions of the syllabus.

Unit approach is bound to make the continuous and comprehensive programme of evaluation of success.

Success of Making Evaluation Programme

Here below are suggested a few steps which will help in making evaluation all successful:

1. Continuous comprehensive evaluation can be made successful if UNIT APPROACH is adopted in teaching and testing. In unit approach, a block of closely related subject matter is taught and thereafter a test is given to the students. It gives continuous feed-back to both the teacher and the taught. So they can improve accordingly.
2. Head of the institutions and the teaching staff should be trained for the purpose of internal evaluation. This job may be entrusted to DIETS set up in different districts. The DIETS should work in collaboration with teacher training colleges, SCERT and N.C.E.R.T.
3. Different criteria may be fixed up for different items. Accordingly assessment of the learners should be made.
4. In each institution, moderation committees be set up with the Head of the Institution as its chairman. Thus all assessment should be subject to the review of moderation committee.
5. Tuition work on the part of the teachers should be banned completely.
6. Any type of evil if spreads anywhere in the institutions, be taken up seriously with strict action against the defaulter. The policy should be to nip the evil in the bud.

Merits

(1) Every teacher knows well about his students. Whatever may be the subject or area of study, only the teacher teaching in the class rooms daily can judge the performance of his students fully and thoroughly. Assessment made by the teacher will naturally be more satisfying and correct.

(2) All the students studying for different courses will become regular and punctual. They will try to do their home assignments and class work to the entire satisfaction of all concerned.

(3) The problem of indiscipline will remain subsided.

(4) Obedience and proper regards for the teacher will revive. It will result into very good academic and homely

environment where teachers will be able to imbibe good qualities in the students.

(5) Erosion of values is a big problem in the youths of today. The main reason behind is fast deteriorating environment all around. It will become easy for the teachers to reinstate all the good things of the past.

(6) Problems like mass copying in the examination will stand ended. When there will be no traditional type of examinations, problems related to that will stand automatically solved.

(7) The job of administrator in educational institutions which is now considered a big challenge, will become respectable and alluring.

(8) The non-academic type of problems will be reduced considerably.

(9) Unlike the present set up of school/college life where students care for academic development only, the students in the newly created environment will start caring for the total personality. They will give equal importance to games, cultural activities, other curricular activities etc. Thus they will be able to have all round development of personalities.

Demerits

(1) Shirkers of work in the teaching profession who are there due to some compulsions of life may not work and the standards in their hands may go down.

(2) Bad things like bribery may increase in number and intensity.

Merits and demerits of everything are always there. Putting things rightly in their true spirit depends considerably upon the Head of the institution. If the staff members in the institutions work as a team and do everything in true spirit with honesty, sincerity and hardwork, internal evaluation will improve everything from almost every angle. Some people might say that when teachers and the education system have already failed to a greater extent in the case of internal assessment, it is no wisdom to entrust those very teachers with the total teaching learning situation where pass or failure of the students will be determined by their own teachers. That is a poor thinking on the part of people which might be there due to some other reasons like jealousy or some personal conflicts. Let the teacher be entrusted with the job of internal evaluators with all good faith and confidence. When the authorities exhibit all faith in them, they will certainly repose their faith in it and come upto the expectations of all concerned with it.

ASSIGNMENTS

1. Only continuous and comprehensive evaluation will improve the standards of English. Discuss.
2. What is the importance of continuous and comprehensive evaluation of English? Explain fully.
3. Write notes on
   (i) Oral Tests
   (ii) Evaluation of scholastic achievement.
   (iii) Importance of Unit Approach.

8

Electic Approach

The learning of language is an important programme in the life of a man. Whatever language we learn, we should be able to communicate efficiently by using that language. Here the linguistic part of it is very significant. Our proficiency in that language is a must. It includes proper use of structures, vocabulary etc. in written as well as spoken form. Efficiency in language is the basis for effective communication. We should be able to use the language in such a way that we are successful in communicating to others.

Every language is mainly to serve the purpose of communication. A person has something in mind and he wants to communicate it to others. It is possible if he knows spoken language. The receiver of information should also know the language specially its listening and speaking. Only then its communication will take place. Verbal communication is possible when both the parties-the giver and the receiver are physically present near each other. Reading and writing skills are needed for communication purpose when there is distance between both the parties. The chief function of language teaching is communication. One who can communicate well, is said to have learned the language well. On other hand, a person, howsoever, qualified he may be, if he can't communicate properly, he is not a master of the language. Let us, therefore, emphasise on this part of language learning.

Basic Assumptions

The basic Assumptions of a person good at different skills are:-

(i) Efficiency in aural-oral aspect of the language.

(ii) Good in the mechanics of reading and writing.

(iii) Correct language habits.

(iv) Command over active vocabulary.
(v) Good at structures.

Communicative Functions

Communicative function of a language plays an important role. A person who cannot communicate is not good at language. The deaf and the dumb are able to communicate through gestures. A person having the knowledge of language needs vocabulary and structures for the purpose of communication. He needs functional grammar and thus he succeeds in passing on the information or his feeling and ideas to others.

Just mastery over vocabulary and structures is not sufficient. One should be able to use them to communicate meaning in real situations. A person visiting some foreign country should be able to communicate. Then only he succeeds there and is able to live well there. He must possess the communicative ability.

Structural aspect of language is important at its own place and its functional aspect is important in its own way. That does not mean that functional aspect is more important than the structural aspect. In fact, the structural aspect is the basis and that is what gives the language its existence and on the basis of the existence, the language functions.

Few Questions

Should a person study literature for the development of communicative skills? Should a person study - linguistics? Should a person study modern grammar? Should a person study language for the sake of language? No. Language should be learnt mainly for communication purposes. Functional effectiveness of the language is important.

The Pre-requisites

Linguistic Competence. The learner of language should have linguistic competence. Then only he can make use of the language as per his needs and requirements.

Different Forms of Linguistics. The learner of the language should understand the different forms of linguistics. Then naturally he can pick up the right one and use it at the appropriate moment.

Develop Skills and Strategies for Using the Language. The language learner should develop all the skills required for learning the language. He should also have training of different strategies which could be applied for using the language in different situations.

Social Setting is Important. For speaking the language effectively, social setting plays a very important role. The speaker should use the language suitable to the requirements of the audience. Then only he is said to have used the language rightly. Suppose the teacher is concerned with the students or a student. He can communicate one thing in the following different ways:

(i) Please help me.

(ii) Could you please help me?

(iii) Would you mind helping me?

(iv) Could I trouble you to help me?

All the above said four ways are linguistic forms where different structures have been used. The first way of communication is more suitable when the teacher is concerned with his students. The same structure cannot be put to use if the situation is between the inspector and the peon. Social situation is important. The user of the language should keep some strategy in mind and then he succeeds in communicating properly.

(a) In the communicative function of the language, the way of speaking also matters a lot. What we say is important but equally important is how do we say that. In a word, all the syllables of it are not equally stressed.

By a shift of stress from one syllable to another, its meanings are changed. A few examples are:

Nouns	*Verbs*	*Nouns*	*Verbs*
Practice	Pra'ctice	'decrease	de'crease
'Insult	In'sult	'desert	de'sert
'Progress	Pro'gress	'increase	in'crease
'Rebel	Re'bel	'refuse	re,fuse
'record	re'cord	'present	pre'sent

The above said words have the same spellings but the way we speak them determine the meanings. Naturally, here the communication will be based on our way of speaking.

(1) In case of a sentence, all the words contained in it are not stressed. The difference in stress changes the meanings of the utterance. Let us take up a simple example to illustrate the point. The sentence 'RAJESH IS MY ENGLISH TEACHER' can be spoken in different ways by shifting the stress. In each way, it conveys a different meaning e.g.

(i) Rajesh is my English teacher. (only Rajesh, not some one else)
(ii) Rajesh 'is my English teacher. (Why do you deny it?)
(iii) Rajesh is 'my English teacher. (mine, not your's)
(iv) Rajesh is my English teacher. (teacher of English, not of Maths or History)
(v) Rajesh is my English 'teacher. (Nothing else than teacher)

(2) While communicating through spoken language, pause, wrong use of pause, lack of pause makes big differences in meanings. For example,

Keep sticking/it praise/its wings/a nice man
Keeps ticking/it sprays/it wings/an ice man

The place where the pause occurs is the only feature of spoken English which can make the difference between the pairs clear.

Advantages

The following are the advantages of being good at communication skills:

1. The person who succeeds in communicating his ideas thoughts and feelings to others is happy, becomes confident, feels, encouraged, is able to impress others through his personality. Everyone says he can communicate well.
2. The user of the language feels satisfied because he succeeds in communicating to others.
3. He wins the confidence of the social gathering or group where he has used the language successfully.
4. It is more practical type of learning the language.
5. It is situational, meaningful, motivating others and is self-rewarding.

In the teaching learning of a language, communication skills play unique role. The teacher as well as the learner should realise their true value and keeping that in mind, all efforts should be made to acquire them right earnestly while aiming at learning the language. Once the habit of right communication is formed, the learner comes out a good speaker and an accurate conveyor of his thoughts.

Eclectic Approach: Eclectic approach means the collections of all the good points of different methods and then using them for teaching something. In teaching English, different methods and approaches have been popular. Each method has some good points and a few draw-backs also. Naturally any one method does not serve the purpose of teaching well for all times and in all types of teaching situations. Moreover, a good teacher does not become a subordinate to any single method. The teacher is expected to handle the methods as per his/her liking. The teacher is the master of the teaching situation and the methods of teaching are tools in his hands.

In this age of competitions, a wise comparison of different things can always help. Besides, in the class different students are able to learn in different ways. One and the same method does not prove successful for teaching to the whole class. Therefore the use of eclectic approach is the most suitable way of teaching English.

Let us pin pointedly see to the extra ordinary merits of different methods and approaches. Then only we shall be able to make use of them in different teaching situations to achieve the desired goals.

In translation method, the students are able to learn many items of English by comparison with mother tongue. That makes learning of the students more clear and firm. Secondly for teaching the meaning of a word or some very difficult line, use of mother tongue helps in proper understanding by the students. Therefore the teacher should be free to use mother tongue in some difficult situations or teaching learning. Bilingual method also advocates the same thing. Not English be taught directly in English medium. Instruction may be given in mother tongue.

The structural approach highlights the importance of teaching structure by creating situations. In teaching English mastery of basic structures is a must. All this will help the students to be good in all the four skills of language learning i.e. listening, speaking, reading and writing. Naturally then the students will be able to communicate well orally as well in written form.

Thus teaching English by combination of different methods and approaches will help the teacher to teach English, effectively in one and all type of classroom situations. The outcomes of eclectic approach will be good learning of English by the students.

ASSIGNMENTS

1. "Communication skills form the basis of learning the language well." Discuss by giving your own views.

2. What are the basic assumptions of Linguistic Communicative Approach? Justify their importance in language learning.
3. What are the pre-requisites of Linguistic Communicative Approach? Discuss briefly.
4. (a) What is Linguistic Communicative Approach?
   (b) What are the advantages of Linguistic Communication Approach?
5. (i) What do you mean by linguistic competence?
   (ii) Write a note on Language learning and Social setting.
6. What is eclectic approach? How is it useful in teaching English in Indian classroom situations.

9

Structural Approach

Heavily debated in the term 'Structural Approach' as it stands, because some people misinterpret it. They believe that it is a method of teaching English. The hard fact is that it is not a method. In a method, we come to know how a particular item is to be taught. In fact, a method is a body of certain techniques. Besides, methods vary from person to person, from place to place and from subject to subject but in case of an approach, we do not have any such type of alternatives. In structural approach, the different structures form the most important thing. Any method can be used for presenting the structures to the learners. Thus we find that the structural approach is not a method but it is an approach which quickens the process of learning a language.

The expression 'Structural Approach' comprises two words 'structural' and 'approach'. The word 'Structural' relates to the structures and 'Approach' literally means coming near. Thus Structural Approach in teaching of English means approaching English on the basis of structures. For this purpose, the structures are well made to teach English. That is called Structural Approach. In this approach, the structures are taught by creating situations. That makes the teaching, learning more effective.

Menon and Patel say in their book 'The Teaching of English as a Foreign Language.' "The Structural approach is based on the belief that in the learning of a foreign language, mastery of structures is more important than the acquisition of vocabulary."

Different Approaches

Different approaches for teaching English are vocabulary approach, grammar approach, structural approach, functional approach etc. In vocabulary approach, the students learn vocabulary items and thereby try to learn English. It is not very effective because words in isolation are not effective for learning the language. In grammar approach, the students are asked to learn the rules of grammar. That does not help much in learning the language. In structural approach, structures are taught by creating situations. All efforts are made to help the students have mastery over the structures. Comparatively structural approach is more effective in teaching a language. In functional approach, functions of the language are given importance. These days communicative function of the language is given the top most importance.

Defining Structure?

The different arrangements in one accepted style or the other is called a structure. The structure may be a complete utterance or it may be a part of some large pattern. The different types of arrangements are called structures. The structures are the tools of a language. Every language has its own tools ; its own pattern of structures. The structures are just like photo frames. Once we get a photo frame, any number of photos can be fitted into it. In the same way, if we learn a structure any number of sentences of the same type can be constructed.

Here below are examples of some structures:

I. S.V.O.

(a) We bought books. (b) She played hockey.
(c) I knew him. (d) The police caught the thief.
(e) You learnt a lesson. (f) He taught English.

II. V.S.O.

(a) Is he a doctor? (b) Are you Geeta?
(c) Is it a flower? (d) Was she a lecturer?
(e) Was it a dog? (f) Was-she a doctor?

III. S.V.O (Negative)

(a) He is not a doctor. (b) You are not Geeta.
(c) It is not a flower. (d) Veena is not a teacher.

IV. V.S.O. (Negative)

(a) Is he not a doctor? (b) Are you not Geeta?
(c) Is it not a flower? (d) Is your brother not a doctor?
(e) Is she not a teacher?

Various Types

There are different types of structures. Basically we may divide them into four different categories:

Sentence Patterns : The sentences may be of different designs e.g., He is my friend. Is he a thief? He has not accepted my proposal. Roshan was not my friend.

Formula : Formula means group of words used regularly on certain occasions e.g., Good evening. Thank You, That's right, Mention not, Good-bye.

Phrase Patterns : The different types of phrases are in the house, out of pocket, under the chair, on the table etc.

Idioms : These are the group of words that must be taught as a whole and not as separate ones, e.g., in the teeth of, in black and white, at sixes and sevens, a snake in the grass etc.

The Concept

Approaching English on the basis of selected structures is called Structural Approach. It is called structural approach because the main emphasis is laid on the mastery of structures or pattern of sentences and phrases and also on the special features of the language which help in the construction of a sentence such as word order, structural words and a few inflexions in English.

In this approach, the use of mother tongue is allowed at the initial stages and that too for explaining a situation when some sentence pattern is to be practised. But it does not allow translation of the structures which are to be practised. The learners are given drill of the structures till they are able to use them automatically without straining their minds.

By teaching the different structures, the aim is to develop certain skills. The different skills are as under:

Ability to (i) understand the spoken language

(ii) speak the language

(iii) read the language

(iv) write the language

In structural approach, the emphasis is on the acquisition of different skills. The person learning the language is able to acquire it through situations. *E.V Gatenby* says: "First follow nature is a good piece of advice for the language teacher. As nature does show us a sure way to success it is only common sense to follow her methods. Where they are followed to-day in the schools of the world, there is very little failure to learn a language."

The Objectives

According to *Menon* and *Patel*, the objectives of structural approach are:

1. To lay the foundation of English by establishing thorough drill and repetition about 275 graded structures.
2. To enable the children to attain mastery over an essential vocabulary of about 3000 root words for active use.
3. To correlate the teaching of grammar and composition with the reading lessons.
4. To teach the four fundamental skills namely understanding, speaking, reading and writing in the order named.
5. To lay proper emphasis on the aural oral approach, active methods and the condemnation of formal grammar for its own sake.

The Principles

The structural approach is based on some principles which are explained hereunder:

Importance of Speech: In the learning of a language, speech is more important than reading and writing, the reason being that language is learnt orally first. Then speech becomes the basis for acquiring other skills like reading and writing. In structural approach, speech is given more importance. It is sheet-anchor of this new approach. This principle is, therefore, very sound as it lays the foundations of language learning. Thus this approach helps in better teaching of the language.

Formation of Language Habits: Structural Approach takes care of the fact that learning of a language is a habit formation process. Here a lot of drill work is given to the learners. The students are given a lot of practice in listening, speaking, reading and writing. Thus the structures are well fixed up in the minds of the learners.

When language learning is based on the principle of habit formation., everything becomes natural with the language learner. It may be of speaking, reading or writing-all these skills are efficiently learnt through practice. Then the language becomes a natural gift with the person who makes use of it.

Pupil's Activity: For learning the language, the students are expected to be very active. In structural approach, pupil's activity is given more importance as compared to teacher's activity. Moreover, the best teaching takes place if both the teacher and the students are actively involved in it. The structural approach takes care of it.

Mastery of Structures: In structural approach, emphasis is laid on the mastery of structures. One structure is taken up as the teaching point. Its listening, speaking, reading and writing practice is given to the learners step by step. The more the aural-oral practice given to the learners, the better would be the result. Actually aural-oral work forms the basis of effective learning of the language material. Emphasis, therefore, need be laid on all the four skills. It will ensure mastery of structures. And mastery of structures results in effective learning of the language.

Meaningful Situations: In structural approach, the teacher is expected to create meaningful situations- That makes the teacher's work interesting. Moreover, the students are able to learn the structures very well. The different types of meaningful situations can be created by facial expressions, by dramatization and by actions. In fact, the resourceful teacher faces no difficulty in creating meaningful situations.

Teaching One Item of Language at a Time: In structural approach, only one item is taken up at a time and taught to the students. In this way, the students are able to grasp it well. A new structure is taught by using the vocabulary already learnt by the students. The second structure is introduced when the learner acquires mastery over the first structure.

Advantages

1. The students remain active throughout in the teaching learning process.
2. This approach helps the students to acquire fluency in their spoken English.
3. It makes the students creative learners. They are able to think a large number of sentences of similar types.
4. The students are able to understand the subject matter fully because teaching is conducted by creating meaningful situations.
5. The learners are able to retain the subject matter in their minds for a longer time because they learn through situations.
6. Learning of the language takes place in a natural way because the students have listening and speaking first followed by reading and writing.
7. It enables the students to have good command over the language.

8. It helps the learners to have good pronunciation. Whereever a student mispronounces a word, there is immediate check by the teacher.
9. Language learning becomes a habit with the student. So the learner is able to speak or write without any stress or strain.
10. The different skills of teaching learning the language are equally emphasised. So the students are good in all the skills i.e. listening, speaking, reading and writing.
11. Structural approach helps all the students of the class to learn the language well. Even the slow learners and the backward children are benefited.

The Limitations

Structural approach, undoubtedly, is of great utility in teaching English to children at all levels. It has worked in the field of English teaching. It has a few shortcomings which are given below:

1. In structural approach, the learners have to be given a lot of practice. This type of teaching might make the process of teaching learning dull and mechanical for a few learners.
2. Teaching by structural approach requires the services of really competent and hard working teachers. But there is dearth of this type of teachers in our country.
3. Teaching by structural approach will be successful only if we have structurally graded syllabus.
4. Now when the emphasis is on communcicative approach, structural approach cannot be given more importance and weightage.

Thus we find that the principles of structural approach are very sound. They are straight way helpful in the teaching learning of a language. But the structures are many and English being a foreign language, it is not an easy job to have mastery over all the structures. So there is need of selecting the structures. It is done on the basis of some principles.

The structural approach is [illegible]ely an improvement upon the traditional methods of teaching English in India. It has made teaching learning scientific. It has also brought a system, variety, life and activity in the teaching of English. Some people still say that this approach has faced an utter failure in the schools. It is quite wrong to say like that. In fact, it needs competent teachers and hard work on their shoulders. For making it a success, *Menon* and *Patel* have suggested in their book 'The Teaching of English as a Foreign Language' Good teachers, smaller classes, provision for up-to-date audio-visual aids, text books written in accordance with the new syllabus are the pre-requisites for the success of the structural approach." To Sum up the structural approach makes the young learners keen and active. It has opened up their lips and justified the truth of the famous Chinese proverb, "Nothing can be taught, though every thing can be learnt."

Selection of Structures

There are large number of structures. Nobody can learn all the structures of a language. Everybody selects structures and then within the selected list, he/she goes on teaching or writing anything. The text book writer also selects the structures. Selection of structure is done on the basis of a few principles which are briefly explained below:-

Principles

Usefulness: While making a selection of structures, we should see that only those structures are selected which are really very useful for the learners. The structures which occur frequently in their reading material and are actively used by them should be given preference. For example, for the VI class students, we will select the structure: 'This is a .... That is a .... and for the VI I Class we must select the structure. 'There is a .... There are .... because these are quite useful for these classes. The students find these structures frequently occurring in their text books. Once they are familiar with these structures, it becomes very easy for them when they come across the structures in their books.

Productivity: By productivity of a structure, we mean that a number of structures can be produced out of it. So in the selection of structures, the productivity of a structure should also be taken into consideration. For example, here are two structures: 'I have to go' the structure to have to do something and 'Boil the water'. The number of sentences that can be made with the first structure is almost limitless. So we will say that it has high productivity. On the other hand, very little can be done with the help of second structure. That structure has low productivity. In other words, we can say that the first structure is more productive as compared to the second one.

Simplicity: The Structures which are quite simple are given preference to the complicated ones. Here by simplicity, we mean that the form and meaning of the structure should be simple. For example; The structure 'He is working' is simpler as compared to the structure, 'No sooner did the bell ring than the boys ran away'. Similarly the structure Although he is poor yethe is honest' is simpler as compared to the above structure where 'no sooner-than' has been used. So it is very essential that the principle of simplicity should be fully taken care of while making a selection of structures.

Teachability: By teachability of structure, we mean that it should be easily- demonstrated in a realistic situation. The structures which are easy from teaching point of view should be given preference. For example, the structure-'I bought this book for ten rupees' can be taught easily but the teaching of the structure 'He comes late every day' is not that easy.

Thus on the basis of the above said principles, the structures are selected. Then they need be graded.

Gradation

Grading implies putting the teaching material in a suitable order. While grading, very simple and common type of structures are kept for teaching at the early stages. Difficult structures are kept for later stages. In short, by gradation we meant which item after which. Thus by gradation, the structures are put in order and then they are presented to the learners one by one in that serial order. *F.G. French* suggests that during the first three years of learning English, the patterns given below should be taken up:

1. Two part patterns.
   Veena/danced.
   The Girl/sang.
2. Three part patterns.
   I/bought/a book.
   Neela/sang/a song.
3. Four part patterns
   The teacher/gave/me/a prize.
   The lady/told/us/a story.
4. The negative forms of the patterns given below.
   ` For example,
   (a) Veena did not dance
   The girl did not sing.

(b) I did not buy a book.
Neela did not sing a song,

5. The interrogative forms of these patterns starting with a verb or question word-what - who etc.
   (i) Did Veena Dance?
   Did the girl sing?
   (ii) Did I buy a book?
   Did Neela sing a song?
6. Command and request.
   (i) Open the door.
   Get out from the class.
   (ii) Please help the poor.
   Meet your boss, please.
7. Hidden subject pattern using 'there and it' e.g.
   (i) There are twenty books on the table.
   (ii) It is a good book.

Thus the different structures form the subject matter or material of structural approach. The approach lays emphasis on the fact that the various structures must be taught to the learners of the language and then there is no reason why a student should fail to come up to the expectations of the teacher.

Many Structures

Now the question arises how many structures or patterns should be learnt to form a good foundation? For this a committee was set up by 'All India Council for Secondary Education.' It suggested a list of 250 structures which can be taught in the first three years of secondary school.

Teaching of Structures

While teaching structures, the teacher should take the pupils through four stages-listening, recognition, imitation and reproduction. Various methods of teaching the structures are given ahead .

Oral Teaching: Aural-oral method is the most suitable for teaching the structures. The teacher may give oral drill to the class in chorus, groups and then to individuals. It will involve speaking both by the teacher and the students. Then reading or writing of the same may be taken up. Pointing out the importance of oral work in teaching structures, *C.C. Fries* in his book, 'Teaching and Learning English as a Foreign Language' rightly says, "The speech is the language. The written record is a secondary representation of the language. To master a language, it is necessary to read it but it is extremely doubtful whether one can really read the language, without mastering it orally."

Situational Teaching: Situational teaching means teaching by creating situations. Anything taught or learnt in a situation is more meaningful than otherwise. It makes teaching or learning more realistic. Moreover, the learner is able to retain the matter for a longer 'time. Situational teaching is therefore, of great value in the teaching of any language.

The best way of teaching structures is by creating situations. The situation makes the structure easily understandable. It establishes a closer and more direct relation between an expression and its meaning. It is very important here that the situation should be appropriate to the structure in hand, otherwise it will lead to confusion.

From the book 'Teaching English' by C.S. Bhandari and others- it is worth quoting. "A structure or a word becomes meaningful for the learner when it is used in an appropriate situation. The teacher should use a particular situation in order (a) to practise the structure and to relate it to its meaning (a) to build up a vocabulary of content words."

Categories of Situations

(a) Situations which the child can see, bear and touch directly in the class room and also through the class room windows.

(b) Situations which the pupil knows from his own experiences in this daily life, family circle etc.

(c) Situations which can be recalled to mind through imagination with the help of pictures, maps, charts, plans, dramatisation and other aids.

(d) Situations which are brought into the minds of the pupils through the spoken or printed word alone.

Creating Situations

The situations can be created in the following ways:-

By using Actual Objects: By showing actual objects inside and outside the class room, we can teach structures like 'This is a window' 'This is a door' 'Ram is here and Sham is there'.

Through Gestures and Actions: For creating certain situations, actions have to be performed. It should be done carefully by the teacher so as to create the right type of situations. For example, 'I am reading'. I am writing.' He is standing.' 'He is sitting.' For all these sentences, situations are created by performing actions and thus they are taught to the students.

By Using Models, Charts and Pictures: There are certain things which in actual form, cannot be brought to the class room. So in such cases, models, charts or pictures can be made use of. For example, elephant, camel, lion etc. cannot be- actually brought into the class room. So we can show their models or pictures and this teach the class about those things.

If the teacher is an expert in blackboard drawing, simple match stick diagrams can be used to create situations. Sometimes, it so happens that the teacher prepares a chart but he forgets it at home. In that case, he should not postpone teaching. He should rather know something of black-board sketching and thus create situations and teach the lesson scheduled for the day.

Verbal Situations: In some cases, physical situation cannot be created by using any of the above said devices. There comes the need of creating a verbal situation. Verbal situation is nothing but creation of a situation by speaking something. Suppose the teacher is to teach the following two sentences:

(a) He is shutting the door.

(b) Neela comes every day.

For the first sentence, physical situation can be created in the class room., but in the case of second sentence, verbal situation will have to be created. How? The teacher will speak a number of sentences like-

The school opens at 9-00 a.m.

Neela came at 9-15 a.m. yesterday.

She came at 9-30 a.m. the day before.

She came at 9-30 a.m. to-day.

Neela comes late everyday.

For teaching the word 'forget' verbal situation can be created as under:

The teacher asks the names of some students; Veena, Sheela, Neena, Leena etc. Then he speaks by pointing towards the students one by one. Your name is Veena. Your name is Sheela. Your name is Neena. Your name .... I forget. This verbal situation makes clear the meaning of the word 'forget.'

Action Chains: Through action chains, the same structure can be drilled very well. For example, a number of continuous actions may be performed by the teacher and the way of speaking: "I am shutting the door. I am opening the door. I am shutting the window. I am opening the window." Then the pupils perform those very actions one by one and speak out whatever they are actually doing.

Substitution Tables

A substitution table is an important aid in the hands of the teacher. The teacher can prepare the substitution table by taking up one structure. He can also involve the students for its preparation.

(a) For example-

1	2	3	4	5	6
He	is	writing	a	letter	
She		reading		book	
Ram					
Veena					8xlx2xlx2=32
The girl					sentences
The boy					
My brother					
My friend					

With the help of the above substitution table, the structure, 'He is writing a letter' can be taught. The learners can be enabled to speak as many as 32 different sentences which are basically of the same pattern.

(b) Suppose the teacher wants to teach the negative form of past indefinite tense. He will write any one sentence of this type and then prepare substitution table e.g.

He	did not		solve	the question
		write		
She			learn	
We				
They				
The boy				
The Girl				

(c) 1	2	3	4	5	6	7	8	9
Why	does	he	come	late	to	the	school ?	
							office	
	she	go						
	the teacher							
	the headmaster							
	the student							
	the monitor							
	your friend							
	your brother							
			8x2x2 = 32 sentences					

The above given substitutions table helps the teacher to teach interrogative sentences or Present Indefinite tense. The farmers can have practice of sentences starting with the questions word 'why. In all, 32 sentences are possible with the help of this substitution.

By using the above given substitution table, 18 sentences can be spoken or written.

Thus the different structures are taught to the learners of a foreign language in an interesting way. Randolph Quirk, writes in his book 'The Teaching of English', "The structural approach brings us nearer to an understanding of the most characteristic human activity and near to linking it up with the rest of man's patterned and systematic behaviour.

Some of the structures briefly illustrated through examples are given below:

S. No.	Teaching Points	Examples
1.	This is....	Touching a table, a chair, a book, a chalk board we may say; This is a table. This is a chair. This is a book. This is a chalk board.
	That is	Pointing towards a table, a chair, a book, a chalk board we may say: That is a table. That is a chair. That is a book. That is a chalk board. By comparison, we may say: This is a book. That is a book. This is a dog. That is a dog.

Contd.

S. No.	Teaching Points	Examples	
.		This is a clock. That is a clock.	
2.	These are ..... Those are	Touching some books and pens, we may say: These are books. These are pens. Pointing towards books and pens, we will say; Those are books.	 Those are pens.
3.	My, your, his, her (Singular Possessives)	This is my pencil. This is my dog. This is his pen. This is his pen.	That is your pencil. That is your dog. That is her pen. This is her book.
4.	Our, Your, Their	These are our pens. These are your pens. These are your pencils.	Those are your pens. Those are their pens. Those are their pencils.
5.	Parts of the body	This is my head. This is my car. This is my mouth. This is my finger. This is my foot. These are my cars. These are my feet.	This is my eye. This is my nose. This is my hand. This is my leg. This is my thumb. Those are my hands. These are my eyes.
6.	Here, There	I am here. My book is here. My dog is here. My house is here.	You are there. Your book is there. Your dog is there. Your house is there.
7.	In, On	The pencil is in the bag. The book is on the, table. The pen is in the inkpot. The inkpot is on the table. The child is in the room. The child is on the cot.	
8.	I am...we are you are...They are He is... she is...	I am a teacher. You are a student. You are students. He is a boy.	We are friends They are teachers. They are friends She is a girl.
9.	_s' (Possessive)	That is Ram's book. This is Mohan's dog. Sita's book is in the bag.	
10.	And (Sentence connector)	This is a boy and that is a girl. This is a chair and that is a table. This is a dog and that is a cat.	
11.	Under, over	A chart may be prepared in which there is shown a river, a bridge, a boat under the bridge and birds flying over the bridge. By showing the chart, we may say: (i) The boat is under the bridge, (ii) The birds are over the bridge. (iii) The bridge is over the boat.	
12.	The, a (When only one	Suppose there is a class room which has walls and a door. By touching walls and	

Contd.

S. No.	Teaching Points	Examples	
	object of a kind is present)	door one, by one, We may say This is a wall. This is a wall. This is a wall. This is the door.	
13.	-ing form (present continuous) She is sleeping. They are reading.	I am playing. He is writing.	
14.	-ing form with objects	I am playing football. He is writing a letter. They are reading books.	
15.	Numbers	This is a flower. This is a tree. This is a man. This is a dog. This is a house.	These are flowers. These are trees. These are men. These are dogs. These are houses.
16.	Commands	Sit down Stand up. Come here. Write your name. Close your books.	 Go to the door. Open your books.
17.	Too (also)	I am going to Delhi. My brother is going too. Veena has come. Her sister has come too.	
18.	Behind, in front of	Our house is behind the school. The school is in front of our house. The garden is behind the post office. The post office is in front of the garden.	
19.	Inverted question forms with 'yes' answer (Simple present)	He is a boy. You are a girl. She is a doctor. They are players.	Is he a boy? Are you a girl? Is she a doctor? Are they players?
20.	Negative Answers (above)	No, he is not a boy. No, I am not a girl. No, it is not a pen. No, it is not a book.	
21.	Short Positive answers	Showing a book a pen, a knife. Is this a book? Yes, it is. Is this a pen? Yes, it is Is this a knife? Yes, it is. Showing a person writing something. Is he writing? Yes, he is., Is she reading a book? Yes, she is.	
22.	Questions with 'ing' form plus object. 'Yes'-'No' answers	He is writing. Is he writing? Yes, he is writing No, he is not writing. They are playing. Are they playing? Yes, they are playing. No, they are not playing.	

Contd.

S. No.	Teaching Points	Examples	
23.	Questions with 'ing' form plus object. 'Yes-No' answers	Is he writing a book? Yes, he is writing a book. No, he is not writing a book. Is she singing a song? Yes, she is singing a song. No, she is not singing a song.	
24.	Past Indefinite Tense, Positive Negative and Question forms	We played. We did not play. Did we play? Did we not play?	They went. They did not go. Did they go? Did they not go?
25.	Past continuous Tense, Positive-Negative and Questions forms.	She was weeping. Was she weeping? She was not weeping.	
26.	'What' question with object.	Showing a book/books, we may say; What is this? What are these?	 What is that? What are those?
27.	What question With verb (ing) Present and Past	What are you writing? What was he reading? What was he singing?	
28.	'Where' questions with object Present and past.	Where is the girl? Where was the book?	Where is the boy? Where was the pen?
29.	'Who' questions. Who is near the black board? Who is your best friend? Who is in the class? Who is out of station?	Who is at the door?	
30.	Question starting.	Whose son is he? Whose book is this?	
31.	Simple Future Tense, positive, negative and question forms.	I will go tomorrow. You will go tomorrow. Will you go tomorrow? Will you not go tomorrow?	
32.	Adjectives of colour (red, green, blue, black).	This is a red book. That is a green shirt. Your pencil is blue. My pen is black.	
33.	Adjectives of size small, short, fat.	A big ball, a small ball; a long line, a short line, a fat person, a thin person.	
34.	Adjectives of Quality (Old, new young, heavy, ugly, beautiful, smart.	that old book This new book. The beautiful girl. The young girl. The heavy goods.	 The ugly boy. The smart boy.
35.	In, on, at (showing time)	They were here in January. He came on Monday. She went at 3-30 p.m.	
36.	Up, down	Ram is up there. Neela is down here.	
37.	early, late	Our train started at 5 a.m.	

Contd.

S. No.	Teaching Points	Examples
	Your bus started at 6 a.m.	
	We started early.	
38.	One, another, (long series).	These are boys. (3 or more). This is one. This is another. That is another.
39.	One, the other (one of two)	These are two books. This is one book and that is the other.
40.	Have, has (Permanent Possession)	I have a shirt. She has a saree. You have a dog.
41.	First-last (Space and time)	Ram is the first boy in this line. Sham is the last boy in it.
	January is the first month in the year.	
	December is the last month in the year.	
42.	Before-after (Time)	January comes before March. May comes after March.
43.	Some, any;	I bought some apples, Did you buy any apple?
44.	A few, a little.	We bought a few books. You bought a few note books. We bought a little milk. She bought a little ink.
45.	More than, Less than	My purse contains ten rupees. Your purse contains five rupees. My purse contains more money than yours. Your purse contains less money than mine.
46.	As much as	This glass has as much milk as that.
47.	As many as	I have as many mangoes as you have. I have as many houses as you have.
48.	As-Adj-as As-big as, as small as)	Your table is big. My table is also big. Your table is as big as mine. Your chair is small. My chair is also small. Your chair is as small as mine.
49.	-ert, -est. more, most	Veena is more beautiful than her sister. This girl is the most beautiful in the class. My younger brother is abler of the two. My younger brother is the ablest of the whole group.
50.	From-To (Time)	(i) I was here from 8 to 9. I was at Simla from May to July. (ii) I am going to the door. I am coming from the door. The child is going to the school. He is coming from the school.
51.	For (Time)	I played for two hours. She sang for fifteen minutes.
52.	Since (Time)	I have been here since 8 a.m. This Principal has been here since January.
53.	Already-yet	Have you read the book already?

Contd

S. No.	Teaching Points	Examples
	Questions and Positive, Negative answers	No, I have not read it yet. Yes, I have read it already.
54.	Too much Too many	There is too much water in the river. There are too many boys in the room. There is too much rush in the bazaar. There are too many naughty pawns in the bazar.
55.	Either-or	In this class, most of the boys are honest. Perhaps Ram is a thief. Sham may also be so. Either Ram or Sham is a thief.
56.	Neither-nor	In the class Veena is generally good. Neela is also good. Neither Veena nor Neela is bad. The table is not bad. The chair is also not bad.
57.	Able +Verb (All Tenses)	I am able to go. They will be able to come.
58.	-ing to -verb (future meaning)	I am going tomorrow. I am going to see him.
59.	About to (Time)	The game is about to start The train is about to come.
60.	About (approximately)	He came about three years ago. I came here about ten minutes back.
61.	In about at about	The paper will finish in about few hours. I went at about I p.m.
62.	If clause (future meaning with one event depending on another)	If Ram comes, I will go. If Ram comes, I will go. If it rains, they will stay at home. If I stand first, I shall give a party.

ASSIGNMENTS

1. "Structural Approach is an approach and not a method." Discuss with reference to its characteristics and describe how it has influenced the teaching and learning of English in India.
2. Describe the meanings of structures and structural patterns. How should these be selected and graded to improve the teaching of English?
3. Describe how structures and structural patterns should be presented and practised in the English class room.
4. What is the importance of situational teaching? How will you create situations for teaching certain things in a class room situation? Write by giving examples.

5. Select three patterns of sentences for the VII class. Explain why you select those and not others. How will you grade and teach them to that class?
6. What is the Structural Approach to teaching of English? How is it an improvement upon the 'Direct Method' of teaching English?
7. What are the essential features of the structural approach to the teaching of English? How dos it differ from the traditional grammar-translation method?
8. 'In learning a foreign language, mastery of structures is more important than mere acquisition of vocabulary' Discuss.
9. How is Structural Approach better than the traditional methods of teaching? Give reasons.
10. The Structural Approach to the teaching of English is a practical way of language. Elaborate this pcint of view with the help of pertinent examples.
11. What are the principles for the selection and gradation of structures or patterns in teaching English? How will you teach the patterns to the students of IX class?
12. What is structural Approach to the teaching of English?
13. What are its characteristic features, merits and demerits?
    (a) What do you mean by a structure? Give two examples.
    (b) Write a note on 'Selection of Structures'.
    (c) What is Structural Approach?
14. (a) How are structures graded?
    (b) Discuss any one method of teaching structures.
    (c) Write two structures for each of the following classes: (i) i (ii) viii (iii) ix

10

Teaching Prose

In literature, prose and poetry are the two forms. Generally in the schools, teaching of prose is considered an easy affair by the teachers. The simple reason being that they feel that it is to be translated into mother tongue. Just translation into mother tongue is not the be-all and end-all of teaching prose. Effective teaching of prose means the attainment of different aims fixed up by the authorities. If this is the case, then the teaching of prose is rather a challenging affair. What type of reading material will be all right for the learner? Easy, interesting and understandable type of matter will suit him the most. In this regard, *Johnson* says, "I will let him at first read any English book which happens to engage his attention because you have a great deal when you have taught him to have entertainment from a book. He will get better books afterwards."

Present Position of Teaching Prose

In teaching of English, prose is always considered important. But the method of teaching it is generally faulty. The following points highlight the glaring defects:

(i) Majority of teachers just translate English prose into mother tongue. In doing so, they feel that they have taught prose well. It is their wrong notion.

(ii) The teachers teach prose just for the sake of prose. They are after finishing the syllabus. And above all, they keep the examination as the main target before them. They rarely teach prose for making the students loam the language.

(iii) Applied grammar or functional aspect of the language are not properly dealt with by the teachers. Generally they leave it to the students. Then they expect that the students should know all these things and they should prepare these items at home. Naturally the students will be compelled to use guides or cheap notes of the market.

(iv) Very limited number of teachers teach prose intensively in the real sense of the word. Such teachers really try to achieve the main aims of teaching prose.

The Aims

(i) To give listening practice to the students.
(ii) To give speaking practice to the learners.
(iii) To give practice of loud reading and silent reading.
(iv) To help them have practice of writing English correctly.
(v) To make them read prose intensively and extensively as the case may be.
(vi) To help the learners add to their vocabulary.
(vii) To enable the learners develop the ability to write independently, accurately and creatively on subjects of general interest.
(viii) To develop the habit of reading for pleasure.
(ix) To make the students library-minded and develop their interest for extra reading.
(x) To give them practice of structures and sentence patterns.
(xi) To improve their pronunciation.
(xii) To make the students interested in English literature.
(xiii) To develop love of the students for English language.
(xiv) To enable the students to read prose effectively and with a reasonable speed.
(xv) To help the students understand the applied grammar contained in prose.

Teaching Intensively

Teaching of prose chiefly aims at comprehension by the students. In teaching prose, the following steps are suggested:

Step I. The teacher introduces the lesson to the students. He tells something about the lesson and something about the writer in simple English. Thus he creates proper environment for teaching.

Step II. The teacher gives model reading of the prose paragraph to be taught. In doing so, he takes care of correct pronunciation. He may give second model reading also depending upon the need and requirement of class room situation.

Step III. The teacher deals with the difficult language items contained in the prose paragraph. He teaches the difficult words by using different methods of teaching vocabulary. Side by side, the teacher goes on giving practice for the use of those language items.

Step IV. The teacher asks the students to do silent reading of the prose paragraph. For this, he prescribes the time limit.

Step V. The teacher asks the students about their difficulties in understanding the prose paragraph. The problems of the students are solved.

Step VI. A few comprehension test questions are put to the students one by one. The teacher enables them to give the correct answers. For this purpose, he gives hints or guidelines for giving the appropriate answers.

Step VII. Lastly, the teacher gives some home work to the students. He may ask them to use the vocabulary items in their sentences at home, or he ask's them to write answers of the comprehension test questions.

Teaching Extensively

Extensive Reading is based on SQ3R formula which is explained below:

Here S stands for Survey, Q stands for Questions and 3R stands for Read, Recite and Review.

The following are the steps for conducting a lesson of extensive reading.

The Survey

Explanation of Key Words: Only very important words ignore the extremely difficult ones.

The Questions

Pre-reading Questions: Teacher gives questions to the students., answers to which they must look for as they read.

More Survey

The teacher mentions main events, characters, ideas etc. These may or may not be written on the black-board.

The Reading

The students read that passage silently. They should be encouraged to read as quickly as possible and not stop over individual difficult words etc. Students should read to answer the pre-reading questions.

Extreme difficulties may be checked up side by side if necessary. However, adequate work in the above three steps should make this necessary.

Recite Reproduction

The students are asked to answer orally the pre-reading questions listed earlier. Whenever the students are unable to answer the questions, the teacher will refer them to the part of the passage containing the answer.

After pre-reading questions are answered, other questions should be asked. These new questions may include, 'Yes-No' type as well as 'Summary' type.

More Review

After satisfactory responses are given to the above questions, the teacher will ask the students to read the passage again silently as fast as they can. To enable the students to know their reading speed, the teacher should announce the limit of time so that the pupils can check the amount of time it takes them to read the passage increasing reading speed be encouraged.

In teaching prose, testing comprehension ability of the learner is cry important. Let us now acquaint ourselves with:

(i) A comprehension Question and its types.

(ii) Way of testing comprehension.

Comprehension Questions

A Comprehension Question is a question put to assess the reader's ability to read and understand a piece of writing. Such a question has a dual function: (i) we can assess the learner's understanding of what he has read, (ii) we can also use it as a device to assist the learner in developing his reading abilities.

Various Types

Broadly comprehension questions may be put into two categories:

(a) Global (b) Local

Global comprehension type question is meant for testing the overall understanding of the paragraph or line read by someone.

Local comprehension type aims at eliciting from the learner his understanding of some important point in the language.

Comprehension Question may be of three types:

Factual Questions

A factual comprehension question tries to find out whether the learner is able to locate the fact occurring in the paragraph. The learner is able to do it if he understands the questions and then he is also able to decide which part of the paragraph contains the answer.

Inferential Questions

Here the learner has to think beyond the answer given in the reading paragraph. He draws a reasonable and valid inference by reading the paragraph. This type of questions form a higher order reading skill.

Evaluation Questions

Here the learner is expected to give a critical thinking to the question and give the answer from his own point of view. Naturally the learner will react to the incident/situation and give a suitable answer. This type of questions are of much higher order as far as reading skill is concerned.

Testing Comprehension

Here below are given some ways by which comprehension ability of the students can be tested:

(i) Simple straight forward questions may be put to the learners.
(ii) Such questions may be put for which the students may have to think over.
(iii) By asking them to write the summary of the passage in a few words.
(iv) By asking them to speak the main idea of the passage in a few words.
(v) Matching type questions may be set. The students will be able to match them correctly if they have comprehended the paragraph.
(vi) By asking the students to write compositions on the topic about, which they have studied the paragraphs.
(vii) Dictionary type questions may be set. For example, some words and expressions may be given and the students are asked to give meanings.
(viii) Multiple choice questions may be given and the students are asked to select the right answers.

(ix) Sentences are written in jumbled form. The students put them in order. Thus word order and meaning are tested.

The students, these days, read the prescribed books only. They read limited material. It is very important to ask them read more and more. Their habits of extra reading should be developed.

Analysis of a Prose Paragraph

On analysing a prose paragraph, the difficulties may be with regard to (i) Vocabulary. (ii) Structures. Let us see how to solve these problems

Words are of two types:

Function Words

These words have no meaning of their own. But they can be used in utterances to signal grammatical relationship. They are also called structural words. They are very simple to look at but it is quite difficult when they are taken up for teaching purposes. For example: auxiliaries (may, will), prepositions (on, to, up), conjunctions (when, whether), the article (a, an, the), degree words (more, most), interogative particles (who, whose), the generalising particle (ever) and special uses of there, it, one.

Content Words

The chief items of a language is the content words. They stand for things, actions and qualities. They are words that have meanings by themselves. For example, book, table (things); sit, sleep (actions), flood beautiful (qualities) etc. Edward Sapir says, "If language is to be satisfactory means of communication we must have objects, actions, qualities to talk about and these much have their compounding symbols in independent words."

Content Words

Class I Words: The words (N)

(i) Simple form of nouns such as pen, book, table, etc.

(ii) Compound forms such as football, book-shop.

(iii) Action words used in grammatical structure as thing words Nouns made of verbs such as failure, discovery, decision etc.

(iv) Quality words used in grammatical structures as thing words. Nouns made of adjectives such as goodness, truth, happiness, etc.

Class II Words: Action Words (Verb)

(i) Simple form of verbs such as run, play, etc.

(ii) Compound form of verb such as run out, play with etc.

(iii) Thing words used in grammatical structure as action words. Verbs made out of nouns such as enjoy, entitle, engage etc.

(iv) Quality words used in grammatical structures as action words.

There are verbs made up of adjectives. For example, weaken, beautify, are.

Class III Words: Quality words (Adjectives)

(i) Simple form of adjectives such as true, good, bad etc.

(ii) Thing words used in grammatical structures as quality words. They are adjectives made from nouns. For example, lovely, rainy etc.

(iii) Action words used in grammatical structures as quality words. They are adjectives made out of verbs. For example, suitable, written etc.

In English we find that there are a large number of words. If we want to understand the meaning of a particular word very clearly, we shall have to see the context and situation in which that word has been used. We cannot get the real meaning by taking up the words in isolation. It is all the more important to notice that there are different kinds of meanings.

Types of Meanings

The students should know it A-cry well that apart from dictionary meaning, there are other meanings of words. In all there are five kinds of meanings which are discussed here under:

Lexical Meaning

By lexical meaning, we mean the meaning of words as given in the dictionary. Suppose we want to understand the sentence: The beautiful girl married the ugly boy. The dictionary tells us that the girl and the boy are beings, the word 'marry' shows the specific action and the words 'beautiful' and 'ugly' indicate the qualities. Dictionary gives us only this much of understanding. It does not tell us whether beautiful refers to the quality of boy or girl.

Syntactical Meaning

Syntactical meaning is indicated by word order in a sentence. Welcome to know the position of words. They help us to have understanding of the sentence. For example, in the sentence referred above, we know that the girl is beautiful and the boy is ugly. The beautiful girl comes before the verb 'marry', so we get the idea that the beautiful girl performed the action and not the boy.

Morphological Meaning

Morphological meaning is indicated by the form of the word. The form of the word 'girl' (as against girls) and the form of the word 'boy' (as against boys) tells us that there was only one boy and one girl. Again the word married shows that the action was performed in the past and not in the present or in the future as will be the case if marries or will marry are used.

Intonational Meaning

Meaning of the words or sentences also depends upon the way they are spoken. The word's 'fire' can be spoken in two ways. By using (i) Falling intonation (ii) Rising intonation. If we use the falling intonation the word 'fire' gives us a warning that there is blaze, but if we use the rising intonation, it seems to ask a question whether there is really fire.

Cultural Meaning

Cultural meaning is taken from the knowledge of background experience of the life of the speaker. It also helps us a good deal in understanding a sentence very thoroughly. Here is an interesting example of a change that is now taking place in U.S.A. specifically. It relates to their culture alone. The use of the word 'bad' is taking up a new meaning. 'That was a bad movie, they say it with an extra stress on the word 'bad'. In this sentence, if taken in the cultural context in which it is developing, the word 'bad' actually means very good. So while speaking this sentence, the person is actually saying. 'That was a A-cry good movie' Spoken outside the cultural area of U.S.A., people would understand the sentence to mean the movie was not good, but in this cultural situation the meaning is different.

Teaching New Words

A number of methods can be used for teaching the new words to the learners. Some of them are briefly discussed here below:

Showing Actual Objects

Words which can be taught by showing actual objects should be taught that way. For example, the words 'Fan', 'Window' can be taught to the students by showing the actual objects. This method is quite useful for the lower classes as it brings variety and life into the classroom situations.

Performing Actions

There are some words whose actions can be performed. For example, walking, writing, jumping etc. That type of words should be taught by actions. Thus there is activity in the class and the students also love to learn those words by that way.

Showing Models

Sometimes the actual objects are not available. In that case; their models can be shown to the learners and thus the words can be taught. For example when we want to teach the words camel, cat, elephant, etc. their models can be shown to the learners and thus those words can be taught.

Using Charts and Pictures

A chart or a picture can be prepared for certain words-may be nouns or action words. Some situations can also be created with the help of charts and pictures. In this way, a sentence or a group of words can be made clear to the learners.

Using a Black-Board

Black-Board is the best type of aid for teaching purposes. If the teacher is an expert in drawing, in that case pictures can be drawn on the black-board. That way some of the words can be taught to the students.

Creating Verbal Situations

Sometimes it so happens that for some words, visual situations are not possible. In that case verbal situations are created. For example; we want to teach the word 'forget'. The teacher may speak the names of the students. Your name is Ram. Your name is Mohan. Your name is .... I forget. When this type of verbal situation is before the students, they will be able to understand that word.

Using Mother Tongue

When all sorts of devices fail for teaching a particular word, it is rather advisable that the teacher should tell the meaning of the word in mother tongue.

Associations

The new words may be associated with the old ones which the child has already learnt. It can be done by asking antonyms, synonyms, past tense, gender etc. as the case may be. For example, while teaching the word 'bad', the teacher may ask. 'What is the opposite of 'good'? Here it will be presumed that the students already know the word 'good'.

Different Levels

Suppose the word 'dog' is to be taught to the beginners who have just started learning the language. If this word is repeated a number of times before the children who have never seen it, it will simply be parrot like repetition of the word 'dog'. To the children it is merely a sound. In order to make the sound meaningful, it should be associated with the animal dog. Once the word has acquired meaning for the child it will go on adding to his knowledge. There will be associations around the word. Thus it will be fixed up in the minds of the learners very thoroughly.

1st Stage

I have a dog. It is my dog. I love my dog. (Here definite concrete relationship is established with one particular dog).

2nd Stage

Veena also has a dog. It is a different dog. Other people have dogs.

(Much later) Dog can be dangerous. All the dogs are not friendly. The dog is a faithful animal. (We have now reached a state of generalisation about dogs.)

3rd Stage

(Much later still). It is a dog's life. Every dog has his day. (An abstract and figurative use of the word 'Dog')

A Few Points

(a) As far as possible, the vocabulary should be presented with the help of the known structures.

(b) Only one meaning of a word should be presented at a time.
(c) In order to communicate meanings, one or more than one device should be used.
(d) Presentation should be followed by repetition and application.

Vocabulary Expansion

Words are our friends, acquaintances and strangers. In our daily life, we meet some people as strangers. If we meet them very often, we become friendly and in some cases, relative like contacts are formed. So does it happen in the case of vocabulary. There is need of expanding the vocabulary. Here below are given some of the methods:

In the learning of a language, expansion of vocabulary is important. Everybody is expected to improve his vocabulary with the passage of time. We can increase the vocabulary of the student in the following ways:

1. Some heading is suggested to a class of students. The learners are asked to speak words concerning that topic. The teacher goes on writing these words on the blackboard. For example: School, Teacher, Headmaster, Class, Monitor, Office, Students etc.

2. The students are asked to prepare lists of related words. Then they learn one list at a time. For example:

Write-Wrote, Written, Writers, Writer.

Book-Books, Bookish, Booking etc.

3. A special black board in the school may be reserved for vocabulary. At the top of this board, it may be written-'Vocabulary for today'. Some body from the school should be asked to write five new words everyday on that blackboard. The students may be asked to learn those words-meanings, usage, spellings etc.

4. (a) Some games may be introduced for the expansion of vocabulary. For example, the class may be divided into two groups. One student from one group speaks a word. Then the students of the second group speak the word starting with the last letter of the word spoken by the first group. In the same way, this game continues and vocabulary of the students will increase. While this game is on, the teacher if he so desires, may ask the students to tell the spellings of the words which they are speaking.

(b) The teacher may write some letter e.g. on the blackboard. Then the students may be asked to speak or write the words starting with that letter. It will help in the expansion of vocabulary.

(c) The teacher may write some word on the black-board e.g. 'picture'. Then the students are asked to form words with the letters 'PICTURE'. Some of the words, thus are CUT, PURE, CURE etc.

5. *Through Homonyms.* The words which have almost the same pronunciation but have different spellings and different meanings may be put in different categories. For example, write, right, rite, flower, flour, floor, etc.

The Practice

Practice is of utmost importance in the learning of every language. After the expansion of vocabulary, practice stage is all the more important. So it should be given due emphasis. The following steps should be kept in mind-

1. The Students should prepare their note-books and they should note down the new words which they have learnt from different sources. While preparing such lists, they should see that the context in which they have learnt the word is also taken down.
2. The vocabulary learnt should be integrated with the structures. Composition may also be developed.
3. The recognition vocabulary should be dealt with only at comprehension level i.e. listening and reading comprehension.
4. The different types of written exercises as mentioned in the previous chapter may also be made use of for practice in vocabulary.

Vocabulary like grammar is a means to an end and not an end in itself. Like grammar, it cannot be taught in vacuum.

Words are functional, but the only functional use to -which they can be put is to use them in meaningful sentences. Whenever any new word is to be introduced, it should be seen that it is presented dramatically and as correctly as possible. A word is a live thing, as it were, and not a museum specimen dead and set in a fixed pose.

Some Facts

1. If we take up any word of English and try to find out its equivalent in mother tongue, we shall fail miserably, the meanings are always approximate.

2. Some people feel that a word has got only one meaning. It is quite wrong to say like that. There are many meanings of the same word in different situations.
3. If we want to get at the meaning of a word, we should not take up the word in isolation, We should remember that context controls the meanings of words.
4. The synonyms of words within the same language are never one and the same thing. They are always approximate.
5. Any word of one language cannot be compared with the word of some other language. None of them is superior to the other. Each one is good at its own place.

Thus we find that in the learning of a language, vocabulary occupies a very important place, Words should not be studied in isolation. They should always be learnt in the context of situations. The fundamental golden principle learn the new words with the help of old structure and learn the new structure with the help of old vocabulary must be kept in mind. That way vocabulary does not pose any problem to the learner. It becomes an easy and interesting affair.

Dictionaries in Use

Teaching-learning of a language needs a lot of improvement. The way it is conducted in the classroom, is not good. The teacher teaches the language and then the students learn it. When the teacher does not teach, the students do not learn. They don't try even to learn at their own. There is a sort of spoon feeding of the learners. This is a wrong habit of learning. This must be checked. The teacher should inculcate among the students the right type of attitudes and help them have good habits of learning. Self-learning is the best habit. The teacher should help the learners team by that way.

In the learning of a foreign language, the student is often confronted with the problem of understanding. The student reads some material and is unable to understand it. On scrutinizing further, the learner feels that if the meaning of some words were known to him, he could understand the subject matter well. Meanings of difficult words can be known by consulting the dictionary. Dictionary is a never failing friend of the learner. It helps the learner in solving the problems of meanings. A good dictionary also teaches him many other things such as noun, verb, adverb-its forms, conjunegation etc. Even for teaching stress, correct pronunciation, dictionary helps.

Concise Oxford Dictionary

It is adopted by *H.W. Fowler* and *F.G. Fowler* from the Oxford Dictionary. The first few pages give a lot of information to the learners. Abbreviations used in the dictionary are given. The students should learn how to locate a word in the dictionary. Every word in the dictionary is arranged alphabetically. Out of a number of meanings given, the student can gradually find out the exact meaning that is needed by him. It would be better if the student spends some time for reading 2 or 3 or 4 lines given by way of meanings, grammatical aspects etc. That will improve his knowledge of language. Thus consulting dictionary helps the learner in a number of ways, Let us now see what are the advantages of consulting a dictionary.

Advantages of Consulting a Dictionary

1. A student becomes a better learner of the language.
2. The learner becomes good in spellings.
3. It improves the knowledge of grammar.
4. It creates good habit of self learning.
5. Knowledge of stress is acquired by the learners.
6. It expands vocabulary of the students.
7. It helps in the improvement of pronunciation.
8. And above all, it gives a lot of confidence to the student and he becomes self-reliant.

The following dictionaries are suggested:

1. The Advanced Learner's Dictionary of Current English by
   A.S. Homby
   EX Gatenby
   H. Wakefield

   Published by: The English Language Society and Oxford University Press.
2. Bhargava's Standard Illustrated Dictionary of the English Language
   (Anglo-Hindi Edition)
   Edited by R. C. Pathak

Published by: Bhargava Book Dept, Chowk, Varanasi.

3. PSUTB English Punjabi dictionary
   Chief Editor Balbir Singh Sandhu
   Former Chief Editor Attar Singh
   Published by : Punjab State University Text Book Board, Chandigarh.

Precautions while Consulting a Dictionary

1. Only a good dictionary should be used.
2. For learning English, English to English dictionary should be used.
3. Dictionary for mother tongue meanings may be used whenever need is felt.
4. In the beginning, the chief purpose for which it is being consulted should be kept in mind. Suppose spellings are to be seen, only spellings should be checked. If meanings are to be seen, one meaning of the word may be taken up at a time. And if time is available, everything concerning the word may be studied from the dictionary.
5. Dictionary should be easily available. It should remain at the study desk of the learner.

Thesaurus in Use

A thesaurus is the opposite of a dictionary. It is needed by the student when he/she has the meaning in mind but the exact word is escaping. One is in a fix to have the word. One has many other words which are not appropriate. Thus a thesaurus comes to assist the student. Surely keeping the thesaurus at the desk of the learner will help him in every situational need. This is also a step towards self-learning by the student. Why should the student always remain on the look out for the teacher's personal help or guidance? The teacher should; in fact, play such a role during teaching that he should equip the learners with this type of self-learning habits. That way then, the student makes progress and marches ahead fully inspired and self-motivated. This is the sure way to help the student learn English well.

Roget's Pocket Thesaurus edited by C.O. Sylvester Mawson assisted by Katharine Aldrich Whiting is recommended for the young learners. This is based on Roget's international Thesaurus.

A Thesaurus makes a person think more and more. Suppose we have got a word with the help of a thesaurus. With that word, the person may become happy first but after sometime it makes the person think of finding out another word.

The Advantages

Using a thesaurus has the following advantages:

(1) It expands and enriches the vocabulary of the student.
(2) It helps the learner have mastery of language.
(3) It helps him to find out synonyms or antonyms of any word.
(4) It helps him to find out suitable word to express some ideas.
(5) It provides new ideas on any given subject.

Thus, we find that a dictionary and a thesaurus are very good in the hands of learner of English. With their help, the learner can learn English well. Only the right use of tool helps in the achievement of desired goal- A good learner keeps this type of tool at his disposal and does not allow them to go beyond control. He makes them his friendly tools and this friendship makes him rich in language learning.

While teaching structures, the teacher should take the pupils through four stages-listening, recognition, imitation and reproduction. Generally the following methods are used for teaching the structures:

Oral Teaching. Aural-oral method is the most suitable for teaching the structures. The teacher may give oral drill to the class in chorus, in groups and then individually. It will involve speaking both by the teacher and the students. Then reading or writing of the same may be taken up. Pointing out the importance of oral work in teaching structures, C.C. *Fries* in his book, 'Teaching and Learning English as a Foreign Language' rightly says, "The speech is the language. The written record is a secondary representation of the language. To master a language, it is necessary to read it, but it is extremely doubtful whether one can really read the language, without mastering it orally."

Using Substitution Tables. A substitution table is an important aid in the hands of the teacher. The teacher can prepare the substitution table by taking up one structure. He can also involve the students for its preparation.

(a) For example:

1	2	3	4	5
He	is	writing	a	letter
She		reading		book
Rajesh				story
Neela				
The girl				
The boy				
My brother				
My friend				
The teacher				
The Headmistress				

With the help of the above substitution table, the structure, 'he is writing a letter' can be taught. The learners can be enabled to speak as many as 60 different sentences which are basically of the same pattern.

(b) Suppose the teacher wants to teach the negative form of past indefinite tense. He will write any one sentence of this type and then prepare substitution table e.g.,

He	did not	solve	the
		write	question
She		learn	
we			
They			
The boy			
The girl			
The student			
My friend			

By using the above given substitution table, 24 sentences can be spoken or written.

Thus the different structures are taught to the learners of a foreign language in an interesting way. Substitution tables can really work wonders in the teaching of structures to the students. They can be given a lot of listening, speaking, reading and writing practice by using the substitution tables. Here all learning by the students is through guidance. There are very few chances of committing errors by the students. *Randoph Quirk* writes in his book "The Teaching of English', "The structural approach brings us nearer to an understanding of the most characteristic human activity and near to linking it up with the rest of man's patterned and systematic behaviour.'

Situational Teaching

Situational teaching means teaching by creating situations. Anything taught or learnt in a situation is more meaningful than otherwise. It makes teaching or learning more realistic. Moreover, the learner is able to retain the matter for a longer time. Situational teaching is, therefore, of great value in the teaching of any language.

The best way of teaching structures is by creating situations. The situation makes the structure easily understandable. It establishes a closer and more direct relation between an expression and its meaning. It is very important here that the situation should be appropriate to the structure in hand, otherwise it will lead to confusion.

From the book 'Teaching English' by C.S. Bhandari and others, it is worth quoting, "A structure or a word becomes meaningful for the learner when it is used in an appropriate situation. The teacher should use a particular situation in order (a) to practise the structure and to relate it to its meaning (b) to build up a vocabulary of content words."

Four Categories of Situations

(a) Situations which the child can see, hear and touch directly in the class-room and also through the class-room windows.

(b) Situations which the pupil knows from his own experiences in his daily life, family circle etc.

(c) Situations which can be recalled to mind through imagination with the help of pictures, maps, charts, plans, dramatisation and other aids.

(d) Situations which are brought into the minds of the pupils through the spoken or printed word alone.

Creating Situations

The situations can be created in the following ways:

Actual Objects. By showing actual objects outside the class-room, we can teach the structures like 'This is a window'; 'This is a door'. 'Ram is here and Sham is there'.

Gestures and Actions. For creating certain situations, actions can be performed. It is done carefully by the teacher so as to create the right type of situations. for example, 'I am reading.' 'I am writing.' He is standing, he is sitting.' For all these sentences, situations are created by performing actions and thus they are taught to the students.

Models, Charts and Pictures. There are certain things which in actual form, cannot be brought to the class-room. So in such cases, models, charts or pictures are used. For example, elephant, camel, lion etc. cannot be actually brought into the class-room. So we can show their models or pictures and thus teach the class about those things.

If the teacher is an expert in blackboard drawing, simple match stick diagrams can be used to create situations. Sometimes, it so happens that the teacher prepares a chart but he forgets it at home. In that case, he should not postpone teaching. He should rather know something of black-board sketching and thus create situations and teach the lesson scheduled for the day.

Verbal Situations. In some cases, physical situation cannot be created by using any of the above said devices. There comes the need of creating a verbal situation. Verbal situation is nothing but creation of situation by speaking something. Suppose the teacher is to teach the following two sentences:

(a) He is shutting the door.

(b) Neela comes late every day.

For the first sentence, physical situation can be created in the classroom but in the case of second sentence, verbal situation will have to be created. How? The teacher will speak a number of sentences like–

The school opens at 9-00 a.m.

Neela came at 9-15 a.m. yesterday.

She came at 9-30 a.m. the day before.

She came at 9-30 a.m. today.

Neela comes late every day.

For teaching the word 'forget' verbal situation can be created as under:

The teacher asks the names of some students: Veena, Sheela, Neena, Leena etc. Then he speaks by pointing towards the students one by one. Your name is Veena. Your name is Sheela. Your name is Neena. Your name.... I forget. This verbal situation makes clear the meaning of the word 'forget'.

Action Chains. Through action chains— the same structure can be drilled very well. For example, a number of continuous actions may be performed by the teacher and he may speak; "I am shutting the door. I am opening the door. I am shutting the window. I am opening the window." Then the pupils perform those very actions one by one and speak out whatever they are actually doing.

Thus we find that situational teaching is of great value in the process of teaching-learning. It makes teaching real, interesting and easily learnable. Surely class-room teaching-learning can improve if situational teaching is used right earnestly.

LESSON PLAN FOR TEACHING PROSE

PT's Roll No .... Dated ....

Class: VIII Subject : English

Topic: The Holidays (Intensive Reading)

Instructional Aids to be Used:

1. A chart showing school campus, class rooms, play grounds, bell, staff room and students standing here and there.
2. Bus stand scene, bus passengers waiting for the bus.
3. Flannel Board, flash cards etc.
4. Flash cards with one comprehension test question on each.

Instructional Objectives in Behavioural Terms

Knowledge- (i) The students acquire knowledge of new words and phrases.

(ii) They can recognize and also recall those words.

Understanding- (i) The learners are able to understand the prose lesson.

(ii) They are able to use those language items.

Skills-(i) The students are able to develop the different linguistic skills such as listening, speaking, reading and writing.

Application-(a) The learners are able to make use of a few new words in their day-to day life situations.

(b) They are able to read the newspaper and other such reading materials in a better way.

Subject Matter. Lesson No. 1—The Holidays (First Paragraph). The summer holidays are over and the school was beginning again. Most of the boys were standing in little groups in the play ground.

They were waiting for the bell. Some boys were already in their class rooms. Some were standing in front of the notice board and looking eagerly at the notices. The teachers were going in and coming out of the teachers room. They were very busy.

Thought Content: The summer holidays were over. The school was re-opening. The boys were standing here and there. Some were looking at the notice boards. The teachers were busy.

Previous Knowledge Testing

1. Name the lessons that have read from your book.
2. What is the meaning of the word "holidays"?
3. Have you read the lesson "The Holidays"?

Announcement of the Topic

Finding a negative answer of the students, the P.T. will say, "Dear students, to-day we shall study the lesson 'The Holidays' from Your Books."

Presentation

Step I. The P.T. will give the model reading of the paragraph. While doing so, he will take care of pronunciation. The students will keep their books open.

Step II. Then he will draw the attention of the students to the difficult words occurring in the paragraph. Those words will be written on the B-B.

Step III. The pupil teacher will create situations with the help of pictures, flash cards- black board drawings and teach the words and phrases. Wherever need arises there to, he will create verbal situations. The students will be asked to use them in sentences. Grammar work will be done side by side.

Summer

(By association) You know the word 'winter'.

The opposite of 'winter' is 'summer'.

Beginning

(By creating a verbal situation).

Your school opens at 9-30 a.m. these days. That is the beginning of the school work.

The new classes start in April. That is the beginning of the classes.

The first form of the word is 'begin'. II and III forms are began, begun.

In little groups

(Asking some students to come forward and stand in small groups).

These students are standing in little groups.

Singular of the word 'groups' is group.

In the play ground

(By showing a flash card or actual situation.)

Some boys are sitting in the class room. Some are standing in the play ground.

Wait for

(Showing a flash card.) It is a bus stand. The passengers are waiting for the bus.

In front of

(Showing the class room situation.)

The teacher is in the class. The students are sitting. The teacher is standing in front of the class.

(Showing flash cards.) The dog is in front of the house. The tree is in front of the house.

Already

(Showing a flash card.) The man is going to his home. His child is already there.

Looking eagerly

The teacher is new for the class. So the students are looking at him eagerly.

(Showing flash card.) The dog wants to cat the sweets. He is looking at them eagerly.

The students of IX class are studying here. They are busy. But the students of VII Class are playing. They are not busy. They are free.

going in—

going out—

(Showing flash cards.)

The postman is going in the street. Now he is going out of the street.

The dog is going in the bazar. Now it is going out of the bazar.

Step IV. The P.T. will ask some individual students to do the loud reading. Corrections if any, will be made with the help of students.

Step V. Silent reading by the class.

Step VI. The P.T. will ask the students if they have any difficulty. The problems will be solved. Mother tongue will be used if the P.T. feels its necessity.

Step VII. In order to test the comprehension of the students, the P.T. will ask the following questions:- (Flash card will be displayed one by one.)

1. Were there holidays in the school?
2. Where were the boys standing?
3. Were all the boys standing them?
4. Why were they standing?
5. Who were looking at the notices?
6. What were the teachers doing?

Wherever the students find difficulty in understanding the questions the pupil teacher mill use mother tongue.

Home work

Use the following words in your sentences:
eagerly, busy, holidays, beginning.

LESSON PLAN NO. 2

Pupil Teacher's Roll No .... Date ....
Subject-English Duration of Period-40 minutes.
Class-IX Topic-The Umbrella Man
(Intensive Reading).

Instructional Aids to be Used:

Chalk board, pieces of chalks, duster, flash cards, a chart shown the picture of pavement.

Instructional Objectives in Behavioural Term:

Knowledge:

(i) The students acquire knowledge of new words and phrases.
(ii) They can recognize and also recall those words.

Understanding:

The students are able to understand the ideas given in the prose lesson.

Skills:

The students are able to develop the different linguistic skills such as listening, speaking, reading and writing.

Application:

(i) The students are able to make use of day to day life situations.
(ii) They are able to read the newspaper and other such reading materials in a better way.

Subject Matter:

Lesson No. 1 'The Umbrella Man' (Paragraph 1-9)
I'm going to tell you about a funny thing...
.... This man had beautiful brown shoes.

Thought Content:

The narrator is a girl of twelve years. She is narrating the incident what had happened with her and her mother yesterday. Yesterday she went with her mother to a dentist. Her tooth was to be filled. The dentist milled her tooth and then they went to cafe. The mother had coffee and the girl took ice-cream- Just when they came out on the street, it began to rain. They looked for a taxi and the mother wished they had a car of their own. Just then an old man of about seventy, came upto them. He looked rich and had a costly silken umbrella over his head. In a very polite and gentle way, he said he was in trouble and he wanted a small help. The mother was always suspicious of strangers. So she looked at him with suspicion. As a rule she did not trust strangers.

Previous Knowledge Testing:

In order to test the previous knowledge of the students, the pupil teacher will ask the following questions :

1. Name the lessons that you have read from your book.
2. What is the meaning of the word 'Umbrella'?
3. Have you read the lesson 'The Umbrella man'?

Announcement of the Topic:

Finding a negative answer of the students, the P.T. will say, "Dear students, to-day we shall study the lesson 'The Umbrella Man' from your books. I

Presentation:

Step I: The P.T. will give the model reading of the paragraph. While doing so, she will take care of pronunciation. The students will keep their books open.

Step II: Then she will draw the attention of the students to the difficult words occurring in the paragraph. Those words will be written on the B.B.

Step III: The pupil teacher will create situations with the help of pictures, flash cards, black board drawings and teach the words and phrases. Wherever need arises there to, he will create verbal situations. The students will be asked to use them in sentences. Grammar work will be done side by side.

(1) Funny:

He is telling .... incidents of his childhood.

(Asking the student to tell some funny incident of his childhood)

(2) Yesterday:

(Asking the student where did they go yesterday)

(3) Already:

Is it 8.30 ....

(Ask one of the student what is the time in your watch)

(4) Gorgeous .... extremely beautiful.

(Sushmita Sen looks very gorgeous)

(5) Pavement:

(By showing a chart)

Pavement .... a hard level path at the side of a road for people to walk.

Step IV: The P.T. will ask some individual students to do the loud reading. Corrections if any, will be made with the help of students.

Step V: Silent reading by the class.

Step VI : The P.T. will ask the students if they have any difficulty. The Problems will be solved. Mother tongue will be used if the P.T. feels its necessity.

Passages for Comprehension

Passage 1

Twenty two centuries ago, Emperor Ashok defined the king's duty as not merely to protect citizens and punish wrong-doers but also to preserve animal life and forest trees. Ashoka was the first and perhaps the only monarch until very recently forbid the killing of a large number of species of animals for sport or food, He went further, regretting the carnage of his military conquests and enjoining upon his successors to find their only pleasure in the peace that comes through righteousness.

Word-meanings :1. defined-explained, 2. preserve-to keep safe, 3. monarch-supreme ruler, 4- forbid-to prohibit, to order not to do, 5. carnage-great slaughter of men, 6. righteousness-uprightness.

Questions based on the above para

1. Name the chapter and the writer.
2. What are the two duties of a king, according to Ashoka?
3. What did he call upon his successors to do?
4. What do you understand by: (a) preserve (b) righteousness?

Hints

1. The name of the chapter is 'Human Environment'. The name of the writer is Indira Gandhi.
2. A king should protect his people. He should also preserve animal life and forest trees.
3. He called upon his successors to find their only pleasure in peace.
4. (a) Preserve keep safe
   (b) righteousness doing what is morally right

Passage-2

Alongwith the rest of mankind, we in India—in spite of Ashoka—have been guilty of wanton disregard for the sources of our sustenance. We share your concern at the rapid deterioration of flora and fauna. Some of our own wild life has been wiped out miles of forests with beautiful old trees, mute witnesses of history, have been destroyed. Even though our industrial development is in its infancy, and at its most difficult stage, we are taking various steps to deal with incipient environmental imbalances.

Word meanings. 1. wanton-serious-grave. 2. deterioration-state of being or growing worse., 3. mute-silent, 4. infancy-early period of existence, 5. incipient-beginning to happen.

Questions Based on the Above Passage

1. Who is the speaker of these lines?
2. What concern is shared by the speaker?
3. Who are the mute witnesses of history?
4. Give the meanings of : (a) flora and fauna (b) mute

Hints

1. These lines were spoken by Indira Gandhi.
2. The speaker is sad over the rapid destruction of our flora and fauna.
3. Beautiful old trees are the silent witnesses of history.
4. (a) flora and fauna Plants and animals.
   (b) mute silent.

ASSIGNMENTS

1. Write a prose paragraph of IX class standard. Prepare a detailed lesson plan for teaching that para highlighting especially your treatment of the difficult words contained in the para.
2. In teaching a prose lesson, vocabulary and structures need be taught thoroughly and grammar work should be done side by side. Discuss what and how by taking up examples.
3. Read the following passage and prepare a lesson plan for teaching it intensively to VIII class students in Hindi medium school:
   Suddenly the man saw a giant. They got frightened. They ran to their boat, jumped into it and rowed away without Gulliver. When Gulliver came back, he did not find either his friends or the boat. He looked for them in vain. Then he said to himself, "I wonder where they are gone or am I looking for them in a wrong place."
4. "Reading comprehension involves understanding-reading of content, vocabulary, grammatical structures, concepts and relationship to ideas." Discuss.
5. State the objectives you would try to achieve through lessons in extensive reading in English. How would these

objectives differ from those of a lesson in intensive reading?

6. "Pave the way to language and find the way to literature." Elaborate the above statement with respect to teaching of English prose to the secondary classes.
7. Think of a prose piece you have taught and outline the steps you employed in teaching it. Mention the class and background of children it was taught to.
8. Outline a strategy for teaching a piece of prose in English to any school class of your choice. Make out a case for the strategy chosen.
9. Outline the various steps in teaching a prose lesson intensively at the secondary stage.

11

Teaching of Poetry

In literature, the poetry and prose reveal glimpses. According to *Chatfield*, "Poetry is the music of thought, conveyed to us in the music of language". Poetry is a thing of beauty because it has beauty of language, beauty of form, beauty of thoughts and beauty of emotions.

Channing says, "Poetry reveals to us the loveliness of nature, brings back the freshness of youthful feelings, revives the relish of simple pleasure, keeps unquenched the enthusiasm which warmed the spring time of our being, refines youthful love, strengthens our interest in human nature, by vivid delineations of its tenderest and softest feelings, and through the brightness of its prophetic visions, helps faith to lay hold on the future life." Poetic language captivates readers and then it attracts them all the more.

Poetry Differs from Prose

Poetry is quite different from prose. *Coleridge* once defined prose as "Words in their best order", and poetry as "The best words in their best order". It is obvious that poetry is a more powerful form of expression than prose. Poetry feeds and waters the desires and passions instead of drying them up. *F. L. Billows* says in the book. 'Techniques of Teaching Language'—"We can compare prose to walking, moving from one place to another on the surface of the earth, getting the word's daily work done: poetry may be compared then to dancing, rising above the surface of the earth, perceiving its relations, getting fuller view of its reality".

Aims and Objectives

Poetry is an important mode of expression in language. Without the study of poetry a person cannot be considered to be well read in language. A subject which cannot captivate a person or arouse his feelings is not a good subject. Poetry is that aspect of language which fundamentally provides entertainment to the readers. We teach poetry with the aims given below:

(i) To give practice of listening to recitation of a poem.
(ii) To help the students recite a poem in proper way.
(iii) To make the students understand the beauty of thought contained in the poem.
(iv) To enable them enjoy music and rhythm of the poem.
(v) To help them improve their power of imagination.
(vi) To enable them to appreciate the poem by awakening in them the aesthetic qualities of appreciation.
(vii) To develop love of the students for English language.
(viii) To make the students familiar with the background of the poem.
(ix) To make the students pick-up the structure or pattern of a sentence.
(x) And above all, to make the students understand the poem.

Present Scene

The present position of teaching poetry in Indian schools is not satisfactory. If we see to the realities of situations, we are astonished. Teaching poetry is not everybody's cup of tea. In a large number of schools, the teacher dictates summary or the main ideas of the poems. The students do not even buy the textbooks. In some cases, the poems are simply translated into mother tongue. Very few teachers are interested in teaching poetry. They are unable to do justice to the teaching of a poem. The details of the situations are as under:

(a) Some teachers ask the children to bring the poetry books in the class room. The teachers just translate the poem into mother tongue. They feel that in doing so they have done their duty of teaching.
(b) The teachers ask the students to learn the summary of the poem from guide. They never ask the children to purchase or study the poetry book. Thus many a time the students pass the examination without having seen even the poetry book prescribed for them.
(c) A few teachers of English dictate notes on poetry to the children. Then they ask them to cram the material and reproduce the same in the class orally or in written form.

(d) A very limited number of teachers are able to teach a poem satisfactorily They can recite the poem well and they are able to give training of poem recitation to the learners. Their teaching attracts the students. They are able to understand the poem really. Only their learners can say with confidence that they have been taught poetry well.

Thinker's Opinion

Seeing this type of pitiable condition, a group of thinkers are of the view that English poetry should not be included in the school syllabus. The different arguments put forth by them are explained below:

Arguments Against

1. The teaching of poetry does not help acquiring mastery over the different skills of language. The reason is that the language used in the poems is widely different from that of prose.
2. Poetry does not help the learners in the expansion of vocabulary.
3. In the poems generally we find that metaphors and similies are used. The school going children find it difficult to understand them. Thus without comprehensive understanding, the poem remains unenjoyed and unappreciated.
4. The social background of English poem is quite different from Indian atmosphere. The school children find it hard to be familiar with it. The result is that they read those poems half-heartedly.
5. Teaching of poetry is not every body's cup of tea. There are very few teachers who have real love for poetry. Only good teachers who love poetry can do full justice to its teaching. All other English teachers just finish the syllabus as far as possible.

Thus on the basis of the above said arguments, one school of thought has formed an opinion that teaching of poetry should be excluded from English syllabus in Indian schools.

Another Opinion

There is another group of people who feel that without poetry, the whole charm of language will be over. That group of thinkers emphasises that poetry in English is very, important and it should he given its due place in the school curriculum. The different arguments given by them in its favour are explained here under:

Arguments in Favour

1. The teacher of poetry creates love for language learning. Without poetry children will be doing language work without putting their heart and soul into it.
2. By studying poems, the students can develop their power of imagination. They also feel aesthetic satisfaction.
3. In the whole of language work, we find that poetry attracts the students. It gladdens their hearts and they feel all the more attracted towards it. They feel the pleasure and appreciate the reality behind the poem.
4. It is English poetry which makes the whole syllabus loveable and attractive. It also adds to the variety in English course.
5. For students who have to memorise a good deal of language material, poetry makes his work easier and simpler to a good extent. The reason is that poems can be memorised easily and quickly as compared to prose.
6. Pattern practice is also possible with the help of poetry. In poetry very often we find that there is repetition of certain patterns or sentences. The readers get a chance of going over them time and again. Thus they get practice and the patterns are registered in their minds.
7. Another important reason for teaching poetry is that it shows the rhythm of English more clearly than regular prose. Stress patterns are regularly repeated. Thus the students can really begin to see the importance of stress and rhythm in English.

Agreed Opinion

The two schools of thought have their varied opinions regarding the inclusion or exclusion of poetry in English syllabus for Indian schools. By comparing and contrasting in arguments of both the groups we can conclude that the arguments put forth by the latter group outweigh those given by the former. Personally I am also of the view that poetry is a must for the learners of English language. So it should be given the privileged position in the school syllabus, and it should form a part and parcel of English syllabus prescribed for school going children in India. *Subrahmanyam* says: The value of teaching poetry in English language course at the secondary school level is immense. It leads to an all-round development of the whole personality of pupils, particularly the emotional, imaginative, intellectual, aesthetic and intuitive sides."

Ryburn is of the view that poetry should not be an examination subject. Pupils should cam poems, recite them and enjoy them. The teacher may not teach a poem which he himself does not appreciate. *Menon* and *Patel* say, "The matter and method for teaching poetry to Indian children should be completely re-oriented, if the teaching of poetry is to be of any value to them."

Easy and Interesting Teaching

Let there be good selection of poems for the students. That will make teaching of poetry easy and interesting. A few suggestions in this regard are as under:

1. The short poems should be given preference over the long ones.
2. The nursery rhymes are the most suitable for the young children.
3. The poems which are philosophical and contain deep ideas should be kept for the seniors.
4. The rhythmic poems appeal more to the children because they can be memorised easily by them.
5. Only poems of that type should be selected which have a universal appeal. They should show variety of form and subject matter so that every body may find his interest there.
6. Only those poems should be selected which are upto the mental level of the learners. The language should be fairly simple so that the learners may not find it hard to grasp the ideas. They should be woven around the ideas which appeal to the students.

Few Examples

A few examples of Poems suitable for the school children are given below:

Nursery Rhymes

1. Jack and Jill
   went up the hill,

To fetch a pail of water,
Jack fell down
Broke his crown,
And Jill came tumbling after.

2. Twinkle, Twinkle, little star,
How I wonder what you are,
Up above the world so high,
Like a diamond in the sky.

3. Laugh a little laugh
Sing a little song,
And you will be happy.
All the day long.

4. Clap hand, clap hand
Till Daddy comes
Daddy will bring
Toffee, chocolate, biscuits
For me alone.

5. Tick tock, tick- tock
Listen to the clock,
The hands go round,
Without any sound,
Round they go
Very very slow.

Simple Poems

6. The teacher beat me
And I slept
Then night came
And I wept,
Rose in the morning
Laughed and played,
Then to school
I went to read.

7. Little star,
Come down little star
Tell me what your are
I love You little star
Will You tell me what you are?
I can see you up there,
Can you see me alone here?
You are up in the sky,

I cannot jump so high,
I don't know why,
The birds too you can't fly
Come down, little star,
Tell me what you are.

A Nations's Strength

8. Not gold, but only men can make,
A people great and strong.
Men who, for truth and honour's sake,
Stand fast and suffer long.
Brave men work while others sleep,
Who dare while others fly ?
They build a nation's pillars deep,
And lift them to the sky.

Why English is Hard ?

9. We'll begin with a box, and the plural is boxes
But the plural of ox should be oxen, not oxes.
Then one fowl is goose, but two are called geese
Yet the plural of moose should never be moose.
You may find a lone mouse or a whole lot of mice
But the plural of house is houses, not mice
If the plural of man is always called men,
Why shouldn't the plural of pan be called pen ?
The cow in the plural may be cows or kine,
But the plural of vow is vows, not vine,
And I speak of a foot, and you show me your feet,
But I give you a boot would a pair be called beet?
If one is teeth and whole set are teeth,
Why shouldn't the plural of booth be called beeth?
If the singular is this, and the plural is these,
Should be plural of kiss be nicknamed kese?
Then one may be that, and three may be those,
Yet the plural of hat would never be hose,
We speak of a brother, and also of brethren,
But though we say mother we never say mothren,
The masculine pronouns are he, his and him,
But imagine the feminine she, shis and shim,
So our English I think you will all agree,
Is the trickiest language you ever did see.

The Vowels

10. We are very little creatures
All of different voice and features;
One of us in glass is set,
One of us you'll find in jet;
Another you may see in tin,
And the fourth a box within;
If the fifth you should pursue,
I call never fly from you.

The Teaching

Someone has rightly said, "Poetry cannot be taught ; the teacher can only create conditions in which a poem has the fullest possible significance for the learners." The teaching of a poem is an art. The teacher of English should try to acquire this. While teaching a poem, the teacher should become one with the feelings of the poet. He should be able to create proper atmosphere for the feelings of the poet. For example, the teacher wants to teach the poem 'Daffodils'. He should make a vivid description of daffodils in such a way that the pupils should think as if the daffodils are before them. This is possible when the teacher has mastery over the language.

The Principles

1. Model Recitation by the teacher is very essential because it helps in attracting the students towards the poem. They are able to grasp the meanings contained in the poem.
2. Detailed explanation of lines or ideas should be avoided.
3. The verbal peculiarities of the language should not be discussed. In the poems, we have words like hath, thou, thee etc. The spellings of some words are written differently. They should not be taken up too seriously as far as the study of the poem is concerned.
4. Paraphrase of the poem should be avoided. It should not be put in the form of prose.
5. The teacher should try to bring enthusiasm and zeal into the teaching of the poem.
6. As far as possible, the poem should be taught as a whole. It should be approached as a total work of art.

Suggested Steps

Step I. The teacher tells something about the poem in simple English. He may show a picture or a chart for this purpose. Thus he creates proper atmosphere for the poem.

Step II. The teacher gives model recitation of the poem. Gestures and actions are performed by the teacher whereever possible. Tape recorder for poem recitation may be used if the teacher feels its necessity.

Step III. Difficult words contained in the poem are taken up and dealt with active participation of the learners. In doing so, the teacher takes up the words and their meanings in simple English.

Step IV. Once again model recitation of the poem is given by the teacher.

Step V. A few students of the class are asked to recite the poem one by one. Mistakes if any, are corrected with the help of other students of the class.

Step VI. The teacher asks the students about their problems in the poem. All the problems of the students are solved as per need and requirement of the situation.

Step VII. The teacher puts a few comprehension test questions to the students. All efforts are made to get appropriate answers from the students. Some hints or guidelines may be provided by the teacher.

Step VIII. Lastly, the students are asked to do some assignments at home. It may be learning of the poem by heart or writing the summary of the poem in simple English.

Teaching a poem is an art. Every teacher of English cannot do justice to the teaching of a poem. Proper atmosphere need be created for it. The teacher who can recite well, is able to succeed in teaching poetry. Tape recorder with recorded poems can surely help the teacher. Practice in poem recitation is needed on the part of English teachers.

LESSON PLAN FOR TEACHING A POEM

PT's Roll No. Date ....

Subject : English Duration of Period: 35 minutes

Class: X

Topic : Stopping by Woods on a Snowy Evening (Poem).

Instructional Aids to be Used : A chart depicting woods covered with snow and a horse with its rider, A pointer, A roller black-board, coloured chalk etc.

Instructional Objectives in Behavioural Terms

Knowledge

(i) The students are able to recognize ideas contained in the poem.

(ii) They are able to recall the thoughts given in the poem.

Understanding

The students get the understanding that duty is more important than enjoyment of life.

Skills

The students are able to develop the different linguistic skills i.e. listening, speaking, recitation and writing.

Application

The students are able to apply the art of reciting a poem in their different life situations. They can entertain themselves and others through recitation.

Subject Matter

Whose woods these are I think I know.
His house is in the village though.
He will not see me stopping here.
To watch his woods fill up with snow.
My little horse must think it queer.
To stop without a farm house near.
Between the woods and frozen lake.
The darkest evening of the year.
He gives his harness bells a shake.
To ask if there is some mistake.
The only other sound the sweep.
Of easy wind and downy flake.
The woods are lovely, dark and deep,
But I have promises to keep.
And miles to go before I sleep,
And miles to go before I sleep.

Thought Content

Robert Frost, the great poet of nature is attracted by the natural beauty and loveliness of the woods. He thinks of enjoying the beauty of the sight. Then he is reminded of certain other engagements. His wife is waiting for him and he has to do important work at his farm. And so he does not stop there any longer. The main idea is that duty is more important than enjoyment of life.

Previous Knowledge Testing

In order to test the previous knowledge of the students, the following questions will be asked:

(i) Name some of the poems that you have read.
(ii) Which poem have you liked most?
(iii) Recite that poem.
(iv) Have you read the poem-'Stopping by Woods on a Snowy Evening'?

Announcement of the Topic

Finding the students' answer to the last question in the negative, the P.T. will say 'Dear students, today we shall study the poem 'Stopping by woods on a Snowy Evening'.

Presentation

Step I. The P.T. displays the chart and tells something about the poem in simple English. He will use mother tongue wherever he needs its assistance. In this way proper atmosphere will be created for teaching the poem.

Step II. The pupil teacher will give a model recitation of the poem. He will use gestures wherever possible. A pointer will also be used to indicate the different aspects of the chart. At this stage, the students will keep their books closed.

Step III. Now the students open their books and second model recitation of the poem will be given by the pupil teacher.

Step IV. A few difficult words contained in the poem are already written on the roller board with coloured chalks and it will be shown to the class. Meanings will he taught with the active participation of the students.

Filled up with snow-covered with snow
queer-strange
downy-soft
flake-light fleecy piece (of snow), thin broad piece.
promise-duties
miles to go-to perform many tasks
Before I sleep-Before I take rest.

Step V. A number of students will be asked to recite the poem one by one depending upon the availability of time. If some student mispronounces a word or a line, it will be got corrected with the help of other students sitting in the class.

Step VI. The P.T. will write the few difficult words contained in the poem on the B.B. Meanings will be taught—with the active participation of the students.

(i) Whisper—To speak in a low voice.
(ii) Grey—Voice like those of the old.
(iii) Anxieties—Worries.
(iv) Luminous—Bright.
(v) Porridge—Softfood made by boiling a cereal.
(vi) Milk of Human kindness—Love and kindness.
(vii) Curry drowed rice—Rice soaked in curry.

Step VII. A number of students will be asked to recite the poem one by one depending upon the availability of time. If some students mispronounces a word or a line, it will be got corrected with the help of other students sitting in the class.

(i) Why do Kalpana's parents worry?
(ii) What do they think of doing for the child?
(iii) What happens to the girl who cats such a rich diet?
(iv) What effect does the poet intend to produce in writing of vitamins from 'ABCDE unto infinity'?

Step VIII. The P.T. will ask the class if they have any difficulty in the poem. Difficult line or stanza pointed out by the students will be explained.

Step IX. In order to test their comprehension of the poem, the following questions will be put to the class.

1. What are the feelings of the traveller while passing through the woods?
2. Why does he not stay and enjoy himself?
3. What is moral of this poem?
4. Why does the poet repeat the last line?

Wherever the students find it difficult to answer, the P.T. will provide guidance.

Home work: The P.T. will ask the students to write the summary of the poem at home.

LESSON PLAN NO. 2

Pupil Teacher Roll No ...... Date ....Duration of Period : 35 min.
Subject : English

Class : IX
Topic : Child or Adult (A poem)
Margaret Lawrence

Instructional Aids to be Used:

Chalk Board, pieces of chalks, Duster, Eight flashcards on which difficult words are written, eight flash cards on which meanings of difficult words are written.

Instructional Objectives in Behavioural Terms:

Knowledge

(i) The students are able to recognize the ideas contained in the poem.
(ii) They are able to recall the thoughts given in the poem.

Understanding

The students are able to understand the state of mind of an adolescent. An adolescent is not able to describe whether still he is a child or he has become an adult.

Skills

The students are able to develop the different linguistic skills i.e., listening, speaking, recitation and writing.

Application

The students are able to apply the art of reciting a poem in their different life situations. They can entertain themselves and others through recitation.

Subject Matter

Am I a child or an adult?
No ! Not a child now-my dolls are gone;
My dream world has rippled away.
I am tall, I understand adult talk,
But does that mean that I am an adult?

Am I an adult or a child?
No ! Not an adult-I couldn't look after myself.
The understanding is just not there.
I pay a half fare on a bus to school,
But does that mean that I am a child?

Am I a child or an adult?
No ! Not a child now-it's not a teddy I love;
His cherished position is taken.
Just because my toys have lost their value,
Does that mean that I am an adult?

Am I an adult or a child?
No ! Not an adult-I do not see
The reason for adult disputes;
I am safe in non-understanding.
But does that mean that I am a child'?

Well, am I child or an adult?
No ! Not one or the other now;
One pace in front of childhood,
And one behind an adult.
Soon I shall stride into a new world.
The world of adult life.

Thought Content

In this poem, the state of mind of all adolescent is shown. She is confused. She does not know whether still she is a child or she has become an adult. She again and again asks this question from herself. In this poem an adolescent asks herself if she is a child or all adult. She tells that her days of playing with the dolls have gone. She loves a teddy bear no more. Toys have lost attraction for her. Her dream world is also gone.

After thinking over the matter, she thinks that she is one step in front of childhood and one step behind adulthood. She is thus in the middle of the two stages. But she shall soon grow into adulthood. This type of questions will not trouble her then. The world of adult life, then will be new for her.

Previous Knowledge Testing

In order to test the previous knowledge of the students, the pupil teacher will ask the following questions:

(i) Name some of the poems that you have read.
(ii) Which poem have you liked the most?
(iii) Have you read the poem 'Child or Adult' by Thargaret Lawrence'?

Announcement of the Topic

Finding the students unable to answer the last question, the Pupil teacher will say, "Dear students, today we shall study the poem-Child or Adult?,

Presentation

Step I. The pupil teacher will tell something about the poem in simple English. She will use mother tongue wherever she needs its assistance. In this way, proper atmosphere will be created for teaching the poem.

Step II. The pupil teacher will give a model recitation of the poem. She will use gestures wherever possible. At this stage, the students will keep their books closed.

Step III. Now the students open their books and second model recitation of the poem will be given by the pupil teacher.

Step IV. A few difficult words contained in the poem which are already written out the flash cards, will be shown to the class,

(1) Adult-a grown up person.
(2) Ripple away-mould in small waves
(3) Understanding-insight
(4) Cherished-much love
(5) Disputes-quarries
(6) Pace-Step
(7) In front of-ahead of
(8) Stride-walk.

Step V. A number of students will be asked to recite the poem one by one depending upon the availability of time. If some student mispronounce a word or a line, it will be got corrected with the help of other students sitting in the class.

Step VI. The pupil teacher will ask the class if they have any difficulty in the poem. Difficult line or stanza pointed out by the students will be explained by the pupil teacher.

Step VII. In order to test their comprehension of the poem, the pupil teacher will ask the following questions from the class:

(i) Can you predict the age of the speaker of these lines?
(ii) What are the three things that have disappeared from the speaker's life at this moment?
(iii) Name the poem and the Poetess.

Home Work

The pupil teacher will ask the student to learn anyone stanza of the poem by heart at home.

LESSON PLAN NO. 3

Pupil Teacher's Roll No .... Date ....
Subject -English Duration of Period-40 minutes
Class-IX
Topic-For Kalpana
(A Poem)
by Nissim Ezekill

Instructional Aids to be Used:

Chalk board, pieces of chalks, duster, flash cards on which comprehension questions are written, a chart depicting the picture of Kalpana.

Instructional Objectives in Behavioural Terms:

Knowledge

(i) The students are able to recognize the ideas contained in the poem.

(ii) They are able to recall the thoughts given in the poem.

Understanding

The students are able to understand that how parents are worried about their children.

Skills

The students are able to develop the different linguistic skills i.e. listening, speaking, recitation and writing.

Application

The students are able to apply the art of reciting a poem in their different life situations. They can entertain themselves and others through recitation.

Subject Matter

How parents worry
When a child is thin
    What shall we do
    What shall we do

they whisper in the right
their voices grey
in the anxieties of love
till the luminous
angel of sleep
leads them softly
(their souls and bodies intervening)
to her own open city
where they see again
for tonic and vitamins ABC
DE unto infinity.
And they watch their child daily eating breakfast
greesy egg-yolk egg-white
jams jelhes toast and porridge
fat with the milk of human kindness
or dinner
of curry-drowned rice
and momentous salad
    eat eat my child
    how thin you are
So the child looks down
distastefully
and eats and eats.

Thought Content

Kalpana's parents worry about her health. She remains thin. They do not understand what they should do. They talk about it in a low murmuring voice at night. Their voices show love and anxiety for the child. Even in dreams they see various bright advertisements of tonics and vitamins. They think of giving these tonics and vitamins to their child.

They watch their child eating daily a rich diet. The child is unwilling to eat all these. They ask her to eat more and more.

Previous Knowledge Testing

In order to test the previous knowledge of the students, the P.T. will ask the following questions :

(i) Name some of the poems that you have read.
(ii) Which poem have you liked most?
(iii) Recite that poem.
(iv) Have you read the poem-For Kalpana?

Announcement of the Topic

Finding the students answer to the last question in the negative, the P.T. will say, "Dear students, to-day we shall study the poem 'For Kalpana'.

Presentation

Step I. The P.T. displays the chart and tells something about the poem in simple English. She will use mother tongue wherever she needs its assistance. In this way, proper atmosphere will be created for teaching the poem.

Step II. The pupil teacher will give a model recitation of the poem. She will use gestures wherever possible. A pointer will also be used to indicate the different aspects of the chart. At this stage, the students will keep their books closed.

Step III. Now the students open their books and second model recitation of the poem will be given by the pupil teacher.

Step IV. The P.T. will ask the class if they have any difficulty in the poem. Difficult line or stanza pointed out by the students will be explained by the P.T.

Step V. In order to test their comprehension of the poem, the following questions will be put to the class;

(i) Why do Kalpana' parents worry?
(ii) What do they think of doing for the child?
(iii) What happens to the girl who eats such a rich diet?
(iv) What effect does the poet intend to produce in writing of vitamins from 'ABCDE unto infinity'?

Homework

The students will be asked to write the summary of the poem at home.

A Stanza from a Poem and Comprehension Questions based on it.

It's a warm wind, the west wind, full of birds cries;
I never hear the west wind but tears are in my eyes
For it comes from the west lands the old brown hills,
And April's in the west wind, and daffodils.

Q. Where is the poet? Describe the feelings of the poet and the reason of his joy.

Ans. The poet is in the western countries and traces the source of his delight. He praises the west wind which has created a warm and cheerful atmosphere all around him. The atmosphere has thrilled the how of the poet.

Q. Explain the meaning of 'full of birds cries.'

Ans. It means that the air is filled with the various sweet and melodious songs of the birds of different types.

Q. Where does the west wind hail from?

Ans. The west wind blows from the western lands. The beautiful and old brown hills are also the source of these winds.

Q. What is meant by the last line 'And April's in the west wind and daffodils.'

Ans. The last line describes the charm and loveliness of the month of April. This month creates the magic of beauty and cheer everywhere as countless flowers bloom over the fields and dance with joy when the winds blow over them. The west wind carries the perfume and jery of these flowers as well as of other objects of nature to the very hearts of the human beings.

Q. Trace the alliteration in the first line.

Ans. 'Its' a warm wind, the west wind point to the art of alliteration as used by the poet to create lyrical atmosphere in the poem.

A Stanza from a Poem

The Charge of the Light Brigade

Word Meanings

Comprehension Questions

"Forward, the Light Brigade
Was there a man dismay'd?
Not tho the soldiers knew
Someone had blunderd
Their not to make reply.
Their not to reason why
Their's but to do and the
Into the Valley of Death
Rode the six hundred.

Word Meanings : 1. 'Forward, the Light Brigade—It was the order given to the Light Brigade by the commander, 2. dismay'd-frightened disappointed, 3. blunderd- made a serious mistake, 4. into the Valley of

Death - in the face of thundering enemy cannon where death was certain, 5. rude-went riding, 6. the six hundred-the six hundred soilders of the Light Brigade.

Comprehension Questions

1. What was the order given by the officer?
2. What are soilders not supposed to do?
3. Why does the Poet say the six hundred rode into the 'Valley of Death'?
4. What quality of the soldiers is shown through these lines?

Answer

1. The officer order was that the Light Brigade should attack the enemy.
2. The soilders are not supposed to question the orders given to them.
3. The poet says so because the death of soilders was almost certain in that attack.
4. These lines show that the soldiers were very dutiful and had rare courage.

Another Stanza for your practice

Cannon to right of them,
Cannon to left of them,
Cannon in front of them,
Volley'd and thunder'd
Storm'd at with shot and shell,
Boldly they rude and well,
Into the jaws of Death,
into the mouth of Hell,
Rode the six hundred.

A Stanza from the Poem 'Lucy Gray'

At daybreak on a hill they stood
That overlooked the moor ;
And thence they saw the bridge of wood
A furlong from their door.

Word-meanings: 1. daybreak-dawn, 2. moor-uncultivated land, 3. overlooked the moor-gave from there a view of the moor from above, 4. thence-from there.

Questions based on the stanza

(a) Who stood on a hill'?
(b) What did they see?
(c) How far was it from their house?
(d) What was the bridge made or?

Answer

(a) Lucy's parents stood on a hill.
(b) They saw a bridge of wood.
(c) It was a furlong away from their house.
(d) The bridge was made of wood.

Another Stanza from the Poem 'Lucy Gray'

They wept and turning homeward, cried,
'In heaven we all shall meet:'
When in the snow the mother spied.
The print of Lucy's feet.

Word Meaning: 1. heaven—the abode of God, 2. spied—saw, 3. Print—impression.

A Few Questions based on the above stanza

(i) Who does 'They' here refer to?
(ii) What did they say weeping?
(iii) What did the mother see in the snow?
(iv) What did they think had happened to Lucy?

Hints

1. The word 'They' here refers to Lucy's parents.
2. They said they would meet Lucy in heaven only.
3. She saw the prints of Lucy's feet in the snow.
4. They thought that Lucy was dead.

One More Stanza

Then downwards from the sleep hills edge;
They tracked the fool marks small;
And through the broken hawthorn hedge;
And by the long stone-wall.

Word-Meaning 1. sleep—rising or falling, 2. tracked—followed the marks. 3. hawthorn— a kind of thorny shrub, 4. hedge—a fence of shrubs.

Questions based on the above stanza

(a) What does 'They' here refer to?
(b) What kind of hill was it?
(c) Whose footmarks did they track?
(d) Where did the footmarks lead them to?

Answer

1. The word 'They' here refers to Lucy's parents.
2. It was a steep hill.
3. They tracked Lucy's footmarks.
4. The footmarks led them through the broken hawthron hedge and by the long stone-wall.

ASSIGNMENTS

1. How will you conduct a poetry lesson in your class so that the aims of teaching poetry in English are fully realised?
2. 'Poetry cannot be taught, the teacher can only create conditions in which a poem may have its fullest significance for the pupils reading it.' Discuss.
3. A Nations's Strength

   Not Gold, but only men can make
   A people great and strong
   Men who for truth and honour's sake,
   Stand fast and suffer long
   Brave men work while others sleep,
   Who dare while others fly
   They build a nation's pillars deep,
   And lift them to the sky.

   Write a lesson plan that you would follow to teach the poem given above to class VIII.
4. State briefly the arguments in favour of and against the teaching of poetry at the school level.
5. Critically review the manner in which English poetry is taught in our schools. How can it be made a source of joy as well as wisdom?
6. (a) What are the aims of teaching poetry?
   (b) Name two Poems for VII class.
   (c) What are the aims of teaching prose?
7. (a) What are the similarities in teaching prose and poetry?
   (b) What are comprehension test questions?

12

Teaching of Grammar

TENSES AND CLAUSES

Simple Present Tense

Here we use is, am, are

Read the following exercises (1, 2, 3)

1. Hari is here.
   My book is here.
   My friend is here.
   My brother is here.
   Karim is there.
   Your book is there.
   Your friend is there.
   My sister is there.
2. This is not a pen.
   This is not a dog.
   This is not a cat.
   This is not my dog.
   That is not a pen.
   That is not a dog.
   That is not a cat.
   That is not my dog.
3. Is this a book?
   Is this a chair?
   Is this a cat?
   Is this not a pen?
   Is this not a cow?
   Is that a book?
   Is that a chair?
   Is that a cat?
   Is that not a pen?
   Is that not a cow?
4. **Fill in the blanks in the following**
   (a) .... here.
   (b) .... there.
   (c) This is not ....
   (d) That is not ....
   (e) Is this ....?
   (f) Is that ....?
   (g) Is this not ....?
   (h) Is that not ....?

5. **Correct the following sentences**

(i) This is a dog.	(iv) That is not cat.
(ii) He is a my friend.	(v) is this table?
(iii) Rajesh is a here.	(vi) Is this not cow.

6. **Read the following exercise (6 and 7)**
   What is this?
   What is that?
   What is it?
   What is here?
   What is there?
   What is Rajesh?
   What is Neela?
   What is the time?
   What is the time by your watch?

7. **It is 6 'O'clock.**
   It is eight.
   It is half past eight.
   It is quarter past eight.
   It is ten minutes past eight.
   It is ten minutes to eight.
   It is quarter to eight.
   It is about to eight.

8. **In the following questions and answers, fill in the blanks**

	Questions	**Answers**
(a)	What is Rajesh?	Rajesh is a ....
(b)	What is Neela?	Neela is a ....
(c)	What is the time?	It is ....
(d)	What is the time now?	It is half .... eight.
(e)	What is the time now?	It is quarter to ....
(f)	What is the time now?	It is about ....

9. **Read the following:-**
   There is teacher in this class.
   There is a dog in this garden.
   There is a pen in my pocket.
   There is a cat in my house.
   There are twenty students in this class.

There are ten teachers in this school.
There are two monitors in this class.
There are no students in this class.
There is one teacher in this school.
There are two teachers in this school.
There is a boy in this room.
There are boys in this room.
There is a dog in this street.
There are dogs in this street.

10. **Fill in the blanks in the following**
    (a) There..................one boy in this class.
    (b) There..................five boys in this class.

Simple Past Tense

Here we use 'was' and 'were'. For example:

1. He was in the good books of the teachers.
   My pen was of red colour.
   Yesterday was a holiday.
   She was in sick bed.
   That was a matter of chance.
   He was a naughty boy in the class.
   Ram was in the teeth of hardships.
   Our Principal was thoroughly gentle.
   My mother was very happy to hear this news.
2. There were dark clouds in the sky.
   The sky was overcast with dark clouds.
   There was peace and order in that country.
   What was the time then?
   What was he to you?
   How was she now?
   How was the weather there now?

A Few Exercises:

Fill in the blanks:

(a) Hari and Karim..................not in the class yesterday.
(b) Our book..................in the press then.
(c) There..................pitch darkness in the street yesterday.
(d) We..................happy but he was not.

Complete the following sentences:

(i) They were ....

(ii) My friend was ....

(iii) Were ....?

(iv) Was ....?

(v) How was ....?

Correct the following sentences:

(1) There was some students in the class.

(2) What he was at that time?

(3) Yesterday is a holiday?

(4) Were not those students happy?

(5) Why that statement was wrong?

Present Indefinite Tense

Read the following exercise:-

1. I like this book. He likes this book.
We like this book. She likes this book.
You like this book. Rajesh likes this book.
They like this book. Neela likes this book.
(a) with I, we, you, they—I form of verb (like)
(b) with he, she, someone—I form of verb+s or es. (likes, goes)

2. I do not write a letter. He does not write a letter.
We do not write a letter. She does not write a letter.
You do not write a letter. Mohan does not write a letter.
They do not write a letter. This a does not write a letter.
The boys do not write a letter. Those boy do not write a letter.

3. Do I sing a song? Does he sing a song?
Do we sing a song? Does she sing a song?
Do you sing a song? Does the boy sing a song?
Do they sing a song? Does the girl sing a song?
Do the boys sing a song? Do the girls sing a song?

4. Do I not play a match? Does he not play a match?
Do we not play a match? Does she not play a match?
Do you not play a match? Do they not play a match?

5. **Fill in the blanks by picking up a verb given in the bracket in front of each sentence:-**

(i) I .... to the lecture. (listen, listens)

(ii) He .... to me. (talk, talks)

(iii) This boy .... out for a walk daily. (go, goes)
(iv) .... he .... a story? (do, does; tell, tells)
(v) The teacher .... well in the class. (teach, teaches)

Read the following exercises:-

6. I meet him every morning.
We get up early in the morning.
We go out for a walk.
The sun rises in the cast.
The sun sets in the west.
He always tells a lie.
She always speaks the truth.

Past Indefinite Tense

Here we use H form of verb e.g.

1. (i) The referee gave a long whistle.
(ii) Our team scored a goal.
(iii) You knew his habits well.

2. Fill in the blanks by using the right form of verb given in brackets in front of each of the following sentences:-

(a) We .... Delhi quite in time. (reach, reached)
(b) She .... very hard near the examination. (work, worked)
(c) Someone .... flowers from the garden. (pluck, plucked)
(d) I .... in this city to-day morning. (come, came)

3. Pick up verbs from below and fill in the blanks in the following sentences:

thanked, stood, helped, lighted, learnt.
(i) The old lady .... a candle.
(ii) He .... me in difficulty.
(iii) I .... my lesson by heart.
(iv) Rajesh .... first in the University.
(v) The Principal .... the guests.

Now read the following exercises:-

4. We did not get the ticket.
Our team did not score any goal.
She did not sing well in the function.
The students did not like this idea.
He did not solve all the questions in the examination.

5. Did the Headmaster take action?
Did you attend the meeting yesterday?
Did your brother take the test?
Did he write a letter to you?
Did the doctor attend the hospital?
Did I finish the paper in time?
Did that teacher write any book?
Did you listen to me?

6. Did he not go with you?
Did the children not pluck the flowers?
Did you not take leave of him?
Did your team not win the match?
Did she not tell a lie?
Did your brother not speak the truth?
Did You not write any poem?

7. Who wrote this book?
Who took your roll call?
Who got the first prize?
Who jumped into the river?
Who punished that naughty boy?
Why did you compel him?
Why did he not take the action?
Why did he fly the kite?
What did he say?
What did you convey?
What did she like?

8. **Fill in the blanks:-**
(a) .... he obey his father?
(b) How .... you find the paper?
(c) Why .... he cheat you?
(d) He .... not come to me.

9. **Correct the following sentences:**
(i) We did not played the match.
(ii) How you liked this picture?
(iii) The dog take a piece of meat.
(iv) Did she know you already?
(v) The old man breath his last.

10. Complete the following sentences:-

(a) Did he ....?
(b) Why did ....?
(c) How did ....?
(d) We did not ....?
(e) What did you ....?

11. Fill in the blanks by taking up the right verb given in the bracket in front of each sentence:-

(i) The gardener .... the plants yesterday. (water, waters, watered)
(ii) Did you .... my message to him? (gives, gave, give)
(iii) Who .... a lie in the class? (tell, told)
(iv) Some students .... in the examination. (rails, failed)
(v) Why did you not .... me? (believes, believed, believe)

Future Indefinite Tense

Use of shall, will and I form of verb.

For example:

1. We shall attend the meeting.
2. He will not listen to you.

Now read the following exercises:

1. I shall complain against you.
I shall leave for Bombay next week.
We shall go to the station to see him off.
My class will take the test tomorrow
His brother will accompany me to the hill station.
They will meet me at my residence.
Neela will sing a sweet song.

2. First of all, the teacher will recite the poem.
You will solve this question.
These boys will make a noise.
The child will weep in the absence of his mother.
The teacher will punish the naughty boy.
The monitor will tell a story.
All the students will pass the examination.
This book will sell like hot cakes.

3. I shall not meet him there.
He will not attend my class.

They will not act upon my advice.
This man will not help me.
She will not agree with me in this matter.
Our team will not play the match now.
We shall not meet him at his place.

4. Fill in the blanks in the following sentences:-
(a) I .... recommend his name for this post.
(b) The teacher will .... take the roll call.
(c) She .... not .... my letter.
(d) The boys .... not .... a match.

Now read the following exercises (5 and 6):–

5. Will you take a cup of tea?
Will you help me in this matter?
Will they not take the test?
Will he not learn his lesson to-day?
Will she not distribute sweets?

6. When will you come back from U.S.A?
When will they visit our place?
Who will solve this question on the black board?
Who will sing a song now?
Why will you not go with me?
Why will he not do the home assignment?

7. Complete the following sentences:-
(a) Will ....?
(b) .... shall ....?
(c) Will .... not?
(d) The boys will ....
(e) When will ....?
(f) Who will not ....?
(g) Why will ....?

Now read the following exercises (8 and 9)

8. I shall go when you come.
The students will stand up when the teacher comes.
The peon will ring the bell when the Headmaster comes.
I will call you if you like.
We shall purchase an umbrella if it rains.
He will not help me if I go to him now.

9. We shall go to see the pictures when you come.
   We shall see the minister if you like.
   I will tend him the book if he asks for it.
   She will sing a song if you request her.

10. Complete the following sentences:

(i) When he comes ....

(ii) If it rains ....

(iii) .... if you like.

(iv) The monitor will call the teacher if the students... ....

(v) The Headmaster .... if you appeal to him.

Present Continuous Tense

Use of is, am, are I form of very + ing

e.g. 1. He is taking tea.

2. I am writing a book.

3. They are studying my book.

Now read the following exercises:-

1. The sun is rising.
   The child is walking.
   It is raining outside.
   The boys are taking a test.
   Miss Neela is teaching us English.
   Our school team is playing a match.
2. This book is selling like hot cakes.
   My brother is working hard these days.
   The students are sitting in the library.
   They are taking tea in the canteen.
   The stars are not shining in the sky.
3. I am not telling a lie.
   She is not speaking the truth.
   They are not attending the classes.
   They are not holding the meeting.
   Rajesh is not flying the kite.
4. This boy is not acting upon my advice.
   The students are not learning their lessons.
   The teacher is not narrating the story.
   He is not building a new house.
   You are not doing your duty.

5. Is the teacher teaching your class?
   Is it raining heavily?
   Is he reciting the poem?
   Is she working in this office?
6. Is he not taking part in games?
   Is she not singing a sweet song?
   Is your child not cutting the teeth?
   Is the train not running to time?
7. Why are you plucking flowers?
   Why is he taking interest in it?
   Why are you going to the function late?
   Why are they not attending the classes?
   Why is he not doing home work?
   Why is your team not playing the match?
8. When are you coming to our house?
   When is he leaving for U.S.A.?
   Who is knocking at the door?
   Who is quarrelling with you?
   What are you doing these days?

9. Fill in the blanks in the following sentences by using the right form of verb:

I am not .... the classes these days. (attend)
I am not .... him to tea party. (invite)
Why are you .... with your brother? (quarrel)
Who is .... you English these days? (teach)
Are they not .... for me? (wait)

10. Complete the following sentences:-

When are you ....?
Why is he not ....?
How are you ....?
They are not ....
I am .... a letter ....

11. Correct the following sentences:

Why your team is not playing the match?
Is not he telling a lie?
How you are behaving with me?
Your brother is not take part in games.
When Miss Neela is leaving for U.K.?

Past Continuous Tense

Use of was, were I form of verb+ing

e.g. 1. The dog was barking.

2. The boys were talking.

Now read the following exercises:

1. The birds were chirping.
   It was raining heavily.
   The students were making a noise.
   They were calling you bad names.
   The teacher was consulting dictionary.
2. The doctor was giving free medicine.
   We were travelling by train.
   The dogs were barking in the street.
   He was writing with a pencil.
   I was doing the whole work in ink.
   The doctor was feeling my pulse.
3. The students were not solving the questions.
   I was not learning my lesson.
   I was all the time helping my brother.
   He was not paying attention to me.
   The children were not flying the kites.

4. Fill in the blanks in the following: The tense should remain the same as in above exercises (1, 2 and 3) :

(a) He .... attending to the people

(b) She was .... a sweet song.

(c) The servant .... tea.

(d) The bus was not .... fast.

(e) The gardener .... the plants.

Now read the following exercises :

5. Were the boys playing in the garden?
   Was the peon ringing the bell?
   Was the washerman washing the clothes?
   Was he not taking care of English?
   Were the children not plucking the flowers?
6. Why were the boys making a noise?
   Why were the two girls quarrelling?
   Why were the students not taking the test?
   Why was he calling you bad names?

What were you doing there?
What was she saying to you?
What was he eating in the kitchen?

7. Which lesson was the teacher teaching?
Which book were you using in the class?
Who was going with you yesterday?
Who was talking to you?
When was she reciting the poem?
When was he sitting in the library?

8. Complete the following sentences. Tense should remain the same as above:

(a) Who was ....?
(b) What was ....?
(c) Why was ....?
(d) Was she not ....?
(e) How was he ....?

9. Correct the following sentences:

(i) Were the boys take the test?
(ii) Which question he was solving?
(iii) Why the doctor was not coming?
(iv) How he was deal with you?
(v) Some students were copy in the examination.

Future Continuous Tense

Use of will be, shall be I form of verb +ing
e.g. 1. We shall be playing a match tomorrow.
2. The child will be crying.

Now read the following exercises:-

1. I shall be preparing for the examination.
We shall be attending the classes regularly.
You will be leaving for Bombay.
He will be looking after the child.
She will be singing a sweet song.
They will be making a noise in the class.

2. I shall not be playing the match.
She will not be attending the classes.
The mother will not be taking rest.
The father will not be going to the bazar.
Some students will not be attending the classes.

3. **Fill In the blanks :**

(a) The teacher will not .... the class.
(b) We shall not be .... here in future.
(c) The gardener will not .... the plants.
(d) The peon will be .... the bell.
(e) The servant will not .... looking after the child.

Read the following exercises :

4. Will the peon be ringing the bell?
Will the mother be looking after the child?
Will the monitor be solving the questions?
Will she not be quarrelling with you?
Will they not be enjoying holidays on some hill station?
Will your brother not be attending the tea party?

5. Why will he not be coming to the class?
Why will she not be going to see the pictures?
Why will they not be staying in the hostel?
What will he be doing now?
What will the teacher be writing these days?

6. When will you be visiting us?
When will they be getting prizes?
When will the gardener be watering the plants?
Which book will he be writing these days?
Which class will the Headmaster be taking now?
Who will be knocking at the door?

7. **Complete the following sentences : See that the tense remain the same as above:**

(a) Will she be ....?
(b) Why will he ....?
(c) Which pen will ....?
(d) Who will be ....?
(e) When will you be ....?

8. **Correct the following sentences;**

(i) When you will be going to Delhi?
(ii) What he will be doing now?
(iii) The teacher will be not going to the class.
(iv) The patient will be take rest.
(v) Will the children be not plucking the flowers?

Present Perfect Tense

Use of has, have III form of verb

e.g. 1. He has stood first in the class.

2. I have taken milk just now.

Read the following exercise :

1. The guest has made a speech.
   She has solved all the questions.
   Rajesh has learnt the poem by heart.
   This boy has completed the home assignment.
   The monitor has solved the questions.
2. I have received your letter.
   They have got into the train.
   We have received the prizes.
   Some students have taken leave today.
   You have done the paper very well.
3. He has not spoken the truth.
   You have not told a lie.
   We have not won the match.
   She has not accepted our invitation.
   They have not called the doctor so far.
4. He has not treated me well.
   I have never taken a revenge.
   They have not solved all the questions as yet.
   Perhaps you have not acted upon my advice.
   She has not spent the whole money.

5. Fill in the blanks :

(a) I have .... tea just now.

(b) She .... the letter in ink.

(c) Your team .... the match by one goal.

(d) She .... never .... a lie.

(e) Rajesh .... always .... the truth.

6. Complete the following sentences

(i) We have ....

(ii) They have not ....

(iii) Veena has not ....

(iv) The monitor has ....

(v) My brother has not ....

Read the following exercises

7. Have you taken the medicine?
   Have you got his address?
   Has she revised her lesson?
   Have the boys taken the test?
   Has the sun risen?
8. Has he not spoiled the whole game?
   Has your brother not won the first prize?
   Has she not given a long rope to her son?
   Have you not missed the bus?
   Has the teacher not taken the roll call?
   Has Rajesh not married Veena?
9. Who have come to school on foot?
   Who has delivered a lecture?
   Who have seen Taj Mahal already?
   Who has seen Taj Mahal already?
   Who has taught you English?
10. What have you said just now?
    What has the teacher taught to-day?
    Why has the Headmaster punished the boy?
    Why has he missed this train?
    How has she solved this question?
    How much money have you spent for this?
11. Who has not solved the question so far?
    Why has he not attended the class to-day?
    Why has he not go?
    How much syllabus have you finished so far?
    How have you got this information?

12. Fill in the blanks :

(a) Has the police not .... the thief?
(b) Have you .... your meals?
(c) Why has he not .... to your letter?
(d) How .... you .... this work so quickly?
(e) What .... you .... in this city?

13. Complete the following sentences

(i) Have ....?
(ii) Has he ....?
(iii) Why have ....?
(iv) How have ....?
(v) They have not ....?

14. Correct the following sentences:

(a) Why he has taken leave for to-day?
(b) What business you have go there?
(c) Has he not invited you to tea party?
(d) Where you have met my brother?
(e) They have appeal to the high court.

Past Perfect Tense

Use of had III form of verb

e.g. 1. The students had plucked the flowers.
2. He had insulted the boy.

Now read the following exercises:-

1. The gardener had watered the plants.
The students had finished the work.
I had mailed the letter already.
Our team had won the match by two goals.
He had copied everything from the book.
2. Veena had sung a sweet song.
They had consulted me already.
The teacher had consulted the dictionary.
We had already seen the Taj Mahal.
I had never seen him before.
3. We had never tasted this dish.
She had not sold the house to anybody.
My brother had not attended the classes.
We had not gone out for a walk.
They had never experienced this difficulty before.

4. Fill in the blanks in the following sentences:-

(a) It had not .... heavily on that day.
(b) They had .... in the examination.
(c) The washerman had not .... the clothes.
(d) The teacher's son had .... first in the class.
(e) I .... already talked to him.

Read the following exercises :

5. The patient had died before the doctor came.
The teacher had checked the note books before I entered the class.
The train had left before I reached the station.

The bus had gone before we reached there.
The rain had started before we came out of the house.

6. We had taken the decision when he came to me.
   She had sung a song when I came there.
   He had finished the lesson when you entered the class-room.
   The sun had already risen before I got up.
   I had received payment before you came there.
7. Complete the following sentences:
   (a) I had bought the ticket before ....
   (b) We had scored a goal before ....
   (c) When you came ....
   (d) They had reached home when ....
   (e) The patient had died before ....

8. Correct the following sentences:

(i) The monitor had solve the question.
(ii) The teacher had taken the roll call when you come.
(iii) The train had stopped when you get out.
(iv) When he comes, I had taken my meals.
(v) She had despatched the papers when the letter comes.

Read the following exercises:-

9. Had he taken part in politics?
   Had you warned him of the danger?
   Had they slept for a while?
   Had we taken the roll call?
10. Had she not solved all the questions in time?
    Had you not taken him into confidence?
    Had the dog not barked then?
    Had the teacher not finished the marking of papers?
    Had they not finished the home work?
11. Who had knocked at the door?
    Who had called your names?
    Who had promised me for help?
    Who had won the match?
12. How had he stood first in the class?
    How had you known him before?
    What had your brother written in the letter?
    What had they purchased from Bombay?
    Why had he not kept his words?
    Why had he not paid attention to you?

13. Complete the following sentences:-

(a) Who had ....?
(b) Why had he ....?
(c) Had she ....?
(d) Had the boys not ....?
(e) What had ....?

14. Correct the following sentences:

(i) Had not the teacher taken the roll call?
(ii) Who had solve the questions?
(iii) What he had thought of?
(iv) Why he had not paid the fee?
(v) My brother had gone to U.S.A. when I reach there.

Future Perfect Tense

Use of will have, shall have III form of verb

e.g. 1. I shall have learn the whole lesson.

2. We shall have finished the syllabus in time.

Now read the following exercises:-

1. You will have played the match.
   We shall have taught him a lesson.
   They will have finished most of the work.
   He will have changed his clothes.
   I shall have paid my fee by this time.
2. Our team will have defeated the other team.
   They will have reached the destination by now.
   Our student will have won the top most position.
   The teachers will have revised the courses in time.
3. The patient will have died before the doctor comes.
   The rain will have started before we reach the home.
   They will have written the book before the session starts.
   He will have helped me before I ask him for that.
   The train will have steamed off before we reach the station.

4. **Complete the following sentences:**

   (a) The doctor will have come here before ....
   (b) The bus .... before ....
   (c) The students will have learn the lesson before ....
   (d) The rain will have stopped before ....

Read the following exercises:-

5. I shall not have given him a word.
   They will not have taken it ill.
   My sister will not have -written a letter.
   You will not have called him names.
   My brother will not have depended upon you.
6. Will she have sung a song by this time?
   Will you have acted upon my advice?
   Will he not have learnt the lesson?
   Will the teacher not have taken the roll call?

7. Fill in the blanks:

(a) He will have .... his duty.
(b) You .... kept the promise.
(c) Will they .... marked the papers?
(d) The doctor will have .... his shop.
(e) They will have .... the house.

Now read the following exercises:-

8. Which book will you have completed?
   Which examination will he have qualified?
   Which question will you not have attempted in the examination.
   Who will have dared to go to the Headmaster?
   Who will have lost the match in the semi-final?
9. What will you have done after passing the examination?
   What will she not have bought from the bazar?
   When will you have met your uncle last?
   When will Rajesh have come back from England?
   Why will he not have attempted the question in the examination?
10. Complete the following sentences so as to have the same tense as above:
    (a) Which pen ....?
    (b) Who will have ....?
    (c) The doctor will have ....
    (d) Why will he not ....?
    (e) What will she have ....?

Present Perfect Continuous Tense

Use of has been, have been I form of verb
Use of since, for
e.g. 1. He has been working since morning.
2. They have been playing for some time.

Read the following exercises:

1. Rajesh has been solving the questions since morning.
Neela has been singing songs since 8 a.m.
Our teacher has been working in the school since 1960.
My brother has been staying with me since January.
These students have been working regularly since Monday.
It has been raining for two days.
2. The foot-ball match has been going on for one hour.
She has been taking medicine for three years.
I have been helping the boy for many months.
He has been writing this book for many years.
3. The gardener has been watering these plants for many days.
The doctor has been treating the patient, since January 15.
I have been putting up with my brother since Sunday night.
My boss has been helping me for a long time.
I have been learning how to swim for some time.

4. Use 'since' or 'for' in the following blanks so as to complete the sentences:

(a) I have been waiting for you .... half an hour.
(b) These days have been quarrelling with one another .... morning.
(c) She has been doing her home work .... three days.
(d) Our Principal has been working in this college .... 1977.
(e) The child has been weeping .... some time.

5. Fill in the blanks in the following sentences:-

(i) I .... writing that chapter .... many hours.

(ii) My friend .... helping me .... two years.
(iii) This student .... attending my class .... January.
(iv) He .... putting me off .... December last.
(v) Rajesh .... reading out letters to the blind .... many years.

Now read the following exercises:-

6. Your son has not been working regularly for three months.
   My watch has not been keeping correct time for one year.
   I have not been using this pen for the last many months.
   He has not been attending my class since Saturday.
7. My brother has been here for many days.
   His son has been in England since 1977.
   The old man has been sick for a few months.
   This shop-keeper has been away since February last.
   Our class monitor has been on leave for three days.
8. Has he been disobeying you for some time?
   Have the boys been reading their lessons for one hour?
   Have you been putting up in this inn for a week?
   Has she been buying books from this ship for six months?
9. Has it not been raining in your city for two days?
   Has she not been knowing you for many years?
   Has the monitor not been attending the classes for some days?
   Has your teacher not been on leave for some days?

Write interrogative sentences of the following on the blanks left:

(a) Mohan has not been coming to me for two years.

....

(b) You have been playing foul in this game for a few minutes.

....

(c) I have not been attending the classes for some days.

....

(d) The children have been plucking the flowers from this garden for a week.

....

Now read the following exercises :–

11. What have you been doing here for two months?
    What has the officer been doing in this office for one year?
    How have you been going on with your job for five years?
    How has the teacher been teaching in this school since January 1950?
12. Why have you been delaying payment since December 1949?
    Why has he not been attending the classes since January?
    Why has the teacher not been teaching your class for two days?
    Why have you been disobeying your parents for some time?

13. Complete the following sentences so that the tense remains the same as above :–

(a) Why has she been ....?
(b) What have they ....?
(c) My brother has been ....?
(d) Has the child not been ....?
(e) How has your mother been ....?

14. Correct the following sentences?

(i) Our Headmaster has been taking action against the naughty boys since two months.
(ii) The farmers have been reaping the harvest from January.
(iii) This book has been selling like hot cakes since many years.
(iv) My mother is there since 1960.
(v) I am working here for December. 1966.

Past Perfect Continuous Tense

Use of had been

Use of since or for I form of verb +ing

e.g. 1. He had been studying here for two years.

2. My brother had been working hard since January.

Read the following exercises:-

1. The boys had been working hard for a few months.

Our teacher had been working for Ph. D. for two years.
It had been drizzling since morning.
They had been playing tennis for one hour.
The washerman had been washing the clothes since 9 a.m.

2. She had not been attending my classes for the last many days.
He had not been writing any letter to me since January.
The children had not been making a noise for half an hour.
We had not been visiting his home for two months.

3. Had she been singing songs for half an hour?
Had you been ironing the clothes since morning?
Had the students not been wasting time for one month?
Had the girls not been cooking vegetables for a few minutes?
Had this book not been selling like not cakes for many years?

4. Fill in the blanks in the following so that tense remains the same as in the above given exercises:

(a) This boy had been telling a lie .... many days.
(b) She .... speaking the truth .... many years.
(c) Had this teacher not .... taking have .... some days?
(d) The old man .... sick .... two years.
(e) He .... to U.S.A .... 1971.

Now read the following exercises:-

5. How had he been passing time for the last so many years?
How had this doctor been earning a lot for two years?
What had he been writing since 1975?
What had this shopkeeper not been doing to earn his livelihood since March?

6. Who had not been paying the fee for the last two months?
Who had not been preparing for the 'examination since January?
Why had you not been visiting us for the last two months?
Why had she not been learning her lesson for two weeks?
Where had he been wandering about for three months?

7. Complete the following sentences:-

(a) Had he been ....?

(b) What had you been ....?

(c) .... since Monday?

(d) Where had .... for two days?

(e) Who had .... since January?

8. Correct the following sentences:

(i) Sunita had been sick since three weeks.

(ii) The old man was crying since morning.

(iii) He had been not meeting us for many days.

(iv) What he had been talking about since morning?

(v) Whom he had been speaking to for the last ten minutes.

Future Perfect Continuous Tense

Use of will have been, shall have been

I form of verb-ing

Use of since or for

e.g. 1. I shall have been correcting the note-books since morning.

2. The dog will have been barking for five minutes.

Read the following exercises:-

1. My son will have been studying in this school since 1978.
   The washerman will have been washing the clothes for three hours.
   She will have been cooking food since '8'0 clock.
   He will have been postponing decision for some days.
   I shall have been taking the roll call for two minutes.
2. That boy will not have been playing for two days.
   I shall not have been meeting him for many days.
   The students will not have been making a noise for half an hour.
   He will not have been writing anything for the last two hours.
3. Will the dog have been barking in the street for half an hour?
   Will the teachers have been sitting in the class for ten minutes?

Clauses

A clause occurs in a sentence. Let us, therefore, understand what is a sentence.

A Sentence is a group of words that make complete sense. For example : Mohan is a good, Sita is my sister. etc.

Kinds of Sentences

According to meaning, there are five kinds of sentences which are very briefly given here below:

Assertive Sentences

A sentence that states something is called assertive.
It may be affirmative or negative. e.g.
She sings a sweet song. (Affirmative)
I do not like bad habits. (Negative)

Imperative Sentence

A sentence that expresses command, request or advice is called imperative sentence. e.g.

Do it just now. (command)
Please help me. (request)
Respect the elders. (advice)

Interrogative Sentence

A sentence that asks a question is an interrogative sentence. e.g.

What is your hobby?
Why are you late?

Optative Sentence

A sentence that expresses a wish is an optative sentence.
For example:
May you be a good person !
May she live long !

Exclamatory Sentence

In this type of sentence, there is a suddent burst of feelings. The feelings may be full of joys, sorrows etc.

For example:
What a good victory
Sentence are of three types

1. Simple sentence 2. Complex sentence 3. Compound sentence.

The simple sentence expresses one single thought. THE CLAUSE

A CLAUSE is a simple sentence which forms part of a longer sentence. e.g- (i) Come in. (one clause)

He is the boy who disturbed me. (two clauses)

Go there, learn your lesson and be good. (three clauses)

DETERMINERS AUXILIARIES AND MODALS PHRASAL VERBS, ADVERBS PREPOSITIONS AND CONNECTORS

Determiners

(i) Articles : a, an, the
e.g. An apple a day keeps the doctor away.
My friend is the best student of the class.

(ii) Demonstratives:
Words that Point towards objects.
e.g. This, that, these, those

(iii) Possessives:
My, our, your, his, her, its, their.

(iv) Numerals:
(a) Definite Numerals : one, two, three .... first second, third .... both.

(v) Indefinite Numerals : some, many, few, a few, several

(vi) Quantitative Determiners:
much, more, little, any.
Any money in your pocket.

Articles

ARTICLES are of two types.

1. Definite Articles ; The used for a specific thing or person.

Examples are:

(a) Used in the superlative degree
the best
the richest
the tallest

(b) I met a girl. The girl was very smart.

(c) The girl with green sari is my sister.

(d) The rich, The poor.

(e) The Taj, The Red Fort.

(f) The Flying Mail, The Himalayan Queen.

(g) The Hindus, The Muslims.
(h) The Tribune, The Hindustan Times
(i) The Bay of Bengal, The Himalayas
(j) The north, the south, the cast, the west
(k) The sky, the earth, the moon, the sun.
(l) The Bible, The Geeta, The Ramayan
(m) All the boys, Both the brothers
(n) Cloth is sold by the metre.
(o) The U.S.A., The Canada, The Russia
(p) Mr. A, the Principal.

2. Indefinite Articiles a, an

(i) a girl, a boy
(ii) 3 ten rupees note, one-eyed girl
(iii) a university teacher
(iv) a Union Government employee
(v) a European doctor

An : an apple, an umbrella, an orange.

An is also used with the words where the first letter is not a vowel but the sound is of the vowel. e.g.

an hour, an honest boy, an M.L.A., an M.P.

Modals are helping verbs because they always come with a main verb. A few Modals are:

shall, will, should, would, can, could, may, might, must, ought to, used to, need.

Properties of Modals

(a) Number, gender or person does not have any effect on the modals

For example:

I can speak English.

She can speak English.

They can speak English.

(b) Modals do not occur alone. They are always used with the main verbs. For example-

May I accompany you?

I shall guide your son.

You can sleep now.

(c) Modals indicate ability permission, request, willingness etc.

(d) With the modals, ought, used-the infinitive 'to' is used.

(e) Infinitive without 'to' -first form of verb is used.

Use of 'Shall'

(i) I shall take his help. (simple future tense)
We shall work hard.

(ii) Shall I take your pen? (Request)
Shall I go with you?

(iii) Sometimes we use 'shall' with the second and third person:

(a) He shall be penalised for his bad behaviour. (Threat)

(b) You shall not tell a lie. (Command)

(c) You shall be given a scooter if you pass the examination. (promise)

Use of 'will'

(a) He will help you. (Simple future tense)

(b) She will go to USA.

(c) I will pray to God day and night. (determination)

(d) We will stand by you. (promise)

(e) I will not harm you. (intention)

(f) We will win the election. (determination)

time or 'should'

should' is the past tense of 'shall'

(i) We should obey the elders. (duty or obligation)

(ii) Should you go to U.S.A. meet my friend Wyne. (conditional sentence)

(iii) She worked very hard lest she should lag behind. (used after the conjunction lest)

Use of ';would'

(a) I told the monitor that I would help him. (Indirect speech)

(b) My son would study regularly. (expresses determination)

(c) If he had worked hard, he would have passed the examination.

(conditional sentence)

(d) He would sit in the street and talk all day. (expresses habit)

(e) Would that I were rich : (expresses wish)

(f) Would you grant me leave? (Polite request)

Use of 'Can'

(a) He can swim very well. (ability/capacity)

(b) Children cannot play here. (Permission)

(c) The Principal of the college can suspend him. (Power)

Use of 'Could'

(i) My friend said that he could help me. (In Indirect speech, can is (changed into 'could')

(ii) He could sing very well when he was young. (ability, past tense)

(iii) Could you please lend me some money? (polite request)

(iv) You could pass the examination if you would. (You can but you do not wish to pass the examination)

Use of 'May'

(i) May I come in, please? Yes, you may. (to denote permission)
May I use your telephone?

(ii) It may rain to-day. (to express possibility)
The officer may not come due to rain.

(iii) May you live long: (to express wish)
May she be blessed with a son:

(iv) They eat well so that they may live well. (express purpose)
He works hard so that he may get a scholarship.

Use of 'Might'

Past tense of 'may' is 'might'.

(i) While converting direct speech into indirect speech, may is changed into 'might'.

My mother told me that she might not come that day,

(ii) I ran fast so that I might catch the train. (purpose).

(iii) If she gets money, she might go to U.S.A. (future condition)

Use of 'Must'

(i) You must pay your debts. (necessity or obligation)

(ii) You must go there. (compulsion).

(iii) My friend must pass the examination this year. (certainty)

(iv) Man must the. (denotes inevitability)

(v) You must not waste time. (Prohibition)

Use of 'Ought'

(i) The employees ought to respect their seniors. (moral duty / social binding)

(ii) You ought to consult some doctor. (suggestion)

(iii) You ought to have consulted some doctor. (past tense)

Use of 'Used to'

(i) I used to go out for a morning walk daily. (habit)

(ii) She used to go to the temple daily. (habit)

(iii) He is used to hard work. (practice)

(iv) She is used to such a chilly weather. (practice)

(v) There used to be a tank at this place. (past-existence of some

Use of 'Need'

(i) I need one shirt more. (used in the sense of requirement or want)

(ii) My wife needs one sari more. (third person singular)

(iii) I need your help in this matter. (main verb)

(iv) This patient needs complete rest. (main verb)

Use of 'Dare'

(i) She dares to face me alone. (affirmative)

(ii) She dares not face me alone. (negative)

(iii) Dare she face me alone? (interrogative)

(iv) Does she dare to go there? (in interrogative and negative sentences, dare is used with 'to')

(v) I don't dare to go there.

(vi) My friend dared me to fight. (challenge or defy)

Auxiliary Verb

An auxiliary verb is a helping verb. It helps the main verb to form the tense. e.g. I shall (auxiliary verb) go there.

The main auxiliary verbs are-to be (is, am, are, was, were); to have (has, had) to do (does, did).

Auxiliary verbs can also be used as Principal verbs.

e.g. I am a teacher here. Do or die.

Use of Auxiliary Verbs

1. The different forms of 'be': is, am, are, was, were, being, been.

(a) God is everywhere.

(b) The dog is faithful.

(c) She sings a song. (Active)

A song is sung by her. (Passive)

(d) The girls were dancing.

Use of 'Have'

(a) I have a friend.
(b) The king had no son. (past)
(c) I shall have the highest degree. (Future)
(d) I have to be there just now.
(e) I don't have money in my pocket.
(f) They have done their duty
(g) I will have learnt a lesson.

Use of 'Do, Does, Did'

(a) Do you take milk daily?
(b) Does she sing every night?
(c) You did well.
(d) We did not play then, but we do now.
(e) She did not sing last year, but she does now.
(f) Don't give me more money. it ill do.

Personal Verbs and Prepositions

Verbs with which we may add prepositions or adverbs to have different meanings are called phrasal verbs. For example; Give is a verb and we may add to it -in' up or away and thus we have phrases having different meanings, give in, give up, give away etc.

Learn the following Phrases. Keep in mind the preposition which is following each word :

Abstain from-	We should abstain from wine.
Abide by-	A student should abide by the rules of the school.
Account for-	It is very difficult for me to account for the loss of money.
Act upon-	I always act upon the advice of my parents.
Accuse of-	My friend was accused of theft.
Agree to-	We agreed to the proposal of our older brother.
Accompany by-	I went to the marriage party accompanied by my wife.
Agree with-	I am sorry, I cannot agree with you in this matter.
Admission to-	That naughty boy cannot take admission to any college.
Afraid of-	The children are afraid of darkness.

Addicted to-	That boy is addicted to gambling.
Alarm at-	We were alarmed at the sight of the thieves.
Accede to-	My friend did not accede to my request.
Apply to-	I applied to the officer for grant of leave.
Amuse with-	My friend is a good singer. He always amuses us with his songs.
Angry with-	The monitor is angry with me these days.
Anxiety for-	My parents have great anxiety for my result.
Angry at-	The teacher got angry at the misbehaviour of a student in the class.
Apologise to-	I apologise to you for coming late in the class.
Approach to-	We should have approach to the minister.
Arrive at-	We ran and arrived at the station in time.
Avail of-	I availed myself of the opportunity.
Attend to-	A good student always attends to the teacher in the class.
Ask for-	You can ask me for money in time of need.
Assign to-	You can assign any duty to me during this function.
Bear with-	Who can bear with this insult?
Beware of-	We should always beware of pick- pockets.
Believe in-	We should not believe in hear-say.
Bless with-	We have been blessed with a son.
Belong to-	The monitor of our class belongs to a noble family.
Blind of-	One student in my class is blind of both eyes.
Born of-	Neela was born of rich parents.
Born to-	A son was born to her yesterday.
Bound for-	That train is bound for Delhi.
Borrow from-	I cannot borrow money from any body.
Bring about-	I want to bring about many changes in the college.
Brought up-	Mahatama Hans Raj was brought up in poverty.
Blow out-	Please blow out the candle now.
Break out-	Cholera has broken out in the city.
Break into-	The thieves broke into his house last night.

Break down-	His health broke down due to hard work near the examination.
Busy with-	I am very busy with my studies these days. Please do not disturb me.
Bring under-	They are trying to bring the fire under control.
Burst into-	When he learnt about his failure, he burst into tears.
Blame for-	He blames others for his own failure.
Charge with-	That man has been charged with the murder of a police man.
Call at-	We shall call at his house today evening.
Call one-	It you like I may call on you tomorrow.
Conscious of-	We should always be conscious of our weaknesses.
Come of-	The monitor of our class comes of a rich family.
Come off-	The marriage of my younger brother came off in December.
Come across-	I came across a monkey on my way io school today.
Carry out-	We should carry out the orders of our parents.
Close to-	My house is close to the school.
Come by-	How did you come by this pen.
Content with-	We should be contented with our lot.
Comply with-	I shall comply with the orders of my boss.
Congratulate on-	I congratulated him on his success in the examination.
Courteous to-	We should be always courteous to others.
Commence on-	Your examination will commence on 1st of April.
Collide with-	Yesterday a tonga collided with a car.
Complaint to,	I will complaint against this clerk to his officer. against
Die of-	That man died of heart attack.
Deprive of-	In the cinema hall, I was deprived of my purse.

Depend on-	He always depends on me for help.
Deal in-	Her father deals in medicine.
Deal with-	I will deal with this student nicely.
Desirous of-	My brother is desirous of going to the United States.
Devote to-	I generally devote much of my time to studies.
Dispose of-	I want to dispose of my old car.
Differ with-	I differ with the Principal on this point.
Due to-	Due-to illness, I could not come to the school yesterday.
Draw near-	Our annual examination is drawing near day by day.
Do Without-	I cannot do without you now.
Duty to-	You should know what is your duty to your country.
Enquire into-	The discipline committee of the school will enquire into the matter.
Exempt from-	The teacher exempted me form fine.
Escape from-	He escaped from the jail at mid night.
Familiar with-	I am quite familiar with the Education Minister of the state.
Famous for-	Our teacher is famous for his gentleness.
Fond of-	The old lady is very much fond of films.
Fill with-	Now that tank has been filled with water.
Friendly to-	My brother is very friendly to his neighbours.
Full of-	This glass is full of milk.
Faithful of-	I shall always remain faithful to my boss.
Fight with-	Please do not fight with your class fellow's.
Faith in-	My brother has full faith in God.
Get through-	Work hard so that you may get through the examination.
Get on-	How are you getting on in the class?
Get up-	I always get up early in the morning and go out for a walk.
Give in-	The enemy tried to succeed but he did not give in.
Give up-	He gave up bad habits and became a good boy.

Give away-	The president gave away the prizes and we came home.
Go through-	Please try to go through this book within a week.
Go off-	When the thief came, the gun did not go off.
Gifted with-	He was gifted with the habit of writing.
Good at-	He worked very hard and now he is good at mathematics.
Guess at-	Please try to guess at the moral of the story.
Grateful to-	I shall be grateful to you for this act of kindness.
Hanker after-	My uncle always bankers after money.
Hatred for-	I have all hatred for greedy persons.
Hope for-	We should always hope for die best.
Hostile to-	The head clerk is hostile to his boss.
Inquire of-	Let us inquire of the station master about the arrival of the train.
Inquire into-	A committee has been formed to enquire into the matter.
Insist upon-	I do not know why he is insisting upon my going there.
Injurious to-	You should know that taking wine is injurious to health.
Invite to-	I have invited all my friends to the tea party.
Inferior to-	Your pen is inferior to mine.
Interested in-	I am greatly interested in teaching of English.
Inform of-	Let us inform the police of the murder.
Intimate with-	That teacher is very intimate with his boss.
Introduce to-	The Principal introduced me to the chief guest,
Impress with-	Everybody was impressed with the personality of the teacher.
Jealous of-	One colleague of mine is jealous of my fame.
Junior to-	He is junior to me in service.
Keep to-	We should always keep to the left while walking on the main road.
Knock at-	Please see who is knocking at the door.
Kind to-	We should always be kind to the poor.
Laugh at-	It is a bad habit to laugh at others.
Listen to-	You should always listen to the teacher carefully in the class.

Live by-	Thanks God that I can live by pen.
Look at-	Please look, at the picture and then answer my question.
Look into-	The officer will took into this matter personally.
Look up-	It seems that price of sugar mill look up next month.
Look for-	I am looking for my lost pen.
Look after-	My son will look after me in my old age.
Look upon-	I always look upon you as my brother.
Leave for-	My friend will leave for U.S.A. next week.
Lay by-	We must lay by something for the rainy day.
Marry to-	Neela was married to Ramesh.
Mistaken for-	At the public meeting I was mistaken for a minister.
Match for-	That girl is no match for you.
Make of-	This table is not made of wood.
Make up-	I have made up my mind to do Ph. D. I shall make up my deficiency by working hard.
Make away with-	The thief made away with the watch.
Need of-	Last year I was in great need of money these days.
Negligent to-	I hate this boy as he is negligent to his duties.
Obedient to-	The dog is very obedient to his master.
Obliged to-	I shall feel obliged to you if you kindly help me.
Object to-	That is a good proposal. I don't object to it.
Occur to-	In the meeting, a very good idea occurred to me.
Overwhelm with-	My brother was overwhelmed with joy at my success in the examination.
Opposite to-	My house is opposite to the post office.
Put on-	It is very cold. You should put on your coat.
Pray to-	We pray to God at the time of difficulty.
Pray for-	I always pray for your bright career.
Put up-	At Simla we shall put up in a hotel.
Partial to-	A good teacher is not partial to any one in the class.
Part with-	These days nobody wants to-part with money.

Prepare for-	Now my younger brother is preparing for his matriculation examination.
Part from-	At last die bride parted from her parents.
Please with-	My officer is pleased with my work.
Participate in-	I am sure one team from our college will participate in the debate.
Prevent from-	He prevented the child from going to the cinema.
Prefer to-	You always prefer milk to tea.
Preside over-	I do not know who is coming to preside over the function.
Provide with-	At the function we were provided with good seats.
Proud of-	The rich man is proud of his money.
Put off-	Do not put off till tomorrow what you can do to-day.
Popular for-	This teacher is very popular for his good behaviour.
Quarrel with-	Let us not quarrel with each other at this time.
Quick at-	My brother is very quick at translation work.
Qualify for-	I am sorry you are not qualified for this post.
Related to-	Perhaps this boy is related to that girl.
Recover from-	Now the patient is recovering from illness.
Refer to-	At last, the matter was referred to the parents.
Remind to-	I shall remind you of your word.
Rescue from-	This man rescued the child from drowning,
Rejoice at-	The boys are rejoicing at their success in the examination.
Refrain from-	We should always refrain from drinking.
Rely on-	He is very selfish. We should not rely on him.
Recommend to-	He recommend me to the chairman for the post of Principal.
Satisfy with-	His officer is satisfied with his work.
Sure of-	I am sure of my grand success in the examination.
Stare at-	Why do you stare at me?
Subscribe to-	Let us subscribe to Haryana flood relief fund.
Sympathise with-	We should always sympathise with the poor.

Stick to-	He will always stick to his words.
Shock at-	He was shocked at the death of my father.
Succeed in-	He worked hard but he could not succeed in the examination.
Stand by-	I shall stand by you through thick and thin.
Send for-	Send for the doctor, please.
Set in-	The rainy season has set in.
Set out-	After the school, we set out to see the film.
Set up-	That old man has set up a shop in the market.
Trust in-	Let us trust in God and do the right.
Take down-	I advise you to take down my words.
Take off-	He took off his clothes and jumped into the river.
Take after-	This girl takes after his father.
Think over-	I shall now think over the matter and then decide.
Take place-	The marriage of my younger brother took place in December.
Taste for-	My friend has no taste for music.
Take to-	His younger brother has taken to drinking and gambling.
True to-	This teacher is true to his word.
Take for-	I took that man for my uncle.
Take over-	I took over as the Principal of the college.
Take up-	He took up Science and Mathematics in the college.
Take care of-	You should always take care of your health.
Tell upon-	Hard work told upon his health.
Think of-	I am thinking of going to some foreign country.
Turn out-	The Principal turned out the naughty boy from the college.
Turn down-	I am sure the officer will not turn down my request.
Unfit for-	That is an old man now. He is unfit for the job.
Versed in-	Our teacher is well versed in poetry.
Vote for-	Many people voted for the Janta Party candidate.

Warn of-	I warned him of the coming danger.
Wait for-	I waited for you yesterday but you did not turn up.
Wait on-	He is a rich man now. Many servants wait on him.
Wanting in-	He is a clerk but he is wanting in commonsense.
Worthy of-	This teacher is worthy of every praise.
Wonder at-	Every body wonders at the success of this lazy boy.
Yield to-	He is very strong. He will not yield to difficulties.
Zeal for-	My friend has a great zeal for work.

Exercises

Use the following phrases in your sentences:-

Act upon, angry with, avail of, deal in, differ with, born of, come off, bound for, ask for, bless with, break- out, draw near, get through, look up, match for

Fill in the blanks by using the words given in the brackets:

(i) I abstain .... wine now. (of, from)
(ii) The child is afraid .... darkness. (from, of)
(iii) He was brought .... in luxury. (of, up)
(iv) Assign any duty .... me. (for, to)
(v) Please blow .... the candle. (off, out)
(vi) His health broke .... due to hard work. (down, away)
(vii) Let us congratulate him .... his success. (at, on)
(viii) She has been deprived .... her purse. (off. of)
(ix) Neela is famous .... her books. (of, for)
(x) My friend bankers .... money. (from, after)

Fill in the blanks by using the words given here below:

To, at, of, to, at, by, for, with, upon, to.

(a) She availed herself .... the opportunity.
(b) We walked quickly and arrived .... the station in time.
(c) You should attend .... the lecture now.
(d) I shall comply .... his order.
(e) Please do not insist .... my going there.

(f) This shirt is inferior .... mine.
(g) We should not laugh .... others.
(h) He can live .... his pen.
(i) She was mistaken .... a doctor.
(j) 1 will not object .... your proposal.

Fill in the blanks:

(A) My friend is jealous .... my grand success. In the examination.
(B) Our Professor will leave .... U.S.A. very soon.
(C) Neela was not married .... Rajesh.
(D) I shall make .... my deficiency during the holidays.
(E) He introduced himself .... the chief guest.

Tick mark (✓) the correct sentences and cross (×) the wrong ones:-

(1) My friend was accused from theft.
(2) She has been blessed with a pen.
(3) Beware from pick pockets.
(4) Do not be hostile for any body.
(5) Veena is good at Mathematics.

Correct the following sentences:-

(i) At last he escaped the jail.
(ii) The President gave the prizes.
(iii) I want to dispose my old car.
(iv) The gun did not go of.
(v) Please listen me now.

Complete the following:-

(a) Grateful .... (b) Laugh .... (c) Fill ....
(d) Beware .... (e) Borrow ....

Complete the following sentences:-

(A) She is blind .... eye.
(B) The thief broke .... house.
(C) Believe .... and do the right.
(D) You can ask .... in time of need.
(E) Please try to get .... examination.

Fill in the blanks by using the appropriate prepositions given in the brackets:-

(i) The Principal is pleased .... my work. (to, for, with, from)

(ii) I am going to preside .... the function. (for, over, to, at)

(iii) Neela is recovering .... illness these days. (from, of, to)

(iv) They are rejoicing .... their victory. (for, of, from, at)

(v) Who will rely .... such a selfish friend? (at, on, in, of)

(vi) Send .... the doctor, please. (in, for, up, to)

(vii) I am sure .... my success in the examination. (of, at, for, from.)

(viii) When are you going to take .... as Principal of your college? (of, up, over, for) as

(ix) What are you thinking .... these days? (from, for, of, at)

(x) He is perhaps wanting .... commonsense (of, in, for, to)

Tick mark (✓) the correct sentences in the following:

1. (a) Please take after these words.
   (b) Please take down these words.
   (c) Please take up these words.
   (d) Please take off these words.
   (e) Please take of there words.
2. (a) Let us be true of our words.
   (b) Let us be true on our words.
   (c) Let us be true in our words.
   (d) Let us be true to our words.
   (e) Let us be true from our words.
3. (a) She will not yield for difficulties.
   (b) She will not yield at difficulties.
   (c) She will not yield to difficulties.
   (d) She will not yield from difficulties.
   (e) She will not yield in difficulties.

Pick up correct sentences out of the following:

(a) I am satisfied for his work.
(b) Who will stand by you in difficulty?
(c) Her marriage takes tomorrow.
(d) Take care for your health.
(e) My sister is well versed in household work.
(f) I availed myself of the opportunity.

(g) Please accede of my request.
(h) Be courteous for all.
(i) Inform him of the case now.
(j) He was deprived of the purse.

Fill in the blanks:

(i) His brother is addicted .... gambling.
(ii) Do not borrow money .... anybody.
(iii) She was charged .... the murder of a man.
(iv) Carry .... the orders of your parents.
(v) I cannot do .... her.
(vi) Are you freindly .... your neighbours?
(vii) The head clerk was hostile .... me.
(viii) I was mistaken .... a minister.
(ix) This idea never occurred .... me.
(x) I shall vote .... the party I like most.

Answers

1. See phrases

2. (i) from	(ii) of	(iii) up	(iv) to	(v) out
(vi) down	(vii) on	(viii) of	(ix) for	(x) after
3. (a) of	(b) at	(c) to	(d) with	(e) upon
(f) to	(g) at	(h) by	(i) for	(j) to

4. (A) of (B) for (C) to (D) up (E) to

5. (1) × (2) ✓ (3) × (4) × (5) ✓

6. (i) At last he escaped from the jail.
(ii) The President gave away the prizes.
(iii) I want to dispose of my old car.
(iv) The gun did not go off.
(v) Please listen to me now.

7. (a) to (b) at (c) with (d) of (e) from

8. (A) of one
(B) into his
(C) in God
(D) for money
(E) through the

9. (i) with	(ii) over	(iii) from	(iv) at	(v) on
(vi) for	(vii) of	(viii) over	(ix) of	(x) in

10. 1 (b) 2 (d) 3. (c)

11. (b) (c) (f) (i)

12. (i) to	(ii) from	(iii) with	(iv) out	(v) without
(vi) to	(vii) to	(viii) for	(ix) to	(x) for

Learn the following keeping in mind the prepositions which are italicised:

I. (a) In Haryana, people abstain *from* wine.
(b) That fellow was accused *of* theft.
(c) How can I agree *with* you *in* this matter?
(d) I availed myself *of* the opportunity.
(e) This train is bound *for* Calcutta.
(f) Cholera has broken *out in* the city.
(g) You blame others *for* your failure.
(h) We should be contented *with* our lot.
(i) You should be courteous *to* others.
(j) My son is desirous *of* going *to* the United States.
(k) She was deprived of her purse *in* the train *at* Agra.
(l) He lives *at* village Barnala in District Ambala.

II. (i) I differed with the whole staff on this point.
(ii) The discipline committee will enquire *into* the matter.
(iii) Her brother is very friendly *to* me.
(iv) You should have full faith *in* your parents.
(v) He is gifted *with* the habit *of* writing.
(vi) The head clerk is hostile *to* his fame.
(vii) His colleagues are jealous *of* his fame.
(viii) You must lay by something *for* the rainy day.
(ix) At the function, I was mistaken *for* a minister.
(x) I am sorry you are not qualified *for* this post.

Read the following phrases carefully :

act upon, angry with, deal in, born of, come off, ask for, draw near, get through, look up, match for, set up, shock at, true to, put on, partial to, popular for, sure of, stare at, refrain from.

Fill in the blanks by using the correct preposition out of the ones given in the brackets:

(i) I abstain .... wine now. (of, from)
(ii) The child is afraid .... darkness. (from, of)
(iii) She was brought .... in luxury. (of, up)
(iv) Assign any duty .... me. (for, to)
(v) Please blow .... the candle. (off, out)
(vi) His health broke .... out to hard work. (down, away.)
(vii) Let us congratulate him .... his success. (at, on)
(viii) She has been deprived .... her purse. (off, of)

(ix) Neela is famous .... her books. (of for)
(x) My friend hankers .... money. (form, after)

Answers

(i) from	(ii) of	(iii) up	(iv) to	(v) out
(vi) down	(vii) on	(viii) of	(ix) for	(x) after.

Fill in the blanks by using the prepositions given below:

to, at, of, to, at, by, for, with, upon, to.

(a) She availed herself .... the opportunity.
(b) She walked quickly and arrived .... the station in time.
(c) You should attend .... the lecture now.
(d) I shall comply .... his order.
(e) Please do not insist .... my going there.
(f) This shirt is inferior .... mine.
(g) We should not laugh .... others.
(h) She was mistaken .... a doctor.
(i) I will not object .... your proposal.

Answers

(a) of	(b) at	(c) to	(d) with	(e) on
(f) to	(g) at	(h) on	(i) for	(j) to

Fill in the blanks:

(i) My friend jealous .... my grand success in the examination.
(ii) Our Professor will leave .... U.S.A. very soon.
(iii) Neela was not married .... Rajesh.
(iv) I shall make .... my deficiency during the holidays.
(v) He introduced himself .... the chief guest.

Answers

(i) of (ii) for (iii) to (iv) up (v) to.

Fill in the blanks by using the appropriate prepositions given in the brackets:

(a) The Principal is pleased .... my work. (to, for, with, from)
(b) I am going to preside .... the function. (for, over, to, at)
(c) Neela is recovering .... illness these days. (from, of to, for)

(d) They are rejoicing .... their victory. (for, of, fro, at)
(e) Who will rely .... such a selfish friend? (at, on, in, of)
(f) Send .... the doctor, please. (in, for, up, to)
(g) I am sure .... my success in the examination. (of, at, for, from)
(h) When are you going to take .... as Principal of your college? (of, up, over, for)
(i) What are you thinking .... these days? (from, about, of, at)
(j) He is perhaps wanting .... common sense. (of, in for, to)

Answers

(a) with	(b) over	(c) from	(d) at	(e) on
(f) for	(g) of	(h) over	(i) about	(j) in.

8. (i) My friend is addicted .... gambling.
(ii) Do not borrow money .... anybody.
(iii) She was charged .... the murder of a man.
(iv) Carry .... the orders of your parents.
(v) I cannot do .... her.
(vi) Are you friendly .... your neighbours?
(vii) The head clerk was hostile ....
(viii) I was mistaken .... a leader.
(ix) This idea never occurred .... me.
(x) I shall vote .... the party I like most.

Answers

(i) to	(ii) from	(iii) with	(iv) out	(v) without
(vi) to	(vii) to	(viii) for	(ix) to	(x) for.

Put cross in the brackets given in front of the following sentences which you feel are wrong:

(a) I am satisfied for his work.
(b) Who will stand by you in difficulty?
(c) Her marriage take to-morrow.
(d) Take care for your health.
(e) My sister is well versed in household -work.
(f) I availed myself of the opportunity.
(g) Please accede of my request.
(h) Be courteous for all.
(i) Inform him of the case now.
(j) He was deprived the pure.

Answers

(a) × (c) × (d) × (h) × (j) ×

Read the following carefully:

(i) I started at dawn and he started in the morning.
(ii) I was sitting in the room when the cat fell into the well.
(iii) Do good to others. My brother is good in English.
(iv) How can I agree with you in this matter?
(v) They prayed to God for his mercy.
(vi) She quarrelled with me over a trifle.
(vii) She placed the purse on the table and came into room.
(viii) She apologized to her friend for the mistake.
(ix) I shall try to bring about improvement in the existing social set up.

Adverbs

An adverb is a word which adds something to the meaning of a verb, an adjective, an adverb, a preposition or a conjunction. A few examples are:

(i) My friend speaks sweetly, Here are the adverb 'sweetly, adds meaning to the verb 'speak'.

(ii) His wife is a very good lady. (Here the adverb adds meaning to the adjective 'good')

(iii) The captain of our team ran very fast. (Here the adverb 'very' adds to the meaning of the adverb 'fast')

(iv) He found the cricket ball just above his head. (Here the adverb adds meaning to the preposition 'above')

(v) My brother did it only because he could not disobey you. (Here the adverb adds meaning to the conjunction)

Kinds of Adverbs

Adverbs are of three kinds:

Simple Adverbs: They modify the words with which they are used. Simple adverbs are of the following kinds:-

(i) Adverbs of Time: e.g. before, after, now, then, today, tomorrow, yesterday, early, late, shortly, immediately etc.

(ii) Adverbs of Place e.g. here, there, up, now, forward, backward, in out, far, near, within, without. etc.

(iii) Adverbs of manner: rightly, wrongly, gladly, slowly, quickly etc.

(iv) Adverbs of number: e.g- firstly, secondly, once, twice, thrice.

(v) Adverbs of quantity: muck more, most, little, less, least, or degree.

(vi) Adverbs of Reason : e.g. therefore, hence, consequently etc.

(vii) Adverbs of affirmative or negative : e.g.,es, no, not, may, etc.

Interrogative Adverbs: This type of adverbs are used for asking questions. e.g. when, where, why, how, how far, how long etc.

Relative Adverbs: They are used to join adverbial clause to main clauses. e.g. when, where, why, how etc.

Examples: I do not know where your father has gone. I can't say why she is happy.

Formation of Adverbs

Read the following:

Adjectives	Adverbs	Adjectives	Adverbs
angry	angrily	faithful	faithfully
brave	bravely	happy	happily
courageous	courageously	kind	kindly
easy	easily	proud	proudly
correct	correctly	greedy	greedily
ready	readily	slow	slowly
successful	successfully	wise	wisely

Connectors or Conjunctions

A conjunctions is a word which joins words, phrases or sentences. Thus it brings about relationships between the elements that are joined.

Main Conjunctions are : and, if, as, whether, either or, neither, nor, but, therefore, unless, through, yet, because, otherwise, lest, when, while, however, since, fill etc.

Kinds of Conjunctions

There are two types of conjunctions:

(i) Co-ordinating Conjunctions.

(ii) Subordinating Conjunctions.

(i) Co-ordinate Conjuctions are those which join together words, phrases or clauses of equal rank. e.g. My friend is poor but he is honest.

Co-ordinating conjunctions are of the following types:

(a) Cumulative Conjunctions: They add one co-ordinate clause to another. e.g. not only .... but also.

(b) Alternative Conjunctions: There is a choice between one statement and another. e.g. either .... or, neither .... nor.

(c) Conjunctions of contrast: e.g. whereas, while etc.

(d) Conjunctions showing inferences: e.g. so, then, therefore.

A few examples :

(i) She is not only poor but also weak.

(ii) He is either a doctor or a lecturer.

(iii) He is a good person whereas his brother is not.

(iv) Subordinate Conjunctions: Those words which connect a subordinate clause and a principal clause.

Examples:

(a) I shall go to his home if he likes it.

(b) She knew that she could not stand first.

(c) Hardly had they gone out when it began to rain.

N.B.

1. Conjunctions showing time e.g. as soon as, as long as.
2. Conjunctions showing condition e.g. if, unless.
3. Conjunctions showing objective e.g. so that etc.

13

Teaching of Composition

ACTIVE AND PASSIVE VOICE DIRECT INDIRECT SPEECH

Change the Voice

When we change active voice into passive voice, subject is changed into object and object is changed into subject. Generally 'by' is used. 'To' is used when the verb is 'know' and 'in' is used when the verb is 'contain'.

Let us now study the change of voice tense wise:

Present Indefinite Tense

A few sentences of this tense are:-

	Subject	**Object**	**Verb**	**Form**
1. I like this book.	I	this book	lie	I Form
2. We like this book.	We	this book	like	I Form
3. She likes this picture.	She	this picture	likes	I Form
4. They read books.	They	books	read	I Form

In active voice, we have first form of verb or first form of verb + s or es. Its conversion into passive voice is : is, am, are and III form of verb. Thus passive voice of the above sentences are

1. This book is liked by me.
2. This book is liked by us.
3. This picture is liked by her.
4. Books are read by them.

Now read the following exercises

		Active Voice	**Passive Voice**
A.	(i)	I take tea.	Tea is taken by me.
	(ii)	We take tea.	Tea is taken by us.
	(iii)	You take tea.	Tea is taken by you.
	(iv)	He takes tea.	Tea is taken by him.
	(v)	She takes tea.	Tea is taken by her.
	(vi)	They take tea.	Tea is taken by them.
	(vii)	Mohan takes tea.	Tea is taken by Mohan.
	(viii)	The girl takes tea.	Tea is taken by the girl.
B.	(a)	I take milk.	Milk is taken by me.
	(b)	We eat rice.	Rice are eaten by us.
	(c)	You see a picture.	A picture is seen by you.
	(d)	They play hockey.	Hockey is played by them.
	(e)	They play hockey daily.	Hockey is played by them daily.
	(f)	He teaches us these days.	We are taught by him these days.
	(g)	We read newspaper daily.	Newspaper is read by us daily.
	(h)	I like this city very much.	This city is liked by me very much.

Fill in the blanks in the following :-

1. I solve the questions daily.
   .... are solved by me daily.
2. Lata sings a sweet song.
   A sweet song .... by Lata.
3. I take the test.
   The test ....
4. She writes stories.
   Stories .... by her.
5. This book contains pictures.
   .... in this book.
6. This glass contains milk.
   Milk .... in ....
7. My book contains essays.
   .... are contained ....

Read the following sentences:-

(i) That book contains beautiful pictures.
Beautiful pictures are contained in that book.

(ii) I know him very well.
He is known to me very well.

(iii) The father tells us a story.
A story is told by the father.

(iv) This teacher teaches us English.
We are taught English by this teacher.

(v) I do my work daily.
My work is done by me daily.

Now fill in the blanks in the following

1. This Pot contains very hot milk.
Very hot milk .... in this pot.
2. He knows me very well.
I am .... very well.
3. She knows radio mechanism.
Radio mechanism ....
4. They distribute sweets to the poor.
Sweets .... to the poor ....
5. We distribute sweets to the children every year.
Sweets .... to the children ....
6. The monitor gets first division every year.
First division .... by the monitor ....
7. God helps those who help themselves.
Those .... by God who help themselves.

Read the following:-

	Active Voice	**Passive Voice**
(a)	Do you take tea?	Is tea taken by you?
(b)	Do the boys play hockey?	Is hockey played by the boys?
(c)	Do we obey the elders?	Are the elders obeyed by us?
(d)	Do you act upon his advice?	Is his advice acted upon by you?
(e)	Do the rich hate the poor.	Are the poor hated by the rich?
(f)	Do I help the poor boy?	Is die poor boy helped by me?
(g)	Do the children make a noise?	Is a noise made by the children?
(h)	Do they play football daily?	Is football played by them daily?

Read the following :-

	Active Voice	**Passive Voice**
(i)	Does she solve the question?	Is the question solved by her?
(ii)	Does he sing a song?	Is a song sung by him?
(iii)	Does Veena paint a picture?	Is a picture painted by Veena?
(iv)	Does the teacher teach English?	Is English taught by the teacher?
(v)	Does Neela like this subject?	Is this subject liked by Neela?

Fill in the blanks in the following

(1) Do you know his habits?
.... known to you?

(2) Does she know your parents?
.... known ....?

(3) Do you sing a song?
.... sung ....?

(4) Does the gardener water the plants?
Are the plants ....?

Read the following:-

	Active Voice	**Passive Voice**
(a)	I do not like this city.	This city is not liked by me,
(b)	He does not like my habits.	My habits are not liked by him.
(c)	The children do not make a noise.	A noise is not made by the children.
(d)	We do not see pictures.	Pictures are not seen by us.
(e)	Do you not learn your lesson daily?	Is your lesson not learnt by you daily?
(f)	Does she not like this subject?	Is this subject not liked by her?
(g)	Why does he hate you?	Why are you hated by him?
(h)	How do you like this picture?	How is this picture liked by you?
(i)	When does he water the plants?	When are the plants watered by him?
(j)	Perhaps he does not like games.	Perhaps games are not liked by him.

Fill in the blanks in the following:-

1. Does he not speak good English?
Is good English .... by him?

2. How do you like the question paper?
How .... liked ....?

3. Why does he not carry out the orders of the parents.
   Why .... not carried out ....?

Read the first three examples and then fill in the blanks:

(i) Who teaches you history?
By whom are you taught History?

(ii) Who helps him in difficulties?
By whom is he helped in difficulties?

(iii) Who knocks at the door?
By whom is the door knocked at?

(iv) Who calls you now?
.... you called ....?

(v) Who makes a noise in the class?
.... a noise ....?

(vi) Who pays her tuition fee?
....................................?

Past Indefinite Tense

Active Voice	**Passive Voice**
II form of verb	was, were III form of verb
use of 'did' in interrogative sentences	

Read the following carefully :–

Active Voice	**Passive Voice**
A. (a) I wrote books.	Books were written by me.
(b) I wrote many books.	Many books were written by me.
(c) I wrote many good books.	Many good books were written by me.
(d) He read some books.	Some books were read by him.
(e) He taught me a lesson.	I was taught a lesson by him.
(f) The teacher appointed me monitor	I was appointed monitor by the teacher.
B. (a) We ate apples and bananas.	Apples and bananas were eaten by US.
(b) My brother wrote a very good story.	A very good story was written my brother.
(c) I finished the marking of papers.	The marking of papers was finished by me.
(d) I posted a letter to him yesterday.	A letter was posted to him yesterday by me.
(e) My son threw a ball towards me.	A ball was thrown towards me by my son.

Fill in the blanks in the following

(i) The mouse jumped at me.
I .... by the mouse.

(ii) She prepared a cup of coffee for me.
A cup of coffee ....

(iii) Yesterday she learnt her lesson by heart.
Yesterday .... was learnt ....

(iv) He treated me very kindly.
I .... by him.

(v) My son got the first position in the university.
The first position ....

Read the following.

	Active Voice	**Passive Voice**
A.	(a) Did you abuse him?	Was he abused by you?
	(b) Did this teacher teach you English?	Were you taught English by do teacher?
	(c) Did she not sing a song?	Was a song not sung by her?
	(d) Did he not call you names?	Were you not called names by him?
	(e) Why did he not obey you?	Why were you not obeyed by him?
	(f) Who taught you Mathematics?	By whom were you taught Mathematics?
	(g) Who stole my pen in this class?	By whom was my pen stolen in this class?
	(h) What did he say?	What was said by him?
B.	(1) Our team did not play the match yesterday.	The match was not played by our team yesterday.
	(2) My friend did not like my suggestion.	My suggestion was not liked by my friend.
	(3) The dog did not bite him at all.	He was not at all bitten by the dog.
	(4) Perhaps he did not behave you well.	Perhaps you were not behaved well by him.

Fill in the blanks in the following:-

(a) Why did he not attend the interview?
Why .... not attended?

(b) Who used unfair means in the examination?
.... unfair means?

(c) Who sang such a sweet song?
.... was ...... sang?

(d) Did you visit our place yesterday?
.... visited by you?

(e) How did she know the question paper?
.... the question paper?

Future Indefinite Tense

Active Voice	Passive Voice
Will be	Will be
I form of verb	III form of verb
Shall	Shall be

Read the following (A & B):-

	Active Voice	Passive Voice
A.	(i) I will catch the ball.	The ball will be caught by me.
	(ii) He will not help me.	I will not be helped by him.
	(iii) We shall speak to him.	He will be spoken to by us.
	(iv) The mother will look after the child.	The child will be looked after by the mother.
	(v) You will keep your promise.	Your promise will be kept by you.
B.	1. I shall not listen to him.	He will not be listened to by me.
	2. Perhaps he will not help me.	Perhaps I will not be helped by him.
	3. Our Principal will give a talk.	A talk will be given by our Principal.

Change the Voice of the following (C & D):-

C. (a) Will you do it? Will it be done by you?
(b) Will he do this job?
(c) Will he do this job for me?
(d) Will Rajesh not visit us?
(e) Will you not cast your vote in my favour?

D. (1) Who will solve this questions? By whom will this question be solved?
(2) Which book will you buy?
(3) Who will not take the test?
(4) When will you visit us?
(5) Why will you not sign this paper?

Fill in the blanks:

(i) I will respect my teacher for all times to come.
My teacher .... by .... for all times to come.

(ii) Where will you read this letter?
.... will this letter ....?

(iii) What will you do after this?
.... done by you ....?

(iv) Will she not teach you grammar?
Will you .... grammar ....?

(v) We will miss you badly after this.
.... badly missed .... after this.

Present Continuous Tense

Active Voice	Passive Voice
Is, am, are	Is, am, are
I form of verb + ing	being III form of verb

Read the following carefully:-

	Active Voice	Passive Voice
A.	(a) He is doing his work sincerely.	His work is being done sincerely by him.
	(b) We are listening to him.	He is being listened to by us.
	(c) This old man is bringing up many orphan children.	Many orphan children are being brought up by this old man.
	(d) Our school team is winning the match.	The match is being won by our school team.

Change the voice of the following (B & C)

B. (i) Are you attending your classes these days? Are your classes being attended these days by you ?

(ii) Am I not telling a he now?

(iii) Is she not singing a sweet song?

(iv) Are you not preparing for I.A.S. examination?

(v) Why are you teasing this innocent child?

C. (1) What are you doing these days? PWhat is being done these days by you?

(2) Who is knocking at the door?

(3) Why are you laughing at him?

(4) How is he befooling you?

Fill in the blanks:

(1) My son is flying the kite.
.... being flown ....

(2) Why are you wasting my time?
Why .... my time being ....?

(3) Why are you telling a lie this time?
.... being told .... this time?

(4) Who is driving this bus?
.... is this bus ....?

(5) That man is doing injustice like me.
I am being ....

Past Continuous Tense

Active Voice	Passive Voice
Was, were	Was, were
I form of verb + ing	being III form of verb

Read the following exercises (A & B):-

	Active Voice	Passive Voice
A. (i)	I was reading the newspaper then.	The newspaper was being read by me them.
(ii)	That boy was abusing me yesterday.	I was being abused by that boy yesterday.
(iii)	The whole class was taking tea a few minutes back.	Tea was being taken by the whole class a few minutes back.
(iv)	The gardener was watering the plants.	The plants were being watered by the gardener.
B.(a)	Were you not paying full fee in the previous class?	Was full fee not being paid by you in the previous class?
(b)	Were you not writing this book last year?	Was this book not being written by you last year?
(c)	Who was plucking the flowers in the garden?	By whom were the flowers being plucked in the garden?
(d)	Why were the farmers not reaping the harvest?	Why was the harvest not being reaped by the farmers?
(e)	When was he practising medicine in the city?	When was medicine being practised by him in the city?

Fill in the blanks in the following:-

1. The barber was cutting his hair.
   His .... being cut ....
2. Why were you troubling him ?
   Why was he ....?
3. Neela was dressing her children.
   Her children by .... Neela.
4. How were you enjoying the holidays?
   How were the holidays ....?
5. Was this teacher not flattering his boss?
   Was his boss .... by this teacher?
6. Was he not teaching the class at that time?
   .... not being .... by .... at ....?

Present Perfect Tense

Active Voice	Passive Voice
Has, have	Has been, have been
III form of verb	III form of verb

Read the following exercises (A & B):-

	Active Voice	Passive Voice
A. (a)	I have passed MA.	M.A. examination has been passed by me.
(b)	Our team has won the football match.	The football match has been won by our team.
(c)	Many students have not done their home task.	Their home task has not been done by many students.
(d)	My brother has never told a lie.	A lie has never been told by my brother.
(e)	We have seen the Taj Mahal many times.	The Taj Mahal has been seen by us many times.
B. (i)	Have you taken your meals?	Have your meals been taken by you?
(ii)	Has she not sung a sweet song?	Has a sweet song not been sung by her?
(iii)	Who has won the first position in the university examination?	By whom has the first position been won in the university examination?
(iv)	Why have you not paid the fee?	Why has the fee not been paid by you?

(v)	How have you done this question?	How has this question been done by you?
(vi)	Who has told a lie in this class?	By whom has a lie been told in this class?
(vii)	Where have you by placed the pen?	Where has the pen been placed you?
(viii)	Has he not wasted the whole money just for nothing?	Has the whole money not been wasted by him just for nothing?

Fill in the blanks:

(a) His result has greatly astonished me.
.... greatly astonished by.....................

(b) She has already posted all the letters.
All the letters..................... posted ....

(c) Have you not invited him to tea party?
Has he..................... to tea party.....................?

(d) Have the children not plucked the flowers from the garden?
Have..................... not been plucked..................... from?

(e) Who has bought a new house?
.... has a new house.....................?

(f) Why have you not taken the breakfast?
.... has the breakfast.....................?

Past Perfect Tense

Active Voice	Passive Voice
Had	Had been
III form of verb	III form of verb

Read the following exercises (A & B) :-

	Active Voice	Passive Voice
A. (1)	He had solved only five questions in the examination.	Only five questions had been solved by him in the examination.
(2)	The teacher had taken the roll call.	The roll call had been taken by the teacher.
(3)	My brother had won the bet.	The bet had been won by my brother.
(4)	Some boys had not taken the test.	The test had not been taken by some boys.

	Active Voice	Passive Voice
(5)	The students had purchased all the books.	All the books had been purchased by the students.
B. (a)	Had you not insulted him?	Had he not been insulted by you?
(b)	Had he not learnt die change of voice?	Had the change of voice not been learnt by him?
(c)	Why had you bought a house?	Why had a house been bought by you?
(d)	Who had broken the slate?	By whom had the slate been broken?
(e)	Who had beaten him?	By whom had he been beaten?

Fill in the blanks:-

(i) They had offered me the job of a Principal.
I had been offered .... by them.

(ii) Where had he placed the books?
.... the books ....?

(iii) Who had locked at my door?
.... had my door been ....?

(iv) Which book had you finished?
Which book .... by you?

(v) Had Neela not deceived Rajesh?
Had Rajesh not been ....?

Future Perfect Tense

Active Voice	Passive Voice
Will have	Will have been
Shall have	Shall have been
III form of verb	III form of verb

Read the following exercises (A & B) :-

	Active Voice	Passive Voice
A.(1)	I will have won the scholarship.	The scholarship will have been won by me.
(2)	She will have finished the paper in time.	The paper mill have been finished by her in time.
(3)	I will have completed book before time.	The book will have been completed before time by me.
(4)	The doctor will have examined him thoroughly.	He will have been examined thoroughly by the doctor.
(5)	Your uncle will have met you at the railway station.	You will have been met at the rail way station by your uncle.

B.(a)	Will the students not have taken the test?	Will the test not have been taken by the students?
(b)	Will Neela not have finished her work by now?	Will her work not have been finished by Neela by now?
(c)	Which team will have won the match?	By which team will the match have been won?
(d)	Who will have narrated the whole story?	By whom will the whole story have been narrated?
(e)	Why will they not have reached an agreement?	Why will an agreement not have been reached by them?

Fill in the blanks in the following:-

(i) My brother will have got the first position in the university examination.
The first position in the university examination .... by my mother.

(ii) Will you not have shaken hands with the Prime Minister of India?
Will .... not .... shaken with .... by you?

(iii) Who will have consoled you in hardships?
By whom will .... consoled in hardships?

(iv) Where will you have forgotten the umbrella?
Where will .... have .... forgotten by ....?

(v) How will you have overcome the problems?
.... have been overcome ....?

(vi) When will you have posted the letter?
When will the letter ....?

(vii) They will have appointed me as Principal of a college.
I .... appointed .... by them.

Miscellaneous–1

Active Voice	**Passive Voice**
can, may, could, must, would, should, might ought	can be, may be, could be. must be, would be, should be, might be, ought be
I form of verb	III form of verb

Read the following (A & B) :-

	Active Voice	Passive Voice
A. (1)	I can talk to him.	He can be talked to by me.
(2)	You may take rest now.	Rest may be taken now by you.
(3)	I could solve this question very easily.	This question could be solved very easily by me.
(4)	One must do one's duty.	One's duty must be done by one.
(5)	She would help me always.	I would always be helped by her.
(6)	You should obey the you.	The elders should be obeyed by elders.
(7)	We might purchase a television.	A television might be purchased by us.
(8)	They ought to respect the parents.	The parents ought to be respected by them.
B. (a)	Can you help me in matter?	Can I be helped by you in this this matter?
(b)	May I talk to you now?	May you be talked to by me now?
(c)	Could you not help him?	Could he not be helped by you?
(d)	Would you not tell me you?	Would I not be told the truth by the truth?
(e)	Should we not take action against him?	Should action not be taken against him by us?
(f)	May God bless you with a son!	May you be blessed with a son!

Fill in the blanks in the following:-

(i) I may help him in difficulty.
He .... helped by .... in difficulty.

(ii) You ought to respect the boss in every case.
The boss .... by you in every case.

(iii) That man would always blame you.
You would .... by that man.

(iv) Should she not play some game daily?
Should some game .... daily?

(v) May God grant peace to the departed soul!
May the departed soul .... !

Miscellaneous–2

Active Voice	**Passive Voice**
Should have	Should have been
Would have	Would have been
Could have	Could have been
Might have	Might have been
III form of verb	III form of verb

Read the following:-

	Active Voice	**Passive Voice**
A. (1)	We should have attended the lecture.	The lecture should have been attended by us.
(2)	By hard work, you would have got the scholarship.	By hard work, the scholarship would have been got by you.
(3)	You could have informed the police before hand.	The police could have been informed by you before hand.
(4)	They might have purchased a card.	A card might have been purchased by them.

Fill in the blanks in the following:

B. (a) Who would have got the first position?
.... would the first position .... got?

(b) He should have written a letter to me.
I .... written a letter to ....

(c) Your team might have scored a goal.
A goal .... scored by ....

(d) We should have known the result before hand.
The result .... known to us before hand.

(e) Should he not have taken your advice?
Should your advice .... by him?

Miscellaneous–3

Read carefully the following:-

	Active Voice	**Passive Voice**
A. (1)	Do it at once.	Let it be done at once.
(2)	Hold your tongue.	Let your tongue be held.
(3)	Call the doctor immediately.	Let the doctor be called immediately.
(4)	Take him to the police station.	Let he be taken to the police station.

(5) Switch off the light.	Let the light be switched off.
(6) Tell him to remain out	Let he be told to remain out.
(7) Never tell a lie.	Let a lie be never told.
(8) Do taste this fruit.	Let this fruit be tasted.
B. (a) Please help me.	You are requested to help me.
(b) Kindly allow him.	Your are requested to allow him.
(c) Get out from the class.	Your are ordered to get out from the class.
(d) Stand up ion the bench.	You are ordered to stand up on the bench.
(e) Let Neela sing.	You are requested to let Neela sing.
(f) Let us play.	It is proposed that we should play.
(g) Let us go out for a walk.	It is proposed that we should go out for a walk.
C. (i) It is time to take the roll call.	It is time for the roll call to be taken.
(ii) It is time to tell the truth.	It is time for the truth to be told.
(iii) It is time to enjoy life.	It is time for life to be enjoyed.
(iv) They say that honesty is the best policy.	It is said that honesty is the best policy.
(v) God helps those who help themselves.	Those who help themselves are helped by God.
(vi) Those who live in glass houses should not throw stones at others.	Stones should not be thrown at others by those who live in glass houses.

Fill in the blanks in the following :-

(1) Do not disturb me now.
Let I be .... now.

(2) Always speak the truth.
You are advised .... always.

(3) Obey your parents.
Let .... be ....

(4) Never deceive anybody.
Let anybody ....

(5) Ring the bell just now.
Let the bell ....

(6) Sit down.
You are requested ....

(7) Let her sing a song.
Let a song ....

(8) It is to pass the examination.
It is time for ....

(9) Take exercise daily.
You are advised to ....

Read the following:

	Passive Voice	Active Voice
(a)	His book has been stolen.	I have stolen his book.
(b)	Is the work being done by me?	Are you doing the work?
(c)	Let it be done.	Do it.
(d)	Could you be helped?	Could he help you?
(e)	Is milk contained in this pot?	Does this pot contain milk?

Fill in the blanks:-

Passive Voice	Active Voice
(i) Were pictures painted by Sita.	.... Sita .... pictures?
(ii) By whom has this book been written?	.... written this book?
(iii) You are requested to help me.	.... help me.
(iv) It can be done even now.	.... do it even now.

Unsolved Exercises

Change the Voice of the following

I. 1. This boy looks after the cattle.
2. How do you like this picture?
3. We do not like gambling.
4. The grandmother tells a story at night?
5. Who does not love his country?
6. What do you want now?
7. Who knocks at the door?
8. Do your know this student?

II. 1. Who taught you grammar?
2. He appointed me as Principal.

3. My brother did not behave me well.
4. Why did you disobey the cider brother?
5. Did this book contain pictures?
6. Where did you disobey the elder brother?
7. How did you like this picture?
8. I solved all the question in time.

III. 1. The teacher will turn me out.
2. I shall not help you there.
3. Will you not help me in this matter?
4. Who will pocket this insult?
5. Which book will you read now?
6. Will he not tell the truth?
7. I will ask her to do so.

IV. 1. The child is cutting the teeth.
2. The dog is barking at me.
3. Are they holding a meeting outside?
4. Is she not keeping good health these days?
5. Is Rajesh flying a kite?
6. These teachers are not doing their duty well.
7. Why are you not attending the classes?
8. Are these boys not killing time?

V. 1. The teacher was not listening to me.
2. She was not telling the truth.
3. Was he not calling me names?
4. What were you doing yesterday?
5. Who was tasing you?
6. Why was he misbehaving with me?
7. Was she taking medicine regularly?

VI. 1. She has passed M. Phil examination recently.
2. Have you not taught him a lesson?
3. I have not come across my boss so far.
4. How much work have you done?
5. Who has lost the match?
6. Why has he not obeyed his parents?
7. Has he not taken leave from the college?
8. What have you written in the letter?

VII. 1. The union had elected me president.
2. Had he not misunderstood you?
3. The teacher had already warned you.

4. How had you missed the train?
5. Had my son not learnt the lesson by heart?
6. Who had beaten that boy?
7. Why had you not solved all the questions?

VIII. 1. I will have corrected her note-book.
2. They will have paid their fees by now.
3. Who will have written this essay.
4. Will you not have bought new clothes?
5. Will she not have taken the test?
6. Why will he not have got the first position in the class?
7. will the farmers not have reaped the harvests?

IX. 1. May I sing a song now !
2. You must do your duty first.
3. Could she not solve this question?
4. Who would do it?
5. May God bless you!
6. You ought to obey him.
7. They should call a meeting sometime.
8. Can I take your scooter?

X. 1. He would have narrated the whole story.
2. You should have learnt the lesson by now.
3. Who would have caught the ball?
4. When would have you done it?
5. Should she not have consulted you?

XI. 1. Show the guest in.
2. Please be seated.
3. Let us talk now.
4. Kindly help me.
5. It is time to speak the truth.
6. It is time to meet the teacher.
7. God helps those who help themselves.

XII. 1. By whom has this letter been written?
2. The test has been taken.
3. Is milk contained in this glass?
4. What is being done?
5. Will I not be liked by him?
6. You are requested to excuse in.
7. The questions are being solved.
8. Can it be done?

Direct and Indirect Speech

One person saying to another directly-Direct Speech.

A person asking someone to convey to the other party/person. Indirect speech.

The speech of a person can be reported directly by using the same words within inverted commas. That is called Direct Speech.

When we report the speech without giving exact words and without using inverted commas, that is called indirect Speech e.g.

Direct Speech: He said to me, "I am late."

Indirect Speech: He told me that he was late.

Understand subject (S) and object (o) in the following reporting verbs:–

(a) He said to me
s o

(b) Mohan said (No object given hare)
s

(c) Said my brother (No object given here)
s

(d) Replied the man (No object given here)
s

(e) He said, "Mohan,.............
s o

Tense of the reporting verb may please be noted in the following.-

(i) He said to me.	Past Tense
(ii) She always says.	Present Tense
(iii) Mohan will say.	Future Tense
(iv) Enquired the boy.	Past Tense

3. (a) When the reporting verb is in present tense or future tense, the whole sentence will remain in the same tense while converting it into indirect speech.

(b) When the reporting verb is in past tense, the tense of the whole sentence will be past while converting it into indirect speech. Thus the changes will be as under:

I form. of verb + s or es is changed into II form of verb.

II form of verb	is changed into	had+III form of verb
has have	is changed into	is changed into had
has been, have been	is changed into	had been
is, am are	is changed into	was, were
was, were	is changed into	had been

can	is changed into	could
will	is changed into	would
shall	is changed into	should or would
may	is changed into	might
had+III form of verb		No change
had been+ I form of verb + ing		No change

Three Persons:-

I me, my;	mine, myself
I Person	We-our, us ours, ourselves
II Person	You-your, yours, yourself, yourselves
	He-his, him, himself
She-her,	her, herself
III Person	It-its, itself
	They-them, their, themselves

I Person in the reporting speech is changed into Subject

II Person in the reporting speech is changed into Object

III Person is not changed.

This	is changed into	That
These	is changed into	those
now	is changed into	then
here	is changed into	there
hither	is changed into	thither
hence	is changed into	thence
today	is changed into	that day
yesterday	is changed into	the previous day
tomorrow	is changed into	the next day
last evening	is changed into	the previous evening
last night	is changed into	the previous night
last month	is changed into	the previous month
next week	is changed into	the following week
next month	is changed into	the following month

Type–I

Simple Sentence-A simple statement.

Such a sentence ends with a full stop. (✓)

It is not interrogative or exclamatory. (×?!)

It does not convey order, advise, request etc. (x order, advise, request, wish)

e.g. I am going to Delhi.

He is my younger brother.

(i) Here 'said to' is changed into 'told'.
says to or say to is changed into tell or tells
(ii) Inverted Commas are replaced by 'that' (" ")
Let us now convert a sentence from Direct Speech into Indirect Speech e.g.
He said to me, "I am going to Delhi to-day."
told that I person that day
I
Is changed into subject (he)
Reporting verb is in past tense,
So Indirect Speech of the above sentence is:
He told me that he was going to Delhi that day.

Now read the following sentences of Direct and Indirect speech:-

(a) He said to me, "I am not feeling well to-day. "
He told me that he was not feeling well that day.
(b) I said to Mohan, " My brother is not here.
I told Mohan that my brother was not there.
(c) You said to him, " I am sick of busy life.
You told him that you were sick of busy life.
(d) She said to her father, " I will now sing a song."
She told her father that she would then sing a song.
(e) The teacher said to us, "Today I am going out of station and shall be back tomorrow."
The teacher told us that day he was going out of station and would be back the next day.

Fill in the blanks in the following:-

(a) They said to me, "We are going to play a match."
They .... me .... they .... going to play a match.
(b) Veena said to her mother, "I want to meet my brother and sister this week."
Veena .... her mother that .... to meet .... brother and sister .... week.
(c) The boy said to me, "My father is out of station these days.
The boy .... me .... father .... out of station ....

Read the following sentences:

(a) Our class monitor said, 'I touch the feet of my parents in the morning when I get up."

Our class monitor told that he touched the feet of his parents in the morning when he got up.

(b) Mohan said, "Mother, I am having a severe headache at this time."
Mohan told his mother that he was having a severe headache at that time.

(c) He said, "Dear friend, we will be leaving for U.S.A. the next month.
He told his dear friend that they would be leaving for U.S.A. the following month.

(d) She said, "Dear father, Rajesh is not solving the questions now."
She told her dear father that Rajesh was not solving the questions then.

(e) He said, "Friend, I am not well these days. I am going out of station and shall be back tomorrow evening."
He told his friend that he was not well those days. He further said that he was going out of station and would be back the next day evening.

Fill in the blanks in the following sentences :-

(a) I said, "Respected brother, I will starting from here early in the morning."
I .... my respected brother that .... early in the morning.

(b) She said, "Mother, I have to go to the college for paying my fee."
She .... that .... go to the college for paying .... fee.

(c) Neela said, "Rajesh, I have to go to England for one year."
.... that .... for one year.

Read the following sentences of Direct and Indirect speech :-

(a) She always says, "I am badly in need of money".
She always says that she is badly in need of money.

(b) The child says, "It is raining outside."
The child says that it is raining outside.

(c) My sister says, "I have done my work."
My sister says that she has done her work.

(d) This old man generally says, "My children do not care for me."

This old man generally says that his children do not care for him.

(e) He says to me, "I am not in the good books of the Headmaster."
He tells me that he is not in the good books of the Headmaster.

Fill in the blanks in the following:-

(a) The brother says, "I have done much for you."
The brother tells us that ....
The brother tells me ....

(b) He tells, "It is the age of science".
He tells that ....

(c) One student in the examination hall says, "I have no pen to write with."
One student in the examination hall says that ....

Read the following sentences:-

(a) She will say, "I don't take tea."
She will say that she doesn't take tea.

(b) He will say, "I am not well prepared for the test."
He will say that he is not well prepared for the test.

(c) The teacher will say, "Rajesh was one of my good students."
The teacher will say that Rajesh was one of his good students.

(d) My wife will say to me, "You cannot please your officer."
My wife will tell me that I cannot please my officer.

(e) He will say, "I shall kill the lion within a second".
He will say that he will kill the lion within a second.

Fill in the blanks in the following :-

(a) You will say, "I do not take tea."
You will say ....

(b) He will say to me, "I have no pen or pencil to write with."
He will tell me ....

(c) The boy will say, "My father is away."
The boy will say that ....

Fill in the blanks sentences :-

(a) The teacher said, "Dear students health is wealth."
The teacher told his dear students that health is wealth.

(b) My friend said to me, "Where there is will, there is a way."
My friend told me that where there is a will, there is a way.

(c) He said, "The sun rises in the east and sets in the west."
He told that the sun rises in the east and sets in the west.

(d) You said to me, "A friend in need is a friend indeed."
You told me that a friend in need is a friend indeed.

(e) The saint said, "God is omnipresent."
The saint told that God is omnipresent.

Fill in the blanks in the following:-

(a) The old man said, "United You stand, divided you fall.,,
The old man told that ....

(b) He said, "Friend greed is a curse."
He told his friend ....

(c) "What cant be cured, must be endured", said he.
He ....

Type–II

Interrogative sentence

A sentence followed by question mark (?)

Here 'said to' is changed into 'asked'.

In reported speech, the question words starting with 'w............h.'

e.g. what, when, where, why, who, whose, whom, how etc. do not take 'if' whereas all other question words e.g. will, can, is, was, has etc. take 'if,.

Now read the following sentences:_

(a) The teacher said to me, "What is your name?"
The teacher asked me what my name was.

(b) He said to me, "Where does Your uncle live these days?
He asked me where my uncle lived those days.

(c) The Principal said to the teacher, "Why are You late to-day again? "
The Principal asked the teacher why he was late to-day again.

(d) They said to her, "Who is Your father?"
They asked her who her father was.

(e) The monitor said to us, "Whose book is this?"
The monitor asked us whose book that was.

(f) The inspector said, "Boys, how did you spend your holidays?"
The inspector asked the boys how we had spent our holidays.

(g) I said to my class-fellow, "When did the teacher come to the class?"
I asked my class-fellow when the teacher had come to the class.

Fill in the blanks in the following :-

(i) She said to him, "What is your father"?
She .... him what .... was.

(ii) "When did you arrive here"? asked I.
I asked him when .... arrived ....

(iii) I said to her, "Who teaches you English these days?"
I .... her .... English ....

(iv) "Why will you report against him?" I asked.
I asked her why .... report against him.
or
I asked him why .... report against him.

Read the following sentences:-

(a) The teacher said to us, "Is the earth stationary"?
The teacher asked us if the earth was stationary.

(b) He said to me, "Was your father in station yesterday?"
He asked me if my father had been in station the previous day.

(c) "May I come in, Sir"? said I to the teacher.
I asked the teacher respectfully if I might come in.

(d) My friend said to me, "Do you know the shortest way to the railway station?"
My friend asked me if I knew the shortest way to the railway station.

(e) She said, "Brother, will you help me in this matter?"
She asked her brother if he would help her in that matter.

(f) The stranger said to me, "Can you tell me the way to some nearest school where I may admit the child?"
The stranger asked me if I could tell him the way to some nearest school where he might admit the child.

Fill in the blanks in the following:-

(i) My sister said to me, "Will you help us in this matter"?
My sister .... me if .... help .... in .... matter.

(ii) Neela said to me, "Did you write a letter to your brother yesterday"?
Neela asked me if .... a letter to .... brother

(iii) He said to me, "Have you ever been to Bombay"?
He .... me .... ever been to Bombay.

(iv) "May I use your telephone"? said I to the shopkeeper.
I .... the shopkeeper if I .... use .... telephone.

(v) "Could you lend me some money"? said he.
He .... me if .... could lend .... some money.
or
He .... them if .... could lend .... some money.

Read the following sentences:-

(a) I said to the students, "Why are you making a noise? Has everybody completed the assignment?"
I asked the students why they were making a noise and if everybody had completed the assignment.

(b) She said to me- "What is the time now? When will you go to college?"
She asked me what the time was then and when I would go to college.

(c) The teacher said to us, "Is everybody present today"? Would you like to go for a picnic tomorrow?
The teacher asked us if everybody was present that day and if live would like to go for a picnic the next day.

(d) The President said to me, "What are your qualifications? Do you study anything these days? What are you doing?"
The President asked me what my qualifications were and if I studied anything those days. He further asked me what I was doing.

(e) The shopkeeper said to me, "How much money have you got? Can you lend me some money?"
The shopkeeper asked me how much money I had got and if I could lend him some money.

Fill in the blanks in the following:-

(i) The doctor said, How is your friend now? Is he all right?
The doctor .... me .... and if he .... all right.

(ii) My elder brother said, "Have you revised the whole syllabus?
Is there any difficulty?"
My elder brother asked me .... and ....

(iii) She said to him, "Do you have a scooter? Can you give it to me for half an hour?"
She .... if .... and if .... for half an hour.

Type–III

Imperative Sentences

These sentences show order, advise, request, wish etc. So we use 'ordered', advised, requested, wished in place of 'said to'. Inverted commas are replaced by 'to'.

e.g. He said to me, "Get out."
He ordered me to get out.

Read the following sentences:

(a) The teacher said to the students, "Don't tell a lie."
The teacher advised the students not to tell a lie.

(b) My elder brother said to me, "Don't waste your time in idle talks."
My elder brother advised me not to waste any time in idle talks.

(c) The officer said to the peon, "Get out from my office just now."
The officer ordered the peon to get out from his office just then.

(d) The doctor said to the servant, "Bring out the first aid box from my office."
The doctor ordered the servant to bring out the first aid box from his office.

(e) He said to me, "Let me complete my work."
He requested me to let him complete his work.

(f) The poor lady said, "Please give her something to eat."
The poor lady requested me to give her something to eat.

Fill in the blanks in the following :-

(i) I said to my friend, "Please give me your book for to-day."
I .... my friend to give .... book for ....

(ii) She said to her boss, "Kindly grant me leave for one day."
She .... her boss to grant .... leave for one day.

(iii) My friend said to me, "Help me in this matter."
My friend .... me to .... in .... matter.

(iv) He said, "Dear friend, count the pages of this note-book, please."
He .... his dear friend .... count the pages of .... note-book.

Fill in the blanks in the following :-

(i) He said, "Get up early in the morning if you want to have good health."
He advised me .... get up early in the morning if .... to have good health.

(ii) My mother said to me, "Do every work in time and never lag behind".
My mother .... me .... do every work in time and never to log behind.

(iii) "Don't quarrel with the neighbour," said I to him.
I .... him .... quarrel with the neighbour.

(iv) The father said,. "Don't feel zealous of others."
The father .... him .... feel zealous of others.

Fill in the blanks in the following:

(i) I said to the peon, "Hurry up".
I .... the peon .... huffy up.

(ii) The Principal said to the servant, "Pack up your luggage and get out from my house."
The Principal .... the servant .... pack up .... luggage ....

(iii) "Count these answer books again," said the Superintendent to the clerk.
The superintendent .... the clerk ....

Type–III-B:

"Let us ...."

Here 'said to' is changed into 'proposed to'

" " .... replaced by 'that'

Let us .... replaced by 'they should'

Read the following sentences:

(a) The boys said to the teacher, "Let us go out for a picnic."
The boys proposed to the teacher that they should go out for a picnic."

(b) She said to me, "Let us solve the questions now."
She proposed to me that they should solve the questions then.

(c) She said, to me, "Let me solve the questions now."
She requested me to let her solve the question then.

(d) The student said, "Let us have a picnic today."
The student proposed to me that they should have a picnic that day.

(e) "Let us wait for the next train," said he to me.
He proposed to me that they should wait for the next train.

Fill in the blanks in the following :-

(i) One of the students said, "Let us all sing together."
One of the students .... me .... they should all sing together.

(ii) He said to me, "Let us take a bath first and then we can take breakfast."
He .... me .... take a bath first and then .... take breakfast.

(iii) She said, "Let Me mark the papers."
She ....

(iv) The child said to others, "Let us enjoy the pleasant weather".
The child .... to others .... enjoy the pleasant weather.

Fill in the blanks in the following:-

(i) The teacher said, "Wait here till the Principal comes.
The teacher ....

(ii) "Kindly help me in this matter, "said she to me.
She .... me to ....

(iii) I said to the shopkeeper, "Weigh these articles as quickly as possible."
I .... the shopkeeper .... articles as quickly as possible.

(iv) My brother said to me, "Don't mix up with bad boys."
My brother .... me .... mix up with bad boys.

(v) "Let us play table tennis now," said he.
He ....

Type–IV

Exclamatory Sentences

These sentences show happiness, sorrow or wonder.

Here the reported verb is changed as:

exclaimed with joy

exclaimed with sorrow

exclaimed with wonder

" " are replaced by 'that'

How is changed into 'very'

e.g. She said, "Oh ! I have passed the examination."

She exclaimed with joy that she had passed the examination.

Read the following sentences :-

(a) The students shouted, "Hurrah! Our team has won the match by three goals.
The students exclaimed with joy that their team had won the match by three goals.

(b) The mother said, 'Oh! My son has come back from U.S.A."
The mother exclaimed with joy that her son had come back from U.S.A.

(c) The Principal said, "Splendid ! Our student is first in the university examination."
The Principal exclaimed with joy that their student was first in the university examination.

(d) The General said, "Bravo ! Our forces are far ahead."
The General exclaimed with joy that their forces were far ahead."

Fill in the blanks in the following

(i) The father said., "Oh ! My son has won the scholarship."
The father .... that .... won the scholarship.

(ii) The leader shouted, "Fine !Our country has become very prosperous."
The leader .... that .... become very prosperous.

(iii) The teacher said to the student, "Splendid ! You have done well in the examination."
The teacher exclaimed .... and told the student .... done well in the examination

Read the following exercises

(a) I said, "Alas ! I lost my father in childhood."
I exclaimed with sorrow that I had lost my father in childhood.

(b) The old man said, "Ah ! I am undone."
The old man exclaimed kith sorrow that he was undone.

(c) "How naughty I have been?" said he.
He exclaimed with sorrow that he had been very naughty.

Fill in the blanks in the following :-

(i) The student said, "Alas ! I have failed".
The student .... that .... failed.

(ii) The old lady cried, "Ah ! My only child is dead."
The old lady exclaimed with .... dead.

(iii) The teacher said, "Alas ! The name of an intelligent boy is missing in the list of successful candidates."
The teacher exclaimed .... that ....

Read the following sentences:

(a) They said. "What ! He has missed the train."
They exclaimed with wonder that he had missed the train.

(b) She said, "What a fine weather it is!"
She exclaimed with wonder that it was a fine weather.

(c) The newly married couple said, "How fine the weather!"
The newly married couple exclaimed with wonder that the weather was very fine.

Fill in the blanks in the following :-

(i) The boy said, "What ! Your roll number is not in the newspaper."
The boy .... that .... roll number .... not in the news paper.

(ii) Neela said, "What a wonderful pen it is" !
Neela .... that ....

(iii) "What a stiff question paper today" ! said the boys.
The boys .... that it was a stiff question paper that day.

TYPE–IV-B

Wish or pray is indicated in some sentences. In those sentences, the reporting verb undergoes a change accordingly. Inverted

Commas are replaced by 'that'. 'Sir' is changed into 'respectfully' 'Good morning' 'wished', Good evening, Good night-bade.

Read the following exercises:

(a) The old lady said, "May God bless you with a son!"
The old lady prayed that God might bless him with a son.

(b) She said, "May you live long" !
She prayed that I might live long.
or She wished that I might live long.

(c) The whole staff said, Thay God grant peace to the departed soul" !
The whole staff prayed that God might grant peace to the departed soul" !

(d) She said to me, "Good morning! How do you do"?
She wished me good morning and asked how I am.

(e) The student said to the teacher, "Good morning ! sir."
The student respectfully wished the teacher good morning.

(f) I said to him, "Good bye!"
I bade him good bye.

(g) "Good evening ! Sir," said the boy to me.
The boy respectfully bade me good evening.

Fill in the blanks in the following:-

(i) The old man said, "May you pass the examination with good marks!'
The old man .... that .... pass the examination with good marks.

(ii) Neela said to me, "May you have all happiness in life" !
Neela wished that .... have all happiness in life.

(iii) The poor boy said, "Would that I were born of rich parents"!
The poor boy .... that the .... born of rich parents.

Fill in the blanks in the following:

(i) He said to his boss, "Good morning".
He .... his boss ....

(ii) They said, "Good bye."
They .... me ....

(iii) "Good morning sir," said the boy to me," Are you going with us?"
The boy respectfully .... me good morning and asked ....?"

Miscellaneous Type

Read the following exercises showing Direct and Indirect Speech:

1. Teacher: "What is you name?"
Student : "Sir, my name is Raju."
Teacher : "Where are you these days?"
Student : "Sir, I am working as a teacher in Germany."
The teacher asked the student what his name was. The student respectfully replied that his name was Raju. Then the teacher asked where he was those days. The student respectfully replied that he was working as a teacher in Germany.

2. Rajesh : "Where have you been for so long?"
Neela : "I was away to England".
Rajesh : "When did you come here? How is everything at home?"
Neela : Only yesterday. All fine.
Rajesh asked Neela where she had been for so long. Neela replied she had been away to England. Then Rajesh asked when she had come there and how everything was at home. To this Neela replied that she had come only the previous day and everything at home was fine.

3. Headmaster; "Did you attend the meeting at D.C. office today"?
Teacher; "Yes, sir."
Headmaster: "What was the most important."
The Headmaster asked the teacher if he had attended the meeting at D.C. office that day. The teacher respectfully replied in positive. Then the Headmaster asked what the most important thing had been in the meeting. To this the teacher said that everything had been important.

4. Monitor: "Good morning, sir, I have a problem."
Teacher: "What is that? Let me know about it."

The monitor respectfully wished his teacher morning and told that he had a problem. The teacher asked what that was. Then he requested him to let him know about it.

5. Father: "Have you done the home task?"
Son: "Yes, I did it at school."
Father: "Didn't you study at home today"?
Son: "No, there was nothing to be done.
Father: "You should study something even if there is no home task given by the teacher."
Son: "All right. I will always do so."
The father asked his son if he had done the home task. The son replied in positive and told that he had done it at school. The father further asked if he had not studied at home that day. The son replied in negative and said that there had been nothing to be done. At this the father advised him that he should study something even if there was no home task given by the teacher. The son assured him that he would always do so.

6. I said to my friend, "Will you forget that we quarrelled with each other lȁst year? Let us be friends again and continue having better relations."
I asked my firiend if he would forget that we had quarrelled with each other the previous year. Then I proposed to him that we should be friends again and continue having better relations.

7. She said, "Rajesh, are you at the door? What brings you here at this late hour? Has your mother also come with you?" She asked Rajesh if he was at the door. She further questioned him what brought him there at that late hour and if his mother had also come with him.

8. The teacher said, "Those who have not done their home task should stand up. You should work regularly and come well prepared in the class. I will not tolerate it in future."
The teacher ordered them that those who had not done their home task should stand up. After this he advised them that they should work regularly and come well prepared in the class. Then he told them that he would not tolerate it in future.

9. He said to me, "What a poor student ! How bad is your writing! You must do something to improve it."
   He exclaimed with sorrow that I was a poor student. Then he remarked that my writing was very bad. After that he advised me that I must do something to improve it.
10. The students said, "Good morning ! May I sit with you for some guidance?" "You are most welcome," said 1.
   The student wished me good morning and asked if he might sit with me for some guidance. I replied that he was most welcome.
11. I said to him, "What is you brother? Where does he live? May I suggest a suitable match for his marriage?" "Please do." said he.
   I asked him what his brother was and where he lived. I further asked if I might suggest a suitable match for his marriage. At this he replied that I should do so.
12. "This teacher is really very hard working. He is bound to reach the heights of glory", said the man. "How do you say like that?" asked he.
   The man told that teacher was really very hard working and he was bound to reach the heights of glory. At this he asked how he said like that.

More Exercises for Practice:

Transform the following into Indirect Speech:

A. 1. The father said, "Dear son, you should always love truth and pardon error."
2. She said, "When the cat is away, the mice will play."
3. "The climate of this place is better than that of Punjab," said he to me.
4. He always says, "I have read this book and now I am going to take another."
5. The doctor said to the patient, "You will soon be better if you continue taking this medicine regularly."

B. (a) You will say, "We are not prepared for the test as yet."
(b) He said to me, "My brother will meet me here tomorrow at this very time."

(c) The mother said, "Dear child, a friend in need is a friend indeed."

(d) The student said, 'Sir, I was going to come to your place yesterday."

(e) The servant said, " I have been working here since 1970".

C. (a) I said to her, "Do you know my younger brother who is a doctor these days?"

(b) The man said, "Why have you come again? What do you want? Should I complain against you to your parents?"

14

Correct Spelling

Undoubtedly English is a foreign language but it has international importance. Hence its study is of unique importance in every nook and corner of the world. The study of this language poses a number of problems for the learners. Moreover, English is not a phonetic language. Its writing system and speaking system are not the same. We write the words in a different way and we speak them in a different way. That is the main reason that many learners of English commit different types of spelling mistakes. A few examples of spelling mistakes are:–

(i) monkey is written as mankey
(ii) cement is written as simint
(iii) rough is written as 'ruff'
(iv) cough is written as 'cuff'
(v) heat is written as 'hit'
(vi) seat is written as 'sect'
(vii) know is written as 'no'

If we analyse the different types of spelling errors, that becomes a sort of humorous situation to laugh at by the linguist and a problem to be tackled wisely and intelligently by the subject teacher.

While writing sentences of English, many students may tend to write patterns of sentences like that of mother tongue i.e. Hindi, Punjabi or Urdu. The structural patterns of English and the above said regional languages are widely different. The errors committed by the learners in structural patterns are as under:

He is a teacher.
Mohan is a good boy.
Geeta is a good girl.
The father is coming.

The following examples are taken from the written English of the school going children. They show clearly that the students are very poor in written English.

More Examples of Mistakes

1. Sentences are being written as:
   - (i) He got to Delhi.
   - (ii) He did not went.
   - (iii) He as well you are busy.
   - (iv) When you are leaving for U.S.A.?
2. Mistakes while giving opposite genders:
   Masculine Faminine
   - (i) Table/Chair
   - (ii) House/Shop
   - (iii) Dog/Dogy
   - (iv) Book/Note-Book
3. Mistakes while writing opposite numbers:
   Singular Plural
   - (i) Child/Childs
   - (ii) Children/Childrens
   - (iii) People/Peoples
4. Mistakes in spoken English:
   - (i) Knowledge
   - (ii) Asked

   'But you are late'

These examples show clearly that the students have not been taught English properly. They do not have knowledge of basic sentence patterns, correct spellings, correct vocabulary etc.

F.L. Bilows says, "Remedial teaching is morale building and an interest building enterprise for the students." Remedial English means improvement in the standard of En". It goes without saying that the students who learn English as a foreign language are considerably poor in this subject. It is very true if we examine a student belonging to the high class of a school or the first year of a college. There are many students in these classes who cannot write even a single sentence of English correctly. If we take into consideration the spoken aspect of the language, there also the condition of the students is rather pitiable.

Now the question arises why this is so. There can be a number of reasons behind it. It is just possible that the students are not interested in learning the language. Another reason can be that learners are careless. But these may be the causes in case of a few children only. The root cause behind this is that teachers of English themselves are not very efficient. Their own English is not perfect. They themselves lack in many respects. So it is very essential that English of the teachers should be improved. The College of Education should see that only the most suitable persons who are good in English should be allowed to take up this subject. And those who are at service may be asked to undergo some training programme. That way they will be equipped with good English. Then, of course, their efforts to improve English of the students will bear fruit.

The worse condition of the students, as far as English is concerned needs a further check. The students should be taught English carefully. They should be given regular guidance by the teacher. The teacher should check up their written work, spoken language etc. frequently so as to improve their condition slowly and steadily. He should not tell the students all of a sudden on the last day of the academic session that he or she is unable to pull on with English. Here it will not be wrong if we refer to Kothari Education Commission report and the suggestion made therein regarding teaching of English. Let English be made an optional subject. Those who are interested in it may take up its study in 5th class and continue onward and those who are not interested in its study may not be asked to study it compulsorily In this way one group of students will have elementary knowledge of it in VII class and those who are really interested in the language will start its study in the 5th class. According to the Commission report, the study of no language is to be compulsory after Matric. Thus only those students will come upto B.A. or M.A. level in English who are already interested in the subject and are capable of teaching this language to others. By following the policy suggested by Kothari Education Commission report the problem of poor English of the students can be solved upto a great extent. It will solve the problems of the teachers as well.

Remedial Measures

Here below are given sonic methods by which mistakes in written English can be remedied:-

1. Drills of sentence patterns may be given. The teacher may take up one sentence at a time, and give simple repetition drill to the class. Then substitiution, completion and

conversion drills can be used for teaching the sentence patterns. After oral practice, they should be given written practice.

2. The incorrect sentences and the corrected sentences may be written on a chart. The students should be asked to consult that chart again and again. Thus they will be able to get rid of incorrect English.
3. There should be frequent tests in order to see whether the students have made some improvement or not.

Thus regular guidance and careful supervision can help the students in the improvement of English.

Some More Practical Suggestions

1. The students should have knowledge of the ten basic sentence patterns given in the chapter on grammar. They should speak as well as write a number of sentences of each pattern.
2. They are advised to study the verb patterns given at the end of the book.
3. They should have thorough knowledge of tenses. For this detailed exercises have been given at the end of this very chapter.
4. For the improvement of spelling mistakes, the learners of English are advised to learn spellings of a few words daily. If they so like, they may have a note-book for writing the spellings of some words daily.
5. They should write a few lines on some topics of common interest. They should make it a point to write a few sentences on one topic daily. Some of the topics for the beginning stages are:-

   My Room, My School, My Teacher, My Brother, My Father, My Class Room.

   My Book, My Friend, My House, My Garden.

   A Dog, A Cow, A Camel.

   My City, My Country.

   The students should write a few sentences daily and get it corrected from someone.
6. Gradually they should take up simple topics from the different chapters of the book and write a few sentences in the same way. For example, English Language, Our National Language, Spellings in English Language, Oral

Work, Written Work, English Teacher, Pronunciation, A Text Book, Examination etc. Practice of speaking or writing of these aspects will improve English and also help them to learn something about the subject matter.

7. One type of sentence may be written. Then the students should think of words which can be substituted for some words given in the specimen sentence. Thus substitution table may be prepared and reading and writing practice on the bases of subsitution table will help the learners considerably. For example:-

Although	he	is poor	yet	he	is honest
	the boy				
	she				
				she	
	the girl				

Thus a substitution table should be completed by the learners themselves and then it can be used for giving practice in reading and writing.

8. As far as possible, the learners should listen to radio news being broadcast in English from B.B.C. They should also listen to some eminent scholars of English. If possible, tape recorder may be used for this purpose.

The study of sonic books is also suggested for this purpose.

1. An Intermediate English Practice Book. By S. Pit Corder.
2. Revision English. By Ronald Forest.

Countable and Uncountable Nouns

The old division of noun is-common, proper, collective and abstract. A more functional division of the same is countable and uncountable nouns. The distinction between the two helps us to know when to use articles, the plural form, much, many, some, any and other words of quantity. By applying rules, it is very difficult to decide which nouns are countable and which are uncountable. Usually the nouns for materials (wood, glass etc.) and for liquids (water, milk, etc.) are uncountable as are abstract nouns (truth, joy, beauty etc.) Some examples of nouns are:-

Countable Nouns:- box, goal, table, books, shoe, river, scene, poem etc.

Uncountable Nouns:- oil, juice, wool, mud, poetry, scenery, air, honesty, weather, dust etc.

Normally, uncountable nouns are not found in the plural form. So it is not possible to express the singular of uncountable nouns. But we can place a suitable countable noun before the uncountable as is shown in the following examples:

advice a piece of advice.
chalk a piece of chalk.
news an item of news.

Some words can be countable or uncountable according to the context in which they are used. For example:-

Countable	Uncountable	
Youth	period of being young	a young man
Change	money in small coins given for large or foreign money	alternation

Objective Type Questions

1. Underline the words with correct spellings:
   (a) Pleisure, pleasure, pleaser, plaisure,
   (b) Savitserland, Svitzerland, Sawitserland, Switzerland.
   (c) Laftinent, lepthinant, lieutinant, laptinent, laftinunt, heutenant.
   (d) askool, skool, school, scool.
   (e) Fashion, Feshion Fashon. Faishon.
   (f) Feithfully, faethfully, faithfuly, faithfully, faithfuly.
2. Underline the mistakes in the following sentences. The mistakes may be of any type. Do as given in the examples:
   Examples: Each boys got a pencils?
   (a) There is some trees in our school.
   (b) He was overjoy then.
   (c) You should have sufficient practice.
   (d) I have not see that picture.
   (e) Although he is poor but he is honest.
3. Re-arrange the words in the following sentences so that they may become meaningful:
   (a) Faster my than horse runs yours.
   (b) Society speech is the of instrument.

(c) Why late your are?
(d) Is my pen here there your is and pen?
(e) There the did collected come thief no sooner all members family than the of the.

4. Tick mark (✓)the correct and cross (✗) the wrong sentences.
(a) The solider married Veena.
(b) The soldier was married by him.
(c) His father is resembled by him.
(d) None of the fighting men were week.
(e) This boy seems to be better from that.

5. Write 'wrong' against the incorrect sentences.
The passive voice of, 'It is time to do that.'
(a) It is time to do that.
(b) It is time for that done.
(c) It is time for that to do.
(d) It is time for that to be done.
(e) It is time for that so that it is done.

6. Tick mark the correct passive voice of the sentences.
(a) **Active Voice.** Did she paint the picture?
Passive Voice: (i) The picture was painted by her.
(ii) Was she painted the picture?
(iii) Was the picture painted by her.

(b) **Active Voice.** I have not done the work so far.
Passive Voice: (i) The work have not done so far by me.
(ii) So far the work has not done by me.
(iii) The work has not been done so far by me.
(iv) The work not has been done so far by me.

7. Write two sentences of the same tense as given in the examples:
(a) Example: The boy is nice. You are not late.
1. ....
2. ....
(b) Example: Mohan was absent yesterday. She was my friend.
1. ....
2. ....
(c) Example: You can go now. Can you help me?
1. ....
2. ....

8. Write one sentence of the same tense as given in the examples. Then convert that sentence into its interrogative.

(a) Neela sings a song. We play football daily.

1. ....
2. ....

(b) She deceived me. He brought more pictures.

1. ....
2. ....

(c) We shall go there. You will help me.

1. ....
2. ....

9. Convert the following sentences into negatives:

(a) That boy is abusing her.

1. ....
2. ....

(b) Were they taking tea?

1. ....
2. ....

(c) We shall be leaving for Bombay.

1. ....
2. ....

10. Form interrogative sentence of the following on the blank space provided:-

(a) The teacher has taught him a lesson.

....

(b) They had gone out of station.

....

(c) Veena will have stood first in the class.

....

11. Form negative sentences of the following on the blank space provided:-

(a) They have been here for two weeks.

....

(b) Had she been weeping for one hour?

....

(c) She will have been working hard since January.

....

12. Convert the following sentences into interrogative forms:

(a) Ram goes to school late.

....

(b) That girl sang a sweet song.

....

(c) I have not been taking rest for many days.

....

13. In each of the following groups, only one of the five alternative is correctly punctuated. Which is it?
Encircle one out of A, B, C, D, or E.

(i)

A. He told me that, he was in the wrong.
B. He told me that, he was in the wrong.
C. He told me that, "He was in the wrong.
D. He told me, " that he was in the wrong."
E. He told me, "That he was in the wrong."

(ii)

A. "Have you seen Veena? Asked I
B. "Have you seen Veena? asked I
C. "Have you seen Veena? asked I?
D. "Have you seen Veena?" Asked I.
E. "Have you seen Veena?" asked I.

(iii)

A. The girl, cannot play badminton at all.
B. thé girl, can't play badminton at all.
C. The girl cant play badminton at all.
D. The girl can't play, badminton at all.

(iv)

A. "What a good picture!'; He exclaimed.
B. "What a good picture ! " He exclaimed.
C. "What a good picture!" he exclaimed!
D. "What a good picture ! " he exclaimed!
E. "What a good picture.!" he exclaimed!

(v)

A. Do you know how to spell transferred?
B. Do you know how to spell 'transferred?
C. Do you know how to spell transferred"?
D. Do you know how to spell transferred'?
E. Do you know how to spell 'transferred'?

14. In each of the following sentences one word is mis-spelt. Give the correct spelling within the bracket provided:
(a) She did the whole work carefully.
(b) This house is bigger than that.
(c) Imediately he entered the room and the boys stood up.
(d) I do not believe him.
(e) He is perhaps the lazest boy in the class.

15. In each of the following questions put the later (A, B, C, or D) of the correct answer in the blanks provided.

(i) "Did you see the boys this evening?
"Yes, I watched them hockey in the grounds,"
A. to play
B. in playing
C. playing.
D. to play.

(ii) " Can you go to see the pictures with us"?
"Sorry, I'm busy, I.... with you."
A. wish I could go.
B. wish I can go.
C. wish I am going.
D. wish I can to go.

(iii) "Do they practise pronunciation much 'T' 'Yes', the teacher makes them... their pronunciation a lot."
A. to pracitce
B. have practice
C. practising
D. practise

16. In each of the following questions, put the letter (a, b, c or d) of the correct answer in the blank provided.

(i) "What were you doing when we came to see you T'
" We ... television.
(a) must have been watching
(b) must have been watched
(c) must have watched
(d) must be watching

(ii) "Did you have time to see this picture?" "No, but I wish sometime to see it.
(a) have had
(b) had had
(c) had have
(d) have have

(iii) "Do you like to take coffee T'
"No, I prefer milk coffee."
(a) than
(b) from
(c) to
(d) on

17. In each of the following questions, put the letter (W, X, Y Z) of the correct answer in the blank provided:-

(i) My brothers were not at home when we went
"They might .... to the movies."
W go
X be going
Y have gone
Z be gone

(ii) "Did you get I wet yesterday?"
"Yes, I did not take my raincoat-it was raining."
W in spite of
X although
Y because of
Z because

(iii) 'Will she take her raincoat
"No-it is raining,"
W unless
X inspite of
Y because of
Z although

(iv) "Are you going to do M.A. in English next year?"
"I expect to do it-time.
W unless I have
X if I had
Y unless I had
Z if I have

(v) "Why did you not visit us last year?'
W would have visit
X will have visit
Y would have visited
Z will have visited

(vi) "Can I see you in the evening to-day?"
"I am sorry. I am-that I won't be free."
W so busily
X too busy
Y so busy
Z very busy

(vii) "They have't seen the owner, have they?"
"No, they"
W have
X having not seen

Y haven't
Z having

18. In the following questions, put the letter (a, b, c or d) of the correct answer in the blank provided:-

(i) "Don't you have to study before dinner
"Yes, I ....
(a) study
(b) have
(c) don't
(d) do

(ii) "When can you go to the movies?"
"As soon as I finish .... this chapter.
(a) write
(b) wrote
(c) to write
(d) writing

(iii) What colour are you going to have your house painted?
"We 'I have
(a) it white painted
(b) it painted white
(c) white it painted
(d) white painted it

(iv) "Why was the monitor late to the class?
.... his note book, he had to go back to his house before class.
(a) having to forget
(b) have forget
(c) having forgotten
(d) have forgotten

(v) "Did the examination seem difficult?"
"Yes, ... the examination is hard work."
(a) take
(b) have to take
(c) taking
(d) have taken

(vi) "Why wasn't she in the class?"
" ...., she stayed at home."
(a) being sick
(b) been sick
(c) to be sick
(d) sick being

(vii) "What are you doing this morning?"
"After breakfast I am going to study history .... I am going shopping."
(a) consequently
(b) then
(c) so
(d) therefore

(viii) "How was your flight to Bombay?
"The weather was very bad .... most of us got sick.
(a) otherwise
(b) consequently
(c) however
(d) still

19. Correct the following sentences and write their corrected form on the lines provided:
(a) It is I who is to blame.
....
(b) He went directly to his village.
....
(c) Such boys who shirk work come to grief.
....

20. Change the following sentences as directed and write them on the lines provided:
(a) A book has been written by him. (Change the voice)
....
(b) Mohan stole his book. (Change into interrogative)
....
(c) She said to the stranger, "Why are you weeping?" (Change the voice)
....

21. Fill in the blanks with appropriate prepositions:
(a) I have nothing to do .... you.
(b) He got .... the examination.
(c) Overwork told .... his health.

22. Use the following in sentences:-
(a) notorious for
....
(b) object
....
(c) part with
....

23. Complete the blanks in the following paragraph. Use the appropriate form of the word or words given in the bracket and any other words that are necessary.

Gulliver found that Lilliputians divided into two parties called High Hills, according to the height of .... (heels shoes), which distinguished one party from the other. They opposed each other and hated each other so much that .... (members, party) would hardly cat, drink or ta!k with those of the other. Although the High Heels were .... (numerous) the Low heels, the Emperor was in favour of the Low Heels. So .... (government be) in the hands of the Low Heels. They were, however, fearful that the young Prince was .... (side of Low Heels) .... (clear) one of his heels was ....: (high, other); and that .... (make limp) when he walked.

24. Arrange the jumbled sentences into a proper order so that they form a meaningful paragraph. Indicate the order by writing the letters A,B,C etc. between the parallel lines under the sentences:

A. The pond is emptied of water.
B. They are put temporarily into small tanks.
C. The goldfish are taken out of the pond.
D. Every year in the city park, the ornamental pond is cleaned.
E. It is cleaned and refilled with fresh water before the fish are put back into it.)

....

....

25. Change as directed:

(a) How can she be manhandled by/her own students: (voice)

....

(b) I will take my raincoat only if it rains. (use 'unless')

....

(c) Our friend said, "Let us have a party." (narration)

....

26. Correct the following sentences:

(a) Whole the family enjoyed the picnic.

....

(b) I shouldn't cut this cake if I am you.

....

(c) Both of my brother-in-laws are very rich.

....

(d) What is the time in your watch?

....

(e) I congratulated him for his success.

....

(f) Neither of the two singers are to be awarded a prize.

....

27. Use the following in sentences so as to bring out the difference in their meaning:-

(a) Walk over ....
Walk in ....
(b) Break into ....
Break off ....
(c) Carry on ....
Carry out ....

28. Fill in the blanks in the following sentences by using the most suitable words from those given in the brackets:-

(a) Although it was from my senior officer .... (turned down, declined, rejected) because it was not .... (suitably, properly, politely) worded.

(b) These days, the .... of the industrial workers are much better than the .... of the school teacher. (Income, salaries, remuneration, wages)

(c) I have a firm .... in the essential goodness of all men and a deep rooted .... that given a chance, they would all grow up to be good law abiding citizens. (faith, trust, belief, opinion)

29. Tick mark (✓)the correct sentences and cross (×) the wrong ones.

(a) The sooner you go, the good it is
(b) It is raining outside for some time.
(c) Hardly I had reached at home when my father came.
(d) I shall have to be here until the Principal does not come.
(e) The elderly person gave me many pieces of advice.
(f) You can solve this question, can't you?

30. Change as directed:

(a) It is time to do that. (voice)

....

(b) No other boy is as good as Ramesh. (Superlative degree)

....

(c) You should work very hard so that you should not fail. (use lest)

....

31. Use the following in sentences:
(a) Make out ....
(b) Get through ....
(c) Call off ....

32. Fill in the blanks with appropriate preposition:-
(a) Nisha is recovering .... illness these days.
(b) Send .... the doctor, please.
(c) I am sure .... my success in the examination.
(d) You must carry .... the orders of your parents.
(e) Are you friendly .... me?

33. Tick mark (✓) the correct sentences and cross (×) the wrong
1. Shiela has been blessed with a son.
2. My friend was accused for theft.
3. At last the prisoner escaped the jail.
4. His father wants to dispose his old car.
5. Neelu is very good at dancing.
6 He was charged with the murder of his wife.

34. Frame sentences so as to distinguish between the meaning of the following pairs of words:-
(a) Scene ....
Seen ....
(b) Principal ....
Principle ....
(c) Weather ....
Whether ....

35. Change as directed:-
(a) "My wife said to me, "My brother will be coming to meet me here tomorrow at this very time." (narration)
(b) Never deceive anybody. (Vocal)
(c) Will you please accompany me to the railway station? (make assertive sentence)

36. Frame questions of which the following are the answers:
(a) No, Sir, I was not absent yesterday.
(b) Bananas come from the South.

Answers

1. (a) Pleasure (b) Switzerland (c) Lieutenant (d) School (e) Fashion (f) faithfully.

2. (a) is (b) overjoy (c) sufficient (d) see picture (e) but.
3. (a) My horse runs faster than yours.
(b) Speech is the instrument of society.
(c) Why are you late?
(d) My pen is here and your pen is there.
(e) No sooner did the thief come there than all the members of the family collected.
4. (a) ✓ (b) × (c) × (d) × (e) ×
5. (a) Wrong (b) Wrong (c) Wrong (d) Wrong
6. (a) (iii) (b) (iii) /
7. (a) (1) Veena is a good girl. (2) You are a nice boy.
(b) (1) I was on leave yesterday. (2) My father was absent.
(c) (1) He can help you in this matter.
(2) You can speak now.
8. (a) He quarrels with me. Does he quarrel with me?
(b) That shopkeeper sold books. Did that shopkeeper sell books?
(c) I shall obey my parents. Shall I obey my parents?
9. (a) That boy is not abusing her.
(b) Were they not taking tea?
(c) We shall not be leaving for Bombay.
10. (a) Has the teacher taught him a lesson?
(b) Had they gone out of station?
(c) Will Veena have stood first in the class?
11. (a) They have not been here for two weeks.
(b) Had she not been weeping for one hour.
(c) She will not have been working hard since January.
12. (a) Does Ram go to school late?
(b) Did that girl sing a sweet song?
(c) Have I not been taking rest for many days?
13. (i) B (ii) E (iii) B (iv) B (v) E
14. (a) carefully (b) bigger (c) immediately (d) believe (e) laziest.
15. (i) C (ii) A (iii) D
16. (i) (a) (ii) (b) (iii) (c)
17. (i) Y (ii) X (iii) W (iv) Z v) Y (vi) Y (vii) Y
18. (i) d (ii) (d) (iii) (b) (iv) c (v) c (vi) a (vii) b (viii) b
19. (a) It is I who am to blame.
(b) He went direct to his village.
(c) Such boys as shirk work come to grief.
20. (a) He has written a book.

(b) Did Mohan steal his book?
(c) She asked the stranger why he was weeping.

21. (a) With
(b) through
(c) upon

22. (a) That boy is notorious for gambling and drinking.
(b) How can I object to his winning over here?
(c) No body likes to part with money.

23. heels
members of one party
more than
the government was
on the side of low heels
clearly .... higher
made limp.

24. D, E, C, B, A
(a) × (b) × (c) × (d) × (e) ✓ (f) ✓

25. (a) How can her own students manhandle her?
(b) Unless it rains I will not take my raincoat.
(c) Our friend suggested that they should have a party that day.

26. (a) The whole family enjoyed the Picnic
(b) Unless it rains I will not take my raincoat.
(c) Both of my brothers-in-law are very rich.
(d) What is the time Your watch?
(e) I congratulated him on his success.
(f) Neither of these two singers is to be awarded a Prize

27. (a) We walked over a distance of two miles and reached a village.
(b) Break into: A thief broke into the house of the rich man yesterday.
Break off, While going to Bombay I shall break off at Delhi.
(c) Carry on You may carry on your work if you like.
Carry out: You must carry out the orders of your boss.

28. (a) decline, properly
wages, salaries
faith, belief.

29. (a) × (b) × (c) × (d) × (e) × (f) ✓

30. (a) It is time for that to be done.
(b) Ramesh is the best boy.

(c) You should work very hard lest you should fail.

31. (a) Make out: I could not make out anything from his speech though I was listening to it very carefully.

    (b) Get through: He worked very hard and got through the examination.

    (c) Call off. At last, the union had to call off the strike.

32. (a) from (b) for (c) of (d) out (e) with

33. 1. ✓ 2. ✗ 3. ✗ 4. ✗ 5. ✓ 6. ✓

34. (a) Scene: the scene at the hill station was worth seeing.

    Seen: I have not seen him for the last two months.

    (b) Principal : He was a lecturer to begin with and then he became Principal of a College.

    Principle: My brother is a man of principle and you can depend upon him.

    (c) Weather: Fair weather friends fall off in adversity.

    Whether: I do not know him whether he is in station or not.

35. (a) My wife told me that her brother would be coming to meet her there the next day at that very time.

    (b) Let anybody be never deceived,

    (c) You will please accompany me to the railway station.

36. (a) Was he absent yesterday?

    (b) Where do mangoes come from?

15

Correct Punctuation

Grammatically punctuation marks are of great importance. Right use of punctuation makes the sense clear. With wrong use of punctuation marks, the sentence may become meaningless or it may give quite different meanings.

Here are the important punctuation marks

1.	Full stop	(.)
2.	Comma	(,)
3.	Semicolon	(;)
4.	Colon	(:)
5.	Question	(?)
6.	Sign of Exclamation	(!)
7.	Apostrophe	(')
8.	Inverted commas	("")
9.	Hyphen	(-)
10.	Dash	(–)
11.	Capital Letters	(A, B, C...)
12.	Parenthesis of Brackets	( )

The use of full stop may be noted in the following:

(a) This is my pen. I bought it for ten rupees. It is a good pen.

(b) M.S. Sachdeva
T.R. Dogra

(c) Mr. Gupta
Dr. Gupta

(d) M.A.
M.B.B.S.
C.I.E.F.L.

(e) Esq.
Max.
Min.
(f) Yes.
(g) "Where is he?" said he.
(h) He said, "I am not well to-day."

The use of comma may be noted in the following:

(a) He gave me a pen, a pencil, a book and many other articles.
(b) This girl wears green, white and red saari.
(c) The Prizes were given to Veena, Neela, Kamla and Monika.
(d) Where are you going, friend?
(e) Dear Sir,
(f) Yours faithfully,
(g) Novermber 25, 1978.
(h) He said, to me.
(i) Yes, you may come.
(j) I Will, of course, come.
(k) All the students, who worked had passed the examination.
(l) The man promised, didn't he?

Use of Semicolon

Read the following carefully

(i) I met the leader yesterday; he is very good.
(ii) We saw that girl in the train ; she is pretty.
(iii) My father seems to be better ; yet the doctor is not satisfied.
(iv) When she went to U.S.A., she was poor; when she came back, she was a rich lady.
(v) The man who has more money is often greedy ; it is the poor who feels contented.
(vi) I hate him ; nevertheless I will shake hands.

Use of Colon

Please read the following:-

(i) The following persons were absent:
(ii) My father's last words were : "Remain united."
(iii) The teacher beat me : I think he was in angry mood

(iv) In this college we find students of different calibre: intelligent, average, below average.
(v) To err is human : to forgive divine.
(vi) Speech is silver: silver is golden.

Question mark or sign of interrogation

Note the use of question mark in the following sentences:

(a) Who taught you English-?
(b) He asked me, "What is your name?"
(c) "What is the time?" Asked the peon.
(d) If you beat me, shall I not beat you?

Sign of Exclamation

Read carefully the following sentences:

(i) Ah ! His father is dead.
(ii) Oh ! You have passed.
(iii) Hurrah ! We have won the match.
(iv) What a fine weather !
(v) How clever he is !
(vi) What a strange happening !
(vii) How nice !
(viii) May you live long!

Apostrophe

The use of apostrophe may please be noted in the following

(i) At 5 O'clock.
(ii) Mohan's leg.
(iii) It's time to work.
(iv) I met him in his 60's.
(v) Can't you reply to my question?
(vi) My teacher says he isn't coming with them. (is not, coming, them)

Inverted Commas

Please see carefully the use of inverted commas in the following:

(a) She said, "How fine it is !"
(b) They shouted, "Fire ; Fire !"
(c) "Where is your brother?" asked he.

(d) "At home," was my reply.
(e) "Who is the monitor?" asked the Headmaster. "Perhaps he is on leave," marked the boys.
(f) "How strange that you are here exclaimed my brother."
(g) "Know thyself," is his advice!

Dash

Please note the use of dash in the following

(i) Men, women, children—'all went to see the circus show.'
(ii) Ram and Shyam—both idiots—have passed the examination.
(iii) She doesn't know—she can't think—she must wait.

Hyphen

Use of hyphen in the following examples may please be noted

(i) brother-in-law
(ii) mid-term
(iii) to-day
(iv) vice-president
(v) forget-me-not

Capital Letters

Please read the following keeping in mind the use of capital letters:

(i) Neela, Veena, Ram, Sham.
(ii) Ambala, Delhi, India, London.
(iii) History Geography, English, Mathematics.
(iv) Sunday, Monday.
(v) January, February.
(vi) (a) A New Approach to Teaching of English in India.
  (b) A Modern Approach to School Organisation and Administration
  (c) Let Us Learn English.
(vii) The Bible, the Vedas.
(viii) Hinduism, Budhism.
(ix) B.A., M.A., LL.B.,
(x) King John, Doctor Jagdish, Uncle Jagdish.
(xi) I, God, Almighty.
(xii) "Where are you going?" asked he.

(xiii) A Rainy Day.
(xiv) The Teacher You Like Most.

Exercise No. 1

Use full stop in the following wherever it is needed

(i) Mr Ram met me yesterday
(ii) Miss Nella narrated a story
(iii) Dr Asija is the Principal
(iv) My brother is a doctor He is M B B S
(v) After M A in English, you can pass some course in teaching of English from CIEFL.
(vi) I am a student of Day school. It is a very good school Students of this school stand first in the whole state.
(vii) Miss Neela is my favourite teacher, she is one of the best teachers of the school. She teaches us English Her method of teaching is very fine. She is very regular. The students respect her very much.
(viii) Tomorrow is your English paper Max marks are 50 Min pass marks are 20 You should try to get good marks
(ix) My name is Rajesh I am M A in English I am working as a Lecturer My younger brother is Jagdish He is MBBS doctor His wife is also MBBS doctor. They are experts in their fields.
(x) I have three brothers We are four brothers. All are very hard working all have risen by dint of hard work Sincerity to work is the basis of all success in life.

Exercise No.2

Re-write the following after inserting comma and full stop wherever they are required :-

(i) He said to me" Let us play."
(ii) "Tomorrow is a holiday" said the teacher
(iii) Mr Jawahar Lal Nehru the first Prime Minister of free India was born on November 14, 1889.
(iv) In Delhi we met Mr. A.B. Vajpaee the Prime Minister of India
(v) I like the company of honest true sincere and hard working persons
(vi) There are different types of persons in this world some are true while some are false- Some are very honest. Some others pretend to be honest.

(vii) Of course I will come to see you on this Sunday.
(viii) To this the Principal promised to pay didn't he?
(ix) At the time of marriage we will visit Lucknow the capital of UP.
(x) Examination Hall
Centre ....
November 25 1978
To
The District Education Officer
Ambala
Dear Sir
Yours faithfully

Exercise No. 3

Use semicolon, full stop and comma in the following :-

(i) I hate him nevertheless I will go to meet him
(ii) I met the Education Minister yesterday he is very good
(iii) We saw that boy in the bus he is very handsome
(iv) When my brother went to England he was matriculate when he came back he was a graduate
(v) The boy who works hard is able to pass the examination it is the shirk worker who fails

Exercise No. 4

Use colon, semicolon, comma and full stop in the following:

(i) The old man's last words were 'Be sincere."
(ii) The teacher praised me very much I think he was in a happy mood
(iii) In this city we find different types of people Hindu Muslim Christian
(iv) The Principal of course will come
(v) To err is human to forgive divine

Exercise No. 5

Re-write the following after putting sign of interrogation, colon, semicolon, comma and full stop wherever needed

(i) Are you in senses
(ii) When are you leaving for Bombay
(iii) Who is there at the door

(iv) If he deceives me shall I not deceive him

(v) He said "Ram what is the time"

(vi) Who is at the door is it Ram or Sham I think it might be Ram

(vii) What will you like to become a doctor or an engineer.

(viii) When are you going to U.S.A. Is Neela to accompany you

(ix) What are you saying we are good friends

Exercise No. 6

Rewrite the following after using sign of exclamation, sign of interrogation, comma and full stop

(a) How fine is the weather

(b) How is the weather

(c) What has he failed in the examination

(d) What has he done so far

(e) May I come in

(f) May I go out

(g) May you live long

(h) Ah -we are all safe

(i) Oh he has stood first

(j) Would that he were a rich man

Exercise No. 7

Use apostrophe, full stop, sign of interrogation in the following where they are needed :

(i) Ram came here at 5 O clock Didn't you meet him

(ii) I wrote to you twice Why didn't you reply

(iii) I am sorry I can't help you in this matter

(iv) Even in his 70 he used to go out for a walk at 5 O clock in the morning.

(v) Wont you reply to my letter

Exercise No. 8

Use inverted commas, comma, sign of interrogation, sign of exclamation, full stop wherever they are needed in the following:

(i) The teacher said what are you not passing the examination

(ii) Who is at the door said he It is I was the reply

(iii) The students said How fine is the weather Let us have a holiday
(iv) When did you come here asked he to me
(v) People shouted fire
(vi) Be sincere to thyself and also to others said the old man

Exercise No. 9

Re-write the following by using dash, comma, full stop, sign of interrogation, inverted commas, apostrophe wherever needed :-

(i) Veena and Neela both intelligent have failed in the examination
(ii) Who want to see the picture asked the Young and old ladies and gents all went to see the picture was the reply
(iii) I don't know I cant think I must wait
(iv) Who when Do you know it
(v) Yes I have done it was the reply

Exercise No. 10

Use hyphen, full stop, dash in the following wherever they are needed :-

(i) He met me to day morning.
(ii) My brother in law sister in law mother in law all am going with me to see the picture
(iii) I think he is the vice President of student union
(iv) Mid term poll takes place next week.
(v) I like him very much He is my father in law

Exercise No. 11

Re-write the following by using capital letters, comma, sign of interrogation, inverted commas, full stop wherever they are needed:-

(i) Neela rajesh came to ambala last sunday
(ii) my friend doctor sunil is not so good in English
(iii) though he is MALLB yet he has no common sense
(iv) my previous book is named as a new approach to teaching of English in India.
(v) do you have any knowledge of the vedas said the inspector to me

(vi) may i take your seat
(vii) what is your name where do you live asked he to me
(viii) twinkle twinkle little star how I wonder what you are

Exercise No. 12

Use parenthesis, comma, full stop, capital letter, and sign of interrogation in the following wherever needed :-

(i) dali i do not know her real name is very pretty
(ii) my second book i do not know whether you know it came last year
(iii) where are your brother sister and parents.
(iv) whom do you want to meet

In a poem,

Jack and Jill,
Went up the hill..
To fetch a pail of water.

Exercise No. 13

Parenthesis or Brackets:-

Read the following examples carefully where brackets have been used :-

(a) Neelu I do not know his real name) is very naughty
(b) My article in the Tribune (I do not know whether you read it) appeared day before yesterday.

Exercise No. 14

thought I don't have enough money yet i feel I am rich said he many people feel they are poor inspite of the fact that they have a lot of money marked his friend.

Exercise No. 15

tomorrow is a big function said the principal who is coming to preside over asked the students a minister was the reply.

Exercise No. 16

what a fine weather shouted the students yes it is will you like to study said the teacher no sir we want a holiday or some picnic said the students

Exercise No. 17

all right ' will come said he will you come alone or your wife will also come asked the friend as you like was the reply

Exercise No. 18

who is there at the door asked I it is I was the reply will you please tell your name asked I sir don't your recognise my voice said he oh no was my reply

Exercise No. 19

(a) she said no my father one gives ones faith but once
(b) thank you boys said the headmaster when everything was ready

Exercise No. 20

mother asked the little boy were you always good when you were a girl I was generally good replied the mother at least when i was asleep

Exercise No. 21

what shall I bring you when I come back from the college said the father to his two daughters and a son one daughter said please bring a pen for me I want a pencil said the second and what would krishan like said the kind father I want to have a baloon said the son shall I get it

Solutions

Exercise No. 14

"Though I don't have enough money yet I feel I am rich," said he. "Many people feel that they are poor inspite of the fact that they have a lot of money." marked his friend.

Exercise No. 15

"Tomorrow is a big function," said the Principal, "Who is coming to preside over?" asked the students. "A Minister," was the reply.

Exercise No. 16

"What a fine weather shouted the students. "Yes, it is. Will you like to study?" said the teacher. "No, sir. We want a holiday or some picnic," said the students.

Exercise No. 17

"All right, I will come," said he. "Will you come alone or your wife will also come?" asked the friend, "As you like," was the reply-

Exercise No. 18

"Who is there of the door?" asked I. "It is I," was the reply. "Will you please tell your name?" asked I. "Sir, don't you recognise my voice? said he. "Oh! No," was my reply.

Exercise No. 19

(a) She said, "No, my father, one gives one's faith but once.

(b) "Thank you, boys," said the Headmaster when everything was ready.

Exercise No. 20

"Mother," asked the little boys, "Were you always good when you were a girl?" "I was generally good," replied the mother, "At least when I was asleep."

Exercise No. 21

"What shall I bring you when I come back from the college?" said the father to his two daughters and a son. One daughter said, "Please bring a pen for me." "I want a pencil," said the second. "And what would Krishan like?" said the kind father." "I want to have a baloon," said the son, "Shall I get it?"

Unsolved Exercises

Exercise No. 22

Punctuate the following:-

(i) why are you late said the teacher to a student I will come in time sir please excuse me this time all right said the teacher

(ii) have your read the tribune to-day said the teacher no sir was the reply of the student did you ever read it questioned the teacher off and on sir was the reply

(iii) good morning sir said the students to their teacher will you distribute our answer books for the house examination no replied the teacher I have not finished their marking so far on what day should we expect them sir asked the monitor of the class.

(iv) what have you failed in the examination said the teacher I have failed by one mark replied the student it is really very sad marked the teacher don't worry work hard and try to get good marks next time all right said the student.

(v) which profession do you like most asked the elder brother to the younger one I like teaching was the reply do you want to become an engineer asked the brother again I don't have any taste for that to be a teacher is my first choice said the younger one

(vi) The teacher got angry in the class and shouted shut up you should behave well don't whisper to the neighbours it is a bad habit at this one of the students got up and said sir we will be careful in future

Exercise No. 23

Punctuate the following:-

(i) amritsar is really worth seeing said a senior student to a junior one what are the different places which can be seen asked the other many places indeed replied the senior student the golden temple is above everything all right I will avail myself of the chance whenever it comes to me was the reply of the younger one

(ii) where do you live asked a man to the doctor in the city was his reply will you please let me know the exact situation as I want to see you at your place no you are not allowed to see me at my residence you can come in the hospital said the doctor all right as you please said the man very humbly

(iii) A I have been pick pocketed said the passenger to the ticket examiner in the train while searching his pockets I had five hundred rupees also in my pocket everything is gone what said the ticket examiner is it a fact may you enquire sir from anybody in this compartment I realised it only a few minutes back vas the reply of the passenger

(iv) how do you like your television set asked the father to the children very good was their reply can you study these days asked the father oh yes replied the children now we learn many things on the TV which we can hardly understand otherwise thats fine marked the father

Exercise No. 24

Punctuate the following

(i) This shopkeeper is a greet cheat said the boy how do you say asked I he weighs less and also charges more was his reply oh then he has been fleecing us all the time lets now avoid going to his shop said I strongly

(ii) a man asked his wife what is there why are people shouting outside oh it is some quarrel was her reply let me go and see said the man let us both go and enquire suggested she all right said the man

(iii) over thirty miles per hour replied the taxi driver cant you slow down a little I said no certainly not sahib said he it is not possible this silenced me for the rest of my journey I only muttered to myself -what rascals these drivers are

(iv) the teacher said mohan can you solve all the questions given in the question paper perhaps was his reply anybody else in the class who can do so asked the teacher who students namely Neela, and rajesh got up and said we can solve all these questions easily to this the teacher said very good all go ahead and solve these questions.

Rhyme and Rhythm

Rhyme : A word that has the same sound or ends with the same sound as another word.

The use of words in a poem or song that have the same sound especially at the end of lines. It is sameness of sound of the endings of two or more words at the ends of lines of verse. (e.g. say, day, play, measure, pleasure, puff, rough)

house rhymes with mouse
school rhymes with fool
beauty rhymes with duty

Rhythm : A strong regular repeated pattern of sounds or movements in speech dancing, music.

It is regular succession of weak and strong stresses, accents, sounds or movements.

The quality of happening at regular periods of time. The rhythm of the seasons.

Simile and Metaphor

Simile : In simile, we have comparison of one thing with another. The comparison may be of a word or a phrase. A few examples are:

It can be an expression making a comparison in the imagination between two things. e.g- childhood is like a swiftly passing dream-

Metaphor : Metaphor can be a word or a phrase. It is used in an imaginative way to describe in order to show that the two things have the same qualities and to make the description more powerful. There is implied type of comparison- e.g. she has a heart of stone. (ii) I shall make him eat his words. (iii) in the roses in her checks.

Alliteration and Pun

Alliteration : The use of the same letter or sound at the beginning of words that are close together. e.g- sing a song of sixpence.

The appearance of the same sound or sounds at the beginning of two or more words that are next to or close to each other. A few examples are:

(i) round the rocks run the river (ii) safe and sound (iii) artful aid

Pun : The clever or humorous use of word that has more than one meaning. It may be words that have different meanings but sound the same.

An amusing use of a word or phrase that has two meanings or of words having the same sound but different meanings. For instarace : (7 days without water make one weak) week.

16

Art of Writing

During teaching of a language, we develop a number of skills in our students. Writing is one of those communication skills. Through writing, a person is able to convey his thoughts or ideas to others who are not present in front of the writer. Moreover, writing makes the record permanent. Whatever is written once remains for ever; unless it is knowingly destroyed. While writing, a person has to be very exact.

In some of the institutions, it is found that too much emphasis is laid down on writing and oral aspect of the language is neglected. No doubt, this type of practice helps the learners in the present day type of examinations but it does not help them in the long run. So the different aspects of language learning should be given due importance.

Teaching how to write involves manual skill-the skill of controlling the small muscles of the fingers, and the wrist and securing co-ordination of the hand and the eye. Secondly, it involves doing various exercises in written work. The exercises cover a vast field ranging from copying the phrases and sentences to composing a long essay.

There are two types of learners who can be taught writing of English language. The first category is of those who have not learnt the writing of any language. The second category is of those who have already learnt the writing of mother tongue. In the first case, the teacher has to explain the learners how the have to sit, how to hold a note book in hand and how to hold a pen. After this, they are given preliminary practice of writing with a pen. Then they are given this type of practice with the help of chalks and small boards which are meant for the students. There are black boards fixed up on the four walls of the class room and they are very near to the floor on which the students are sitting. By using two type of black boards, the students may be given practice of drawing straight lines. In the beginning, the lines may not be straight. By and by, they should be given practice in drawing short lines, in one direction and then in another direction.

After this they should be given practice in drawing circles, semi-circles etc. This type of practice should continue as long as the students are able to move their fingers and wrists according to the writing specimens. It will be all the more useful if the students are asked to study drawing as a compulsory subject at this stage. All that will be fully helpful in the learning of writing. This much practice will pave way for teaching the writing of alphabets. The second category of students who have already learnt the writing of mother tongue, are already at this stage when writing of English alphabets is introduced to them.

Choice of Script

In the writing of language we can have two types of scripts: (i) Print Script (ii) Cursive Script. In print script, each letter stands distinct as if in print form. But in cursive script, all the letters of a word are joined. Now the question arises which script out of these two should be followed by the beginners. The print script is suggested for them because it is more convenient for the learners. Of course, they have gradually to shift over to cursive script and they have to continue with that throughout their lives. But at the initial stages print script is useful. Given ahead are the advantages of using print script:-

(i) In the books, writing is done by using print script. If the students use print script in their own writing it will be more convenient for them because they will look at the written symbols of the books exactly in the same fashion.
(ii) By using print script, the writing stands clear and distinct.
(iii) It helps in keeping the maxim of going from easy to difficult.

Choice of Language Material

The language material to be used in writing by the students should be the same which they have practised orally. Nothing new with which they are unfamiliar should be taken up for writing purposes. This will give a little bit of revision of words and structures already learnt orally. Besides, the problem of spelling is solved upto some extent.

Choice of Slant

In writing, there are three types of slants: (i) backward slant, (ii) forward slant, (iii) erect position. The students should always be discouraged to use the backward slant while writing anything. The forward slant and writing in erect position are highly recommended.

Different experts of languages put forth different opinions about it. The generally accepted opinion is ..... after oral teaching, reading from black board or flash cards is started. In case of flash cards, those very language items are written on the blackboard in print script. When all the pupils can read those language items quickly and correctly, writing' should be introuduced. During the first three or four months writing is restricted to copying. Pupils copy from the black board the material which they can read.

In some schools, we notice that writing is introduced alongwith reading. Moreover, they do not give any practice of listening and speaking. This is a big drawback.

Teaching of Writing

While teaching writing, the teacher should not start from a, b, c, and go upto z. The alphabets are taught according to the convenience of the learners so that they may not face any problem all of a sudden and above all, their interest in learning is also kept in mind.

Capital Letters or Small Letters

Capital letters should be taught first because they are easy for the small children. The small letters should be taught afterwards.

While teaching capital letters, it will be more convenient if the different letters are taught category wise. First of all those letters should be taught which can be written with one or two strokes e.g. 1, L, T. Y. X, V etc. Then the letters with three strokes, four strokes and so on, can be taken up, e.g.

Style of Handwriting

Gradually letters which are written with circle or semi-circle and letters with strokes and circles should be taught.

Freeman in his book - 'Teaching of Handwriting' recommends the following six groups:-

(i) i, u, w,
(ii) n, m, v, x,
(iii) a, e, o. c,
(iv) r, s,
(v) d, p, q, t,
(vi) i, b, h, i, g, y, z, f

Alice E, Stephens has suggested the following groups:-

First groups involves the stroke from top to bottom:-

i, n, t, p, w, v, in, n, r.

Second group implies a round stroke as

or a, d, c, e, q,

Third group includes loops as:

b, f, y, i, k, i, z.

Fourth group is as under:

s, x.

For capital letters, F.G. French has suggested the following groups:

Round Capitals (each filling one circle)

O, Q, C, D, G.

Square Capital (each filling one square)

H, N, M, T, Z, A, X, U, T. W.

Half square Capitals (each filling half a square)

F, E, L, X, L I.

Half circle

S, P, B, R.

The above said groups are the suggestions of the different experts. Further it depends upon the individual teacher that he may form certain groups out of the alphabets depending upon the teachability of the letters or their learnability.

Some other Techniques

By over writing. The teacher writes something with a pencil on the note-books of the students. The students are asked to overwrite it. It can also be done by prescribing English writing note books in which letters or words or sentences are written with dots. In this way, the students can have overwriting practice.

With the help of flash cards. Something is written on the flash cards and they are given to the students. By consulting the flash cards, the students write down the same thing in their note books.

With the help of black-board. Something is written on the black-board. Then the students are asked to observe it carefully and copy it down in their note books.

By teacher himself. The teacher writes the first line in the note books of the students. Then the students are asked to complete the whole page by consulting the first line.

By using substitution table. The teacher prepares a substitution table on the black board or on a chart. He makes them dwriting of students should be displayed in oom. It will help improve the handwriting of ents.

y stages, the students should be encouraged to of four-lined note books. The use of fountain d be discouraged.

ting is very essential for every student. Both the udents should make efforts for it. The above ds can work wonders in improving the ol going children. The school authorities should ce to good handwriting. Good handwriting of also have its impact on the personalities of the

ng of writing, there is one big problem which is learners of English language. The problem is of

s in every language are very important. English is nguage. So there are more chances of committing es. By writing-wrong spellings, the writer can be understood. Here under are given a few samples of spelling mistakes:

rite)

That)

e him (I love him?)

you police sin hear. (Will you please sign here?)

me across a mankey (I came across a monkey)

pe of writing, one can be completely misunderstood. ng of a language correct spellings are very essential. spellings depend on the cultivation of visual memory nborn quality in a person.

, *F.J.* writes in his book 'Backwardness in the Basic pelling is a complex sensory motor process the efficiency ased on repeated motor reactions to sensory stimuli. In mastery in spellings is possible when proper auditory mpressions fuse with articulatory and graphic motor

ngs in English are most irregular and illogical. The guist *Max Muller* once said. "English spelling is a isfortune to England and an international misfortune to

understand how they have to consult it for speaking or writing purpose.

By and by the teacher is to enable the students to write without consulting the book flash cards or the black-board. The teacher should see that the students have good hand writing.

Very often, it is found that the students have poor handwriting. It is first and foremost duty of a language teacher that he should help the students have good handwriting. By good handwriting, we mean legible writing which is clear to others. It does not mean decorated one.

Good Handwriting

Writing is one of the important skills in the teaching learning of the language. Good handwriting is an asset with the learner. By good handwriting, people understand differently. Some people say that good handwriting is very beautiful to look at. It is full of ornamentations throughout. An intelligent person interprets good handwriting in another way. By this, he means legible writing. That writing which does not strain the mind of the reader. The reader can read it easily, nicely and fluently. Some people say that handwriting is linked with the mental efficiency of a person. Surely good handwriting is the replica of one aspect of the personality of an individual.

Good handwriting makes the learner good. The learner of the language is called poor with bad handwriting. Therefore, every teacher of English must have attractive handwriting. It is all the more essential for the teacher who teaches the, beginners. Both the teacher and the learner should aim at having good handwriting. Simultaneously, the speed of writing should be maintained.

Quality of Handwriting

A good handwriting is a composite of some characteristics. To know about the characteristics of good handwriting is an interesting process. Let us, therefore, visualise the main characteristics of good handwriting. The following are the characteristics of good handwriting:-

Distinctiveness. Every letter of a word is distinct. It is clearly visible. It can be recognised easily by every type of learner of the language. Thus each letter is joined with the neighbouring letters of a word.

Proper spacing. There is proper space between the different words of a sentence. Whenever a new paragraph is started, some space is left. That is maintained throughout the writing. Some space is also left while starting a new sentence.

Size of the letters. The size of the letters is according to the age group of the learner. It is neither too big nor too small. The same proportion is kept in the whole writing.

Simplicity. A good handwriting is simple to look at. The different letters of a word are written in a simple way. There are no unnecessary strokes.

Straight lines. Good handwriting runs in straight lines. That is all parallel to the top of the page.

Principle of four lined note book. The principle of writing on a four lined notebook is always kept in mind. That gives uniformity to the writing.

Position of letters. While writing, the position of letters is very important. The letters may be in erect positions. They may also be in forward slant positions. Backward slant positions are to be avoided.

Good punctuation marks. Good punctuation marks are also essential in writing beautifully. The punctuation should be correct. The shape of different signs of punctuation marks should be beautiful. They can make or mar the beauty of writing.

Importance of Good Handwriting

In every language, handwriting of the learners is considered very important. In fact, every student of the language is expected to have good handwriting. By good handwriting we mean legible and fully clear type of writing. The following points show the importance of good handwriting:-

1. A good handwriting impresses others, especially the reader for whom it is meant.
2. A good handwriting communicates the thoughts and ideas accurately.
3. It is easily understandable. There is no scope for any type of misunderstanding.
4. It helps in creating interest of the students in language learning. Good handwriting once acquired becomes an asset with the learner.
5. Handwriting of a person speaks to a considerable extent about the personality of an individual. Thus, from good handwriting of a person we can judge about him or her.

6. Goo
and
7. A goo
for ot
feels i
handw
privileg

Present Position

These days, many
'The main reasons a

(i) Many tea
students i
(ii) The teache
handwritin
(iii) Ball-pens ar
ballpens spo
(iv) Four lined no
only.
(v) No credit is gi
very good.

Improvement of Handwri

(i) The teacher shou
at the early stage
go the students ac
of writing. Any s
should be nipped i
(ii) The teacher's writ
students. When he
students should be as
and fingers.
(iii) Then the students sh
matter from the black
may write the first line
students and ask them to
at the first line. And if ne
is done with dots may be
asked to overwrite it.
(iv) There should be frequ
handwriting. The winners

(v) Good han
the class r
other stud
(vi) At the ear
make use
pen shou
Good handwr
teacher and the st
explained meth
handwriting of sch
also give importa
the students will
students.
In the teach
confronted by the
English spellings

Spellings

Correct spelling
not a Phonetic la
spelling mistak
completely mis
writing having
1. rit (w
2. dat (
3. I low
4. Will
5. I ka
By this ty
So in the writ
In fact, correc
which is an i
Schonell
Subjects': "Sp
of which is b
other words
and visual i
responses."
Spelli
famous lin
national m

the rest of the world." *Bernard Shaw,* the great dramatist and humourist of English has made fun of English spellings. According to him if a learner of English language has limited knowledge of words and their spelling and he is asked to write another word, there is possibility of committing blunders. He explains his point by giving an example. Suppose a person knows only three words and he makes a note of the sounds underlined in the words rough, woman, nation. Then he is asked to write the word 'Fish'. That person having limited knowledge will write it as 'ghoti'. The word 'ghoti' in place of fish is a cent percent different word. It is a jugglary of spellings in English language. The reason why spellings of English language are difficult is that it is a mixed language. Main words have been borrowed from other languages like Greek and Latin. A few examples of difficult and confusing spellings are given below:-

(a) Ph is pronounced as 'F' in English. Some of the words are philosophical, photo.
(b) Ch is pronounced as 'K'. Some of the words are character, chorus.
(c) 'H' is silent in some words like hour, honour.
(d) 'K' is not sounded in some words-Knife, Knowledge.
(e) 'T' is silent in some of the words-listen, hasten.
(f) 'B' is silent in some of the words like comb, tomb.
(g) 'Gh' is not sounded in the words-bought, night, height, sight, flight, plight.
(h) 'Gh' gives the sound of 'f' in some of the words like cough, laugh, tough.
(i) Some sounds but written differently. Some of the words are way, weigh, whey.
(j) Types of errors may also include:

omissions	(wether)
additions	(waite)
insertions	(similiar)
substitution	(tence)
transposition	(recieve)
Phonetic error	(they in place of Day)

Methods of Teaching Spellings

W.S. Tomkinson says in his book 'The Teaching of English', "Spelling is caught rather than taught. Teaching of English Spelling is not an easy job. There are different types of students and so thev learn spellings in different ways. Some students are touch-minded. They learn spellings when the teacher asks them to write the spellings of the words again and again. The second category of students is called car-minded. They are able to pick up spelling when they listen to the spellings of the word. There are still other students who are called eye-minded. These students are considered to be superior to other types of students. They are able to understand spellings simply by looking at the word." So we shall have to make use of different methods for the different types of students. A few methods of teaching spellings which are commonly used, are explained here under:-

1. One method of teaching spellings may be summed up 'look, say and write'. The teacher writes on the black board and speaks the words alongwith the spellings. Then the students speak the word alongwith spellings and copy it down in their note books.
2. Drills of different types play a significant role. Oral drill, motor drill and visual drill can be used.
3. The students may be encouraged to group together words which are almost of the same type in speaking. For example, rat, cat, bat, sat pat, etc., or tin, pin, bin, etc. This type of association exercises are useful for teaching correct spellings.
4. Different letters are written on the flash cards. They are mixed together. Then the students are asked to frame words by using the various letters written on the flash cards.
5. The teacher writes wrong spellings of the words on the blackboard. Then the students are asked to come to the black board one by one and correct the spellings.
6. The commonly mis-spelt words are written on a chart and that chart is hung at some important place in the class. The students consult that chart again and again and learn spellings.
7. There are gramophone records available on which the words along with spelling are spoken. The record player is one and the students listen to the records.
8. Some interesting games may be introduced for teaching spellings. A few words are written on the black board. The students look at the words for some time. Then one student is asked to speak words alongwith spellings by

keeping his back towards the board. It is repeated by a number of students. For this, class can also be divided into two groups and competition may be held.

Writing skills are very important for the learner of the language. Sometimes some defects are seen in the writing skills of children. A few examples of such defects are:

(a) Writing small alphabets first and afterwards learning capital letters;

(b) Backward slant in their writing;

(c) Using cursive script first;

(d) Not caring for the principle of writing on a four lined notebook;

(e) Writing carelessly and committing spelling errors.

(f) Wrong posture of sitting for writing;

(g) Wrong holding of pen, notebook etc while writing;

All the above said defects need be fully cared for by the learners of language from the beginning. They should see that none of these defects is allowed to linger on. These must be carefully rectified with sincere efforts. The teacher should see that small letters are taught afterwards and capital letters first because capital letters are easy in writing. The learner should be enabled to use print script first and cursive script afterwards. Principle of writing on a four lined notebook and sitting in a right posture are important and their importance should be well known to the learners of language. The learner must be discouraged in the use of backward slant in writing. Thus timely guidance and proper encouragement by the teacher must be there when the budding children are taught the skills of writing. That will equip them with good writing skills.

ASSIGNMENTS

1. When should writing be introduced? What are the initial difficulties in the way of teaching writing? How will you overcome them?
2. Explain the mechanics of writing. How should the beginner be initiated into writing?
3. What are the different types of writing scripts? Which scripts would you make your students to follow in the beginning and why?
4. What are the chief characteristics of good handwriting? How would you help the beginners to write more beautifully? Give suggestions.

5. "English spellings is often unreliable" Comment. What steps will you like to ensure that your students spell correctly?
6. What are the causes of bad handwriting? How will you help your students to write legibly?
7. Spellings of English pose a big problem to Indian students. How then the teacher help the students overcome this problem?
8. (a) What are the characteristics of good hand writing?
   (b) Dictation is a good aid to writing. Discuss.
9. (a) Write a note on characteristics of good hand-writing.
   (b) Suggest 2-language game for improving the English spellings of your VII class students.
   (c) What script of English should be taught to the beginners in writing? Give reasons in support of your choice.

17

Art of Reading

Any language is taught with a view to develop certain skills. The right approach to it is the natural one. Listening and speaking skills should be developed first. After giving sufficient practice of listening and speaking, then reading and writing skills should be introduced. These skills are inter-related. Good reading definitely depends upon a lot of practice in listening and speaking. If a person has learnt spoken language carefully, he will not face any problem while reading. A good speaker is always a good reader.

Skill of Reading

Bacon said, "Reading make a full man, writing an exact man." Reading skill is, undoubtedly of unique importance in the learning of a language. *A. W Frisby* says. "Reading for those who have been guided to appreciate it, is one of the most important activities of life to bring to us not only a pleasant way of spending the time, but a way of entering into the life of the world and helping us to contemplate spiritual matters. Many of those who do not approach reading in this life have probably not received in their youth the right encouragement." Thus we find that the ability to read well is very much expected from every person..*R. S. Trivedi* and *D.A. Ghanchi* write in their books 'Teaching English' .... "In fact, the education of a child is imperfect, unless he is equipped with ability to read, to decipher, to interpret and to understand properly the contents of a reading material. The intellectual advancement of a child is strictly limited if he is unable to read."

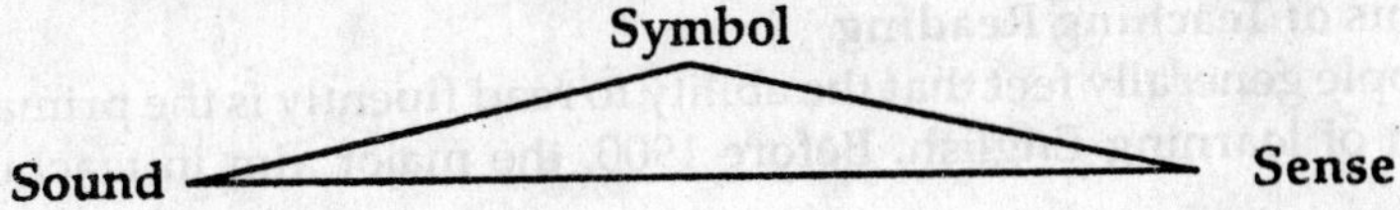

Reading involves recognition of sound and written symbols. Recognition of sounds is needed for listening or speaking of the language. Recognition of written symbols is important for reading purposes. Let us first of all, study what is meant by reading.

Meaning of Reading

Reading is a process of looking at a written or printed symbol and translating it into an appropriate sound. This spoken symbol is further associated with an object for which it stands. Thus reading consists of three elements ..... the symbol (written or printed), the sound and the sense. For example, the child reads the word 'dog' in his reader. First of all, he looks at the symbol, translates it into a specific sound which stands for some animal called 'dog' and at the same time he visualises the concrete object or idea for which the said symbol stands.

Reading in fact is the ability which enables the pupils sooner or later, to read with the purpose of extracting from the printed page, the thoughts, facts and information that it has to give him. We are enlightened by reading. By reading our written message is interpreted by the other person.

Mechanics of Reading

When a person reads anything his eyes go on moving alongwith the printed or written symbols. If we watch carefully, the eyes do not move smoothly in one even movement. They move by jumps separated by short stops. He reads when the eyes are having a pause and not when the eyes are in movement. The number of words read in one complete movement of the eyes is called the Eye-Span.

While reading, we do not look at the various letters of a word. We rather look at the words as a whole e.g. (Chair not c-h-a-i-r) The cc span can help develop the art of reading, There are fast readers and slow readers. The reason behind it is that a fast reader has a wider eye-span, whereas a poor reader has short eye-span.

While reading, some students put their fore fingers under every word. It is a bad habit because it has adverse effect on the speed of reading. So the teacher should check this bad habit at the initial stages.

Aims of Teaching Reading

People generally feet that the ability to read fluently is the primary aim of learning English. Before 1900, the major aim in teaching reading was just word recognition. But in due course of time, the concept underwent a change. In the modern times, there have been many social changes and so the purposes of teaching reading have increased. So much so is the change that even the methods of teaching reading have been modified accordingly. At present reading is taught so that a person is able:

(i) to recognise words.

(ii) to understand the meanings of words.

(iii) to react to what has been read. In other words, the child laughs, feels sad, waits for the ending etc. as the case may be. And he will disagree on false statement.

(iv) To change ideas and behaviour of the students.

Reading of mother tongue and reading of a foreign language are fundamentally the same processes. The learners face problems in both the cases. However in case of mother tongue, the problems are few because he has already learnt listening and speaking at home. In case of a foreign language, practice in listening or speaking is given in the school. Comparatively, the learners have less practice in aural-oral aspect of the language. Besides, English is not a phonetic language. Its spelling system creates problems in reading. So it is very essential that reading should be started after giving sufficient practice in listening and speaking.

Where to Start ?

Reading should not be introduced to the students unless they have acquired the ability to speak well. Now the question arises how much time should be spent for developing the speaking ability of the learners. *Thompson* and *Wyatt* write in their book, 'The Teaching of English in India'. "The Indian boy is eight or nine when he begins the study of English and he can already read his mother tongue fluently... In teaching him to read English, therefore, we need not be concerned with creating in him the right attitude of mind towards the printed (or written) word."

Different linguists give different opinions about it. Some of them say that reading should be started after one year of oral practice. Some others advocate that six months oral practice is very essential. No doubt, the opinions given by experts are based on observations made in experiments. But it is an admitted fact that we can't fix up the period for oral practice. The reason is that the period of practice will vary from place to place and from class to class. The following are the factors which determine the time to be spent on oral practice:

(i) Age of the learners.
(ii) Class in which the study of foreign language is introduced.
(iii) The ability of the students to understand and imitate the spoken language.
(iv) Ability of the teacher to maintain interest without books.
(v) The community to which the students belong.

So it is a decided fact that the time to be spent on oral work, will be different in different cases.

Present Day Situation

These days, we find that teaching of reading is started on the first or second day of schooling. It is a great draw-back. There may be a number of reasons behind but it is cent percent a wrong step. So it is absolutely necessary that some times must be spent on aural-oral practice.

Preparatory Reading

Preparatory reading means preparing the students for reading from the books. When the students come to the school, they should not be taught reading on the first or the second day. Rather they should be given language training in listening, and speaking for some days. Thus oral work and its practice of one type or the other should continue for a number of days.

In preparatory stage, the teacher should teach the students how to produce certain sounds. They should be taught how to speak the words. Those words should be taken up in oral work which the students will conic across in their books at the later stage. This stage when the students are prepared for the stage of reading is also called pre-reading stage.

Thus we notice that preparatory reading is of utmost importance in the teaching of a language. The following steps are suggested for conducting it:

1. By showing actual objects, the teacher tells the names of the things. In case of verbs, actions are performed and the teacher speaks the words. The students simply watch and listen carefully.
2. The teacher makes use of charts or pictures for those items which cannot be actually shown by their sketches or diagrams can be drawn easily.

3. Flash cards can also be used for this purpose. On one flash card the name of the object is written and on the other, sketch is drawn. The teacher shows the flash cards and makes the students speak the words. By and by, he makes the picture disappear. It helps the students to have some recognition of the words or letters as the case may be.
4. In case the flash cards are not available, the black-board can be used for the same purpose. Some of the pictures may be drawn and words or sentences describing them are written. Then the pupils are asked to read them, Later, only words or sentences may be written and pupils are helped to read them.
5. Some drills of words or sentences may be given in chorus, in groups and then to individuals.
6. By using black-boards or, flash cards, simple comprehension drills may be conducted as mentioned below:
   (a) The learners may be asked to pick up one of the objects provided.
   (b) Some pictures may be provided, and the learner is asked to find one mentioned by the teacher.
   (c) First halves of a few sentences may be written on the black board. The second halves may be written on the flash cards. The students may be asked to pick- it the corresponding halves on the flash cards.
7. Some of the reading games may be introduced. These games are of two types: (i) Recognition games. (ii) Comprehension games.

Recognition Games

(a) Flash cards of some words in duplicate are prepared. One set is displayed on the board in front of the class and the second set is given to the students. The pupils are asked to match the words.

(b) Flash cards of some words in duplicate are prepared. Then the class is divided into two parts. One set of flash cards is distributed in one group and the other set is given to the students of the second group. Thus each student holds one flash card in his or her hand. One student stands up and shows the flash card to the other group. The students of the other group read it out. Thus competition between the two groups is held. Of course, when the students have to speak the word, the time factor is controlled by the teacher.

Comprehension Games

The shop game. Each team is given a number of mixed flash cards containing the names of things to be found in three or four shops. The students sort them out properly shop-wise.

Read and do games. The teacher writes a number of sentences about actions on the blackboard and he numbers them. Thus he calls out the number of sentence and the name of a student. The student reads the sentence silently and does the action.

Methods of Teaching

Different methods of teaching reading have been popular from time to time. The methods even differ from country to country. Some of the popular methods are explained here below:

The alphabetic method. It is an old method of teaching reading. In this method, the students are taught the alphabets i.e. A, B, C—of the language. Here the unit of teaching is a letter. Later the students learn words by combining the alphabets.

It is a dull and boring method because the students are learning the alphabets A, B, C etc. which are meaningless. The small children do not feel interested in it. The teacher should try to make it interesting. *Walton* writes in his book. 'Principles and Methods of teaching'—"The Alphabetical Method insists upon a child attending separately to a dog's legs, tail etc. before allowing it to apprehend and name the animal as a whole." It is not a good method because it is lengthy and tedious. Moreover, there is too much emphasis on learning by rote.

The phonic method. It is a method of teaching reading in which each word is broken up into basic speech sounds. It really facilitates reading. Here the students are taught the different sounds first. They learn the alphabets afterwards. In other words, we can say that here the teacher teaches English through the phonetic script.

It is a very common method used in U.K. The only difficulty in its application is that there is need of expert teachers. That is one reason why this method did not become popular. In the words of

T.K.N. Menon and *M.S. Patel*, "The Phonic Method was adopted when it was realized that the sounds of letters, not their names when uttered rapidly produce the word. It was also assumed that once these sounds had been learnt, they should be combined into syllables and words, then into larger language units. The method is most effective for languages in which the forms of letter invariably correspond with their sounds."

The word method. *P.C. Wren* calls it 'The One and Only Rational Method' of teaching to read. It is called Word Method because the unit of teaching is a word. Moreover, pictures are also used with the words. The students look at the picture and they say whatever they see. That is why, this method is also called 'Look and Say' method.

It is a very popular method of teaching reading. The learners remain motivated by this method. The only drawback in this method is that a good many pictures have to be used here. It is difficult to have pictures for some words such as a, the, to, of, from, at, etc. But this single drawback—remains nothing as compared to the good point of this method.

So we find that this method remains a distinguished method in comparison with other methods.

The phrase method. In this method, the unit of teaching is a phrase. The students learn phrases and they learn the alphabets afterwards. According to *Menon* and *Patel*, "The Phrase Method is based on the assumption that phrases are more interesting than words and place emphasis on meaning. It is believed that since good readers recognise group of words at each fixation of the eyes, the phrase method should foster rapid growth in efficient reading."

This method cannot be used for all types of children. The reason is that the weak—students can hardly pick up one word at a time. They find it hard to learn two or three words at a time.

The sentence method. In this method, the unit of teaching is a sentence. The students learn words and alphabets afterwards. This method cannot be used for all types of children. The reason is that average child cannot pick up one complete sentence at a time. This method can be used only in that case when the children are exceptionally good. *Schonel, Free I.* writes in his book, 'The Psychology and Teaching of Reading', "One of the greatest values of the sentence method lies in the help it offers to the pupil from the context and from the continuity that can be embodied in material."

Best Method

Out of the above mentioned methods of teaching reading, we find that none of them is perfect in every respect. So it is rather difficult to conclude that this method or that method is more useful and better than the other. Taken from the realities of class room situations point of view, we can say that we have to depend upon the combination of methods. So it is obvious that one and only one method cannot serve purpose in all types of situations and for all times to come. We have to be very careful while making the selection of a method for teaching purposes. Generally we make use of the -Word method' or 'Look and Say Method' which is a via media approach.

Thus by using the different methods, reading is taught to the students. At the initial stages, the learners may not be good readers but gradually the teacher is to enable them to read accurately and correctly by taking care of pauses.

Development of Proper Eye-span

The teacher himself should present model reading to the learners by having proper eye movement. He should divide the sentence into phrases which are to be read together without any pause. Then he can give practice to the learners by setting time limit for reading any paragraph.

Reading Defects and Their Cure

While learning to read English, there may be many problems which the students will face. Some of the problems may be timely which will be solved automatically in due course of time. Thus at the initial stages, some of the letters which are slightly different in written representation may confuse the learners. For example, the letter m, n; c, e: It, k; y, z. This problem remains no problem when the learner will look at these letters again and again and be familiar with them. But there are some other problems which are not easy to tackle. This problem continually frightens the learners. Some students who are actively interested in the language, are able to get over those but others remain ill the grip of difficulty which may be a little bit or more. A few sounds of English which are different from the sounds of mother tongue may be misunderstood by the learners. For example /v/, /w/. They will produce both the sounds like Hindi sound. They will also confuse English sounds with Hindi and Punjabi sounds. Another problem in their way will be the problem of English spellings. English is not a phonetic language, but gradually they will tend to speak according to the written representation of the language. Then it will give rise to innumerable mistakes in reading. At the early stages, it is just possible that they may read the words in a funny way. For example, hat, and hut and shut and knife.

But these problems will not remain problems if sincere efforts are made to overcome all these difficulties. *A.W. Frisby* in his book 'English Teaching' has pointed out. There is no difficulty in teaching children to read. Many will teach themselves if we give them the right preparation, the right material and let them help each other. The young teacher should bear in mind that it is easier to teach pupils to read a new language than to speak it. At the same time, children should not be rushed into learning to read. The basis of sound reading method is that it presents in the form of signs material about which we have spoken and we must see that this principle is maintained. The material of reading follows the material of speech and when the pupil finds that he already knows that material and has only to learn to recognise the printed symbols for it, he will soon demonstrate his ability to read, to write labels for his pictures and attempt to read new. There must be ample language background before reading is attempted in earnest, and the richer the background is, the more easily will the pupils learn to read, apart from other considerations such as physical and intellectual equipment. Reading fits on the background of language experience. If this background is not there, learning to read will be a painful and frustrating experience of the pupil and the teacher. The background must be supplied by the agency of both home and school and will take the form of stories, discussions on pictures and a wide variety of conversation on ordinary experiences of life."

There are two types of learners who can be taught writing of English language. The first category is of those who have not learnt the writing of any language. The second category is of those who have already learnt the writing of mother tongue. In the first case, the teacher has to explain to the learners how they have to sit, how to hold a note book in the hand and how to hold a pen. After this, they are given preliminary practice of writing with a pen. Then they are given this type of practice with the help of chalks and small boards which are meant for the students. They are black boards fixed up on the four walls.

Types of Reading

Prose may be read:

1. Loudly
2. Silently

Loud Reading

Loud Reading means reading a book by producing sounds audible to others. This type of reading is useful during the first three or four cars of language learning. The reason is that the students are beginners and there is possibility of committing errors. Sometimes the learners are hesitant to reveal their shortcomings. So loud reading plays a very significant role in the teaching of a language. It is advantageous at the early stages but it will be nothing less than luxury if it is carried on at higher stages of learning the language.

Reading aloud by the teacher can help the students in the improvement of their listening ability. They are also able to sharpen their recognition of different sounds. Moreover, they can watch the movements of organs of the teacher when he is presenting model reading to the learners. Some of the words which the students find difficult to speak are well understood by them. Pronunciation of the students is also improved considerably. So reading aloud by the teacher helps the learners in a number of ways.

Thus we find that reading aloud is of great advantage at the early stages of learning a language. According to *A. W Frisby*, "The danger of too much reading aloud as a method of teaching reading is that it may lead to the short circuiting of the meaning whereby the written word does not convey meaning but becomes merely a symboi for a collection of sounds and is translated straight in sounds."

Silent Reading

Silent reading means reading something without producing sounds audible to others. In this type of reading, the learner of language reads everything quietly. He is not expected to move his iips even. This type of reading is useful at the advanced levels of learning a language. The reason is that at this stage the learner of language has to read a number of books. Sometime the reader is busy in reading a novel. In such cases it will be worth-while to make use of silent reading. Only then the reader will be able to go through a lot of reading material.

Silent reading is not of any use if it is carried on at the lower stages of learning a language. But at the higher stages, it is highly ıas etc. He tries to understand anything and everything contained he paragraph.

Extensive Reading. In extensive reading, the aim is not uistic. Here the reader is concerned with getting the overall ning or idea of the passage. He is not to bother about the detailed guage items contained in the paragraph *W.M. River* says in his k. 'Teaching Foreign Language Skills', "The purpose of extensive gramme will be to train the student to read directly and fluently e foreign language for his own enjoyment, without the aid of eacher."

Generally in the lower classes, books are prescribed for ısive reading. But in the higher classes, extensive reading on part of the students is as important as is intensive reading. In ısive reading the student cannot ignore the meaning of any l. He has to follow each word or structure contained in the graph. But in extensive reading, he can skip over a line or a l or a structure which he fails to follow.

The prescribed books in different classes are meant for sive reading. Read and Learn Series is a set of books prescribed e first three years of learning English. The students here cannot e anything. Similarly in Prep. class, 'Poems for the Young' is a ribed textbook for intensive reading. The students can be asked ite context and explanation in the examination. Even a critical ion can be put on anything contained in the lesson.

'n extensive reading, one is concerned with the over-all ings contained in the book or chapter. Let us take up a single ple. Intensive reading of a newspaper, says, 'The Tribune', ıas to be done extensively otherwise one will lag far behind. xtensive reading breaks the dull and monotonous reading of tbook. Moreover, the reader is not required to strain much in ive reading.

tant Type of Reading

ı't say that of these two types one is better than the other and more important. The fact is that both these types of reading portant in their own ways.

ı Indian schools, we find that more stress is laid on intensive g. The extensive reading is encouraged in a very few schools. ive reading should serve as a means to extensive reading.

recommended. *A. W. Frisby* says, "While reading alou
few pupils will have much need of it when the lea
must teach the skill of silent reading as soon as poss
useful to our pupils throughout their lives." *Handschi*
reading inculcates love for reading and is pleasurab
the pupil a feeling of power and achievement.

Silent reading is both an end and a means in
means to achieve the following objectives:

Intellectual. The students are quickly able to
or thoughts contained in the subject matter.

Literary. The students get both enter
enlightenment.

Linguistic. It aims at the expansion of pupils

W.S. Tomkinson very beautifully explains l
distinguishing between silent reading and loud r
quotes two sentences (i) Culture is reading and (ii
noble exercise by the first is meant that they should l
both accurate enough to turn the print into corr
tender its logical content and expressive enough
the beauty or word and their emotional significan
we mean reading nicely which is good and nobl

Silent Reading : The Greater Need of Learners

Silent reading is needed by all types of learners of
reading aloud is useful at specific moments alon
the students will almost never be called up
Moreover, reading aloud prevents the student
understand the meaning of a sentence even whe
one word in the sentence. It prevents him from
he is forced to struggle with the word in order
aloud. Reading aloud can easily be done with n
all. Allowing the students to read silently, enco
for understanding rather than finishing th
reading the students can more easily work a
pace or speed.

Reading may be done (i) Intensively (ii) I

Intensive and Extensive Reading

Intensive reading. Intensive reading means
passage. In this type of reading, the reader has
different language items i.e. words, grammar,

Skimming

Skimming of a lesson means gathering together salient facts contained in it. Skimming of a prose paragraph means going through it and collecting the main points contained therein. Surely the reader is able to take out the best contained there in the lesson or the paragraph.

Practice of skimming is very important for the senior students. It gives them a lot of confidence. The main purpose of the person is to assemble main things contained therein.

Scanning

Scanning of a book or a lesson or a paragraph means collecting detailed information contained in the subject matter. The reader goes through the subject matter with searching looks. He/She examines every thing very closely. So much so that the reader is not allowed to ignore even a single difficult word contained there in. In scanning, everything good or bad is pointed out. Every thing very objectively and in a A-cry scientific manner is highlighted.

Scanning of materials is recommended for the senior students. It teaches them to call a spade a spade. It also develops the habit of working hard. It also helps them in developing scientific attitude in thinking and understanding things which is very important in life. They tend to read the subject matter cautiously and carefully.

Developing the Reading Habits

These days, we find that the students are not in the habit of studying extra books. The, study only those books which are prescribed for the different classes. If the students continue like this, then the real aims of teaching the language will be missed. It is the duty of all concerned that they should make efforts to improve the deteriorating conditions. The examination system should also be changed. The question paper and the syllabus expect the study of some other books. For extra reading, *Prof Rajagopalan* says: "We should concentrate all our attention on the pupils now in schools and make them more and more book-minded. We should create in them a real love for books and not only a good taste for reading." The following steps in this direction are suggested:

(i) The teacher should explain to the students the utility of library reading. They should be given knowledge about different types of books lying in the library.

(ii) As far as possible, the books should be easily accessible to the students. For this a small library in the class-room may be started. Open shelf system may be introduced if possible.

(iii) Sometimes the teacher may tell a part of the story contained in some books. As soon as the students feel interested in it, the teacher may say that they should read the rest of the story from the books lying in the library. In such cases, it is expected that the library will have a number of copies of the book.

(iv) There should be competitions for extra reading. Thus the winners may be given prizes.

(v) In the examination, there should be some questions for which the students may be required to make use of the subject matter acquired through extra reading.

(vi) During the school hours, one period should be prescribed for library studies. It will be all the better if open-shelf system is introduced in the library.

(vii) In order to draw the attention of the students and make them feel interested, some books of common interest may be placed in the canteen. The students in their free time will be able to have a look at them.

(viii) Sometimes there may be discussion on books and the students who show extra knowledge of books should be given either special certificates or special credit for that.

(ix) The library should have suitable type of books for all the students. There should be banks for the children, the grown ups, the teachers, the geniuses, the dullards etc.

(x) The library and the reading room should be well decorated. It will attract the readers.

(xi) The newly arrived books in the library should be notified on the notice board. If possible, the covers of those books should be exhibited on a special board meant for this purpose.

(xii) A library association of the students may be formed. The students may be involved for doing social service in the library. The students will come to know about the various books lying in the library. Thus they will be attracted towards reading some of them.

(xiii) The class teacher or the subject teacher himself should be interested in reading extra books from the library. This example of the teacher will have its effect on the students. They will also becom: interested in library books.

(xiv) The teacher should announce in the class the names of the students who are doing extra reading. It will give recognition to those students. Moreover, it will attract the attention of the students to library.

Thus developing the reading habits of school going children should be dealt with on priority basis. In the words of *Prof Rajagopalan*:

"We can never hope to improve the standard of English of our pupils and help them derive full benefits out of learning a difficult foreign language unless and until this desirable habit is formed among our students first."

ASSIGNMENTS

1. What are your suggestion for developing the reading habits of your students in secondary schools?
2. "Pave the way to language and find the way to literature." Elaborate the above statement with respect to teaching of English prose to the secondary classes.
3. "Reading comprehension involves understanding, reading of content, vocabulary, grammatical structures, concepts and relationship to ideas". Discuss
4. State the objectives you would try to achieve through lessons in intensive reading in English. How would these objectives differ from those of a lesson in extensive reading?
5. Outline a strategy for teaching a piece of prose in English to any school class of your choice. Make out a case for the strategy chosen.
6. Bring out clearly the difference in the procedure of a lesson on 'Intensive Reading' and that on 'Extensive Reading'.
7. In what ways is the teaching of extensive reading different from that of intensive reading? Give examples in support of your answer.
8. Think of a prose piece you have taught and outline the steps you employed in teaching it. Mention the class and background of children it was taught to.

9. (a) Reading comprehension does not mean only skill in reading but something more.' Explain.
   (b) Distinguish between the aims of intensive and extensive reading.
   (c) How will you as a teacher, satisfy yourself that your pupils read with comprehension?
10. Write a note on:
   (a) Model reading by the teacher.
   (b) Importance of Silent Reading.
11. (a) Suggest ways to expand the reading habits of your students.
   (b) Comment on Silent Reading and Loud Reading.
   (c) Write a note on the importance of Silent Reading.
12. What are comprehension questions? Describe various types of comprehension questions.